BAPTISE EVER

Baptise Every Baby?

The story of one vicar's struggle to treat baptism as if it mattered

CLIFFORD OWEN

MARC

EASTBOURNE

*Front cover photo by Peggy & Drummond Chapman
Cover design by Ron Bryant-Funnell*

British Library Cataloguing in Publication Data

Owen, Clifford
Baptise every baby?
I. Title
265.12

ISBN 1-85424-131-1

Printed in Great Britain for
MARC, an imprint of Monarch Publications Ltd,
1 St Anne's Road, Eastbourne, E Sussex BN21 3UN by
BPCC Hazell Books, Aylesbury, Bucks.
Typeset by Nuprint Ltd, Harpenden, Herts

To Avis
in memory of that day when you came into the
kitchen of the curate's house with the baptism
register in your hand, turning the pages and exclaiming,
'Where are all these people?'

ACKNOWLEDGEMENTS

I am grateful to the following for their help in making this book more interesting than it would otherwise have been:

Avis, my wife, for constant reading, correcting and encouragement with the manuscript and for assistance with typing it.

Anne Gayden, of Clifton-on-Teme, for typing chapters 4, 5 and 6.

Mrs Joan Muxlow, widow of Arthur, my first vicar, at Stowmarket, for reading the draft of Chapter 2, suggesting alterations and supplying additional material.

Mrs Sally Puddick of Bordon, Hampshire, for writing her testimony which I have used at the end of Chapter 5.

Bishop Philip Goodrich, Bishop of Worcester, for writing a foreword.

Bishop Colin Buchanan, President of MORIB, for writing an epilogue.

Bishop Paul Barber, Bishop of Brixworth, for permission to quote from previous correspondence between us.

Richard Inkpen, Vicar of St Matthew's, Blackmoor,

for permission to use his baptismal policy and for his letter updating me on its progress.

Raymond Dent, Vicar of Emmanuel, New Brighton, for permission to use his questionnaire and survey results from the Diocese of Chester.

The Petersfield Post for permission to use the newspaper articles relating to the launch of the Headley/Bordon baptismal policy.

The Times for permission to reprint Clifford Longley's articles.

The Sunday Telegraph for permission to reprint the article by Minette Marrin.

The Grapevine, the newspaper of the Bath and Wells Diocese, for permission to use the article by Bishop George Carey.

And last but not least to Derek Head, Michael Powell, John Cherrill and all my former clergy colleagues in the Headley/Bordon team ministry with whom I have discussed baptism over the years.

CONTENTS

Foreword by the Bishop of Worcester   11
Author's Preface   13

Chapter 1   When Did I Become a Christian?   19
Chapter 2   Stowmarket By-pass   36
Chapter 3   A New Town   52
Chapter 4   Getting Them to Church   65
Chapter 5   Fruit for Labour   82
Chapter 6   Hurdles and Hostility   99
Chapter 7   The Baptismal Richter Scale   116
Chapter 8   Differing Neighbours   132
Chapter 9   Do We Really Refuse?   150
Chapter 10   The Mystery of Faith   167
Chapter 11   Baptism and Evangelism   181
Chapter 12   Dear Bishops...I'm Re-writing the
             Canons   196
Chapter 13   'I Don't Like the Feel of This Place'   211
Chapter 14   National Press   226
Chapter 15   Rural Postscript   239

Epilogue by Bishop Colin Buchanan   252

Appendices:
1. Parish Magazine articles from Headley in 1988   267
2. Newspaper cuttings from the local press   274
3. Suggestions for group discussion   280
4. Clifford Longley's article from *The Times* of
   29th October 1988   282

FOREWORD

by the Bishop of Worcester

I commend this book written by an incumbent of this Diocese of Worcester of which I am bishop. To begin with I commend it because the author, still young and with much of his ministry in front of him, has taken the trouble to reflect on his experience in a way which is workmanlike and thorough. You may not agree with all that he writes; nevertheless each chapter would make an excellent basis for discussion for a clergy group or even better, for a parish house-group.

Clifford Owen, though a member of the Movement for the Reform of Infant Baptism, is no fundamentalist. His capacity to grow in his understanding in the light of his experience is too patent for that. He also has the self-discipline to live with anomaly and imperfection. This is close to what we lightly call a sense of humour. It is also a sense of proportion. It is God-given. It is the prerequisite to bringing the best out of a situation which all parish priests inherit. It is none of their making. As he says in Chapter 15, 'I have furnished plenty of evidence already that if too strong a line is taken on baptism and you "lose" then it sets back the work pastorally by some years.' The 'wise bird of necessity' must brood over all our pastoral work.

Chapter 13 will make interesting reading to many clergy who have had parishes, even parish churches, which do not 'feel right'. Frequently the liturgy of the church, as in the celebration of a cheerful and victorious Eucharist or the Easter ceremonies, and plenty of sanctified common sense are better remedies than spook-hunting. The latter can in itself become a form of neurosis and unbalance with Christian protestations.

In all, I hope this book will be well received, even if sometimes critically. Few can minister in the Church of England, especially in the rural areas, without sometimes being provoked to anger by the way people want to use the church for their own convenience. Even those of us who dislike hard and fast lines which put some favoured souls in the church and others outside it, must share with Clifford Owen and others a desire to rescue the prime sacrament of baptism from being a mere social occasion. In the Decade of Evangelism we want to grow in depth, in involvement in society and in numbers. If that is so, although we will totally reject sectarianism, we must also look to our missionary and church strategy. This book is going to be a great assistance in that enterprise.

+ Philip Worcester

Hartlebury Castle
Kidderminster
11th December 1990

AUTHOR'S PREFACE

Like many books, this one has turned out rather different from my original conception of it. I thought that my interest in reforming infant baptism began in a low profile way in my first curacy. I discovered however as I sat down to recall facts and marshall material that it had been on my mind for years without me being very conscious of it. Indeed it may run in my family. I recall my late grandfather, who was a sidesman and regular worshipper in his local Anglican church, saying one day with passion, 'It's all wrong you know...these folk who only turn up for christenings, weddings and funerals! They should be either in or out!'

What precisely grandfather had in mind to do by way of altering the situation he never disclosed, but I take his point. Every baptismal reformer walks a narrow ledge: on the one hand, he wants discipleship to be real and the sacraments to be received rightly, and on the other he realises that many outside the church, not yet ready for Christian commitment, want some form of ritual expression at key points in their lives.

The point at issue for those of us within the church is whether we should now come clean and clearly delineate these two separate needs. This book contains the account of my experience of trying to do just that within the framework of the Church of England's present rules. I also make suggestions for mapping out new territory where the present rules fall short. Only by so doing do I believe the church will be equipped to witness to Christ more clearly and to carry out his mission in the world.

The book is not an autobiography, but it contains a great deal of my life story. That is because I believe the reader will better understand what I am trying to say if he knows more about me. It is very easy to find yourself labelled 'unorthodox', 'unwelcoming' or 'rigorist' in the area of baptismal reform. I hope at the end of this work none of these labels will stick to me! I hope also that the particular kite which I fly in Chapter 13 will not cause the reader to dismiss the rest of the book.

David Pawson once said to me that when you start to study the theology of Christian baptism you will discover that practically every other theological issue in the church branches off from it. So far I have found that to be true.

For whom is this book intended? Baptism is an issue for every Christian at some point in their lives, and this book provides food for thought whether your own baby is to be baptised, or your non-Christian neighbour's baby, or your teenage son wants to be baptised by immersion. There is another group who need to consider the issues around infant baptism in a more objective way, and they are the members of the Parochial Church Council. It is the PCC members of our Anglican parish churches who have such a part to play in the effective outreach of our churches in the next few years. By a careful and considered study of the issues surrounding the administration of infant baptism, leading to baptismal policies which are right for a particular parish at a particular time, church councils could experience the joy of real church growth. But I do not leave the buck solely with PCC members. There are issues of baptismal reform which can only be dealt with at a church-wide leadership level across the country. My chapter addressed to the House of Bishops spells these out.

I have tried to write this book with a lightness of touch which I hope will sustain interest. If you detect a sense of humour then I have been faithful to my naval training!

Finally I hope that this offering will be part of my contribution towards the Decade of Evangelism.

The Rectory,
Clifton-on-Teme
November 1990

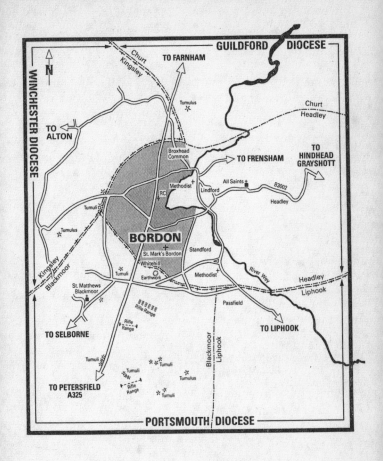

+ — + — Diocesan Boundaries

— · — · — Parish Boundaries

░░░░░░ The L.E.P. area of Bordon

Chapter 1

WHEN DID I BECOME A CHRISTIAN?

I was driving back one Sunday evening in 1968 from my home in Warwickshire to *HMS Ganges* in Suffolk, and I had arranged the journey to take in the evening service at the Church of the Holy Sepulchre in Cambridge (the 'Round Church'). The Round Church had been one of my favourite spiritual feeding points during my under-graduate days a few years before and this special affec-tion caused me to stop off for Evensong. The curate's sermon on that occasion answered a question for me. His subject was baptism, or, more specifically, re-baptism: should a Christian who has come to a personal faith in Christ go through a re-baptism in water or will his infant baptism, assuming he had one, suffice?

The question was appropriate. For some years I had been periodically assailed by Christians, usually Brethren, Baptists or Free Evangelicals, who felt that believers' baptism was part of Christian obedience. I had grown accustomed to their dismissive attitude towards Anglicans in general and infant baptism in particular.

'No, you don't need to go off and get re-baptised if you've made a commitment to Christ,' preached the curate. 'Your infant baptism was done in good faith by parents and godparents, and your conversion was entirely what was presupposed when you were sprinkled at the font.' He then went on to expound what I now know as covenant theology, that baptism is the covenant sign in the New Testament equivalent to circumcision in the Old Testament. The importance of believing parents had a high profile in the sermon. I completed my journey to Suffolk relieved that I no longer needed to worry that I should be baptised again as a believer.

However, that sermon didn't answer all my questions about infant baptism. It didn't get near an answer to a nagging problem. Where precisely did we come into the Christian fold? At infant baptism? At confirmation? At conversion? Some were further complicating the question with the issue of a 'second blessing' of the Holy Spirit, often called 'baptism in the Holy Spirit'.

The early sixties in Cambridge were exciting and controversial days, and to someone who had never travelled further east than Leicester, the ambience of Cambridge was captivating. The very atmosphere seemed charged with the excitement of learned and enquiring minds. Every issue was open for discussion. Even in my engineering course I discovered that what had been certainties at 'A' level were now only first approximations. 'Cambridge has more churches than pubs' was one of the few certainties. During my first year as an undergraduate I was to visit more of the latter than the former!

I had not come straight from Grammar School to University, but had spent two years in the Royal Navy being honed as a cadet and midshipman in preparation for a permanent commission in the Senior Service. In John Winton's *We Joined the Navy*, there is a famous utterance by a senior naval officer at the Admiralty Interview Board. When addressing the Board before a series of young hopeful men appeared before them he said: 'Now remember the Navy is not looking for intelligent men. If they were intelligent they wouldn't be here. No, the Navy is looking for half-wits. The Service will add the other half in its own good time!' At Cambridge I felt like the half-wit upon whom the Service had so far failed to add that other half!

Ironically, it was in the Navy that my quest for certainty and truth received an unexpected boost. One morning in the spring of 1961 the Captain of the Royal Naval College at Dartmouth[1] came onto the parade ground and asked for the parade to be stood at ease. That usually meant trouble.

'The number of you who attended church yesterday morning could be counted on the fingers of one hand. Now I know a number of you are anxious about exams, but if you are to be successful naval officers then you need to get your priorities in the right order, and worship of Almighty God ought to come first.' The Captain then asked the parade commander to 'carry on'. Inwardly I felt a glow and a question. A glow, because I had been one of the few in church the previous Sunday (and being in the choir at Dartmouth Naval College took precedence over everything except punishment!), and a question, because I stood there in the midst of a parade ground of apparent doubt and felt myself at the same time to be part of that doubt. Maybe those other cadets were simply more honest than me...maybe my attendance at worship was mere routine. Certainly I could not begin to articulate my belief in any terms remotely similar to the Apostles Creed which I gaily recited as part of the service.

Two things happened as a result of that parade ground 'stand easy'. Firstly, in our eight-berth cabin in the college that week there followed a most interesting and heated debate about the truth of Christianity. It seemed to centre on the Person of Jesus Christ. Who was he? What was a Christian? Of the eight cadets in the cabin four or five carried on a discussion for two or more hours. I took no part. One cadet, I remember, was a

Buddhist from the Ceylon Navy. I felt simply quite out of touch with any religious convictions I might have possessed. When my head hit the pillow that night my one certainty was my uncertainty of my own religious convictions.

The other thing that happened on the parade ground as the Captain delivered his 'blast' was that standing in the rank behind me was a cadet who muttered: 'He only goes on like this because he's in the Officers' Christian Union.' The name of that group stayed in my mind as if imprinted. When I arrived in Cambridge in October 1962, among the many invitations in my pigeon hole was an invitation to attend the Officers' Christian Union. Another invitation was to attend the freshmen's sermon at Great St Mary's Church[2] and another to attend the college Christian Union.[3] I duly attended all three!

The service at Great St Mary's made a deep impression on me; not least because the preacher was no less a man than Archbishop Michael Ramsey. Though that great man had a slight stammer in his delivery, his countenance and conviction came over with clarity and firmness. I was moved at the sight and sound of a great archbishop preaching orthodox certainties with 600 undergraduates listening intently. But as yet that certainty was not inside me.

Two weeks later I prepared to attend the CICCU[4] freshers' sermon in Holy Trinity Church just along the road from Great St Mary's. I had persuaded another naval officer to come with me, but we decided to go out for a drink first. Then just as we were finishing our beer to walk down to the church, another naval officer entered the pub and he persuaded us to stay until closing time! History could have been different had I reached that sermon!

My freshman's interview with the College Dean also exposed my lack of conviction. The Dean was one Hugh Montefiore[5] who asked me at the end of a pleasant

interview if I was a practising Christian. 'Yes,' I replied
in a half-baked way. I am glad he didn't press matters
further. When our paths crossed again twenty-five years
later Hugh's razor-like memory caused him to remark,
'Yes, I remember you. You didn't go to chapel much,
did you?'

It was when I began to admit my doubts that things
started to happen in my religious thinking. I read John
Robinson's *Honest to God* and found it interesting, but it
didn't mean much to me. I went to another university
sermon in Great St Mary's and was conscious that the
preacher was airing doubt rather than certainty.

About this time I began to get a strong desire to go on
the Norfolk Broads for an Easter sailing holiday. I had
always been a keen sailor and wanted to try and keep my
'sea-legs', so it was a strange coincidence when a friend
said to me one morning, quite out of the blue, 'Would
you like to come and hear this chap speaking in Trinity
College?[6] He is looking for people to come sailing on the
Norfolk Broads'! The holiday turned out to have a Christian basis to it. 'There'll be a bit of Bible-bashing but
don't let it worry you,' my friend said. 'Just enjoy the
sailing.' It didn't worry me and I did enjoy the sailing.
Indeed the whole organisation of committed Christians
left a deep impression on me. I enjoyed their company
but they must have detected something missing in me
because after I had taken breakfast prayers one morning
on the yacht, I was politely not asked to take them again!

During the summer term of 1963, panic over first-year
examinations set in and I started to slide into depression.
The initial glamour of Cambridge had faded and I felt
suspended between a desire to find the living God and a
fear that I might not find him or even want him if I did
find him. All the academic goals up until then in my life
had been achieved, and I faced for the first time the
possibility that I could fail an exam. I was also uneasy
about the thought of the next thirty years in the Navy. I

went to see the secretary of the Officers' Christian Union in King's College and asked him to tell me where he got his Christian certainty from.[7] He did! Two weeks later he visited me in my rooms in Gonville and Caius College and brought with him a friend from the Caius Christian Union, plus Bibles, and then very quietly proceeded to explain the certainties of evangelical conviction. They left me with the indelible impression that I would get nowhere in my religious search unless I made a 'step in faith of commitment to Christ'. I didn't know what that meant at the time, other than that it had to be done. I was 'strongly encouraged' to attend the going-down sermon[8] to be given by the Revd David Watson. A posse from the Christian Union was lovingly arranged to escort me to the sermon to ensure that I got there! David Watson's sermon had a clarity and power that I had never come across from a pulpit before. (What a great loss to the Church of England was caused by the untimely death of this great man.)

So it came to pass that over that summer I threw in my lot with the Christian Union. Somewhere along the way I must have made a faltering commitment to Christ as requested by my friends. My 'conversion' was not dramatic, heralded. I would have liked to have kept it totally private but these things have a way of filtering through and soon I was numbered among the brethren! Very tentatively I joined in with the Christian Union meetings and gradually became versed in CU language, attitudes and thought forms. I made my first faltering attempts at private personal prayer and found reading the Bible very difficult.[9] I settled down and gained spiritual height. I knew God was there and I had peace for a season.

It wasn't long before the inevitable questions arose. Christian Union types didn't generally attend college chapel because it was thought either 'unsound', 'unsafe' or both; and evangelicals didn't need Great St Mary's because they had everything they needed elsewhere. As for the Faculty of Divinity, that was a veritable temptation to infidelity, and should never be entered without the backing of a prayer group! These safety ground rules naturally caused me to ask about the status and validity of all the previous Christian influences in my life. Infant baptism, for example, didn't figure in any sound Christian scheme of things. It was irrelevant to them. Yet the Prayer Book suggested, and the Church of England taught, that baptism was the beginning of Christian life. How could this square with what evangelicals called 'conversion', by which they meant the beginning of conscious personal Christian commitment. I tried to force the question out of my mind but it continued to bother me.

Meanwhile there was another confusing factor to disturb my new spiritual state. In the mid-sixties there was a renewed interest in the Person and work of the Holy Spirit, and this was creeping into Christian Union circles as the divisive 'neo-Pentecostalism'. Within a few months of my finding a secure home for my faith among the members of the Christian Union I became aware that within the group all was not the undivided bliss that appeared at first sight. Some Christian students were claiming that the normal pattern of Christian initiation—receiving Christ as Saviour and thereby being simultaneously born of the Holy Spirit—was in fact only a first step. These students taught that a later work of grace, known as the 'second blessing' or the 'baptism of the Holy Spirit' was available to Christians for the asking and ought to be sought after. As a tangible sign that one had received this second blessing, you would speak in tongues. This infiltration of neo-Pentecostalism into Christian Union circles was viewed with much suspicion and hostility, particularly when the adherents went as far as to suggest that you weren't a real Christian until you had received the baptism of the Holy Spirit and spoken in tongues. This, of course, was anathema to orthodox IVF[10] Christian Union students.

Few of my friends were theologians, but certain theological questions were now having to be faced. The neo-Pentecostals were shifting the basis of faith from the Word of God written to an observed Christian experience—or at least that was the accusation. This of course was not quite true, because the neo-Pentecostals (they weren't called 'charismatics' until a few years later) appealed to Scripture to authenticate their experiences of the spiritual gifts. The orthodox evangelical, on the other hand, believed in his acceptance by Christ because the Word said so. Faith was believing the Word and a man is justified by faith alone. God could be trusted because he had written his Word in the form of Holy Scripture and if we disbelieved that Word then we made God out to be a liar. Such reasoning was the meat and bedrock of evangelical security as we students understood it, and it is easy to see how this rock was shaken by the suggestion that Christians ought to manifest the reality of their faith by the exhibiting of some spiritual gift.

The alarm caused by the 'tongues movement' was widespread and it was not long before direction was coming from on high to protect the minds and souls of the faithful. John Stott's booklet *The Baptism and Fullness of the Holy Spirit*[11] sought to inform and comfort the minds of anxious Christian students, arguing clearly from Scripture against the idea of a 'second blessing'. The booklet made scant reference to water baptism.

Yet one of John Stott's curates, Michael Harper, was to be a leader in charismatic renewal, and through the Fountain Trust[12] was to channel a growing renewal movement in the historic denominations.

Echoes of this division were heard in Cambridge also. At the Round Church David Watson was reported to have come into this 'speaking in tongues thing' and as a result was both under suspicion and by the same token intriguing to listen to. David symbolised CICCU orthodoxy. He was an outstanding university missioner and the effect of his freshers' sermon and addresses in the 1965 mission left an indelible impression upon me. Looking back I can see that there was some very special anointing upon him: the addresses were to form the basis of one of his books, *My God is Real*. But as well as having absorbed this new spiritual experience he continued to be a loyal and faithful member of the team at the Round Church where the vicar was the warm-hearted (now late) Mark Ruston, to whom countless Cambridge undergraduates must owe their faith.

Where did I stand in all of this?

One member of the Christian Union invited me to coffee in his room one evening to explain how I could be baptised with the Holy Spirit, and then offered to lay hands on me with prayer. I declined at the time but felt that what he had to say carried some conviction. Not long afterwards I was reluctantly taken to some meetings at a Pentecostal church in the Newmarket Road. There I saw worship of a kind I had never seen before—a mixed congregation of town and gown, punctuating every few minutes with 'Hallelujah' and 'Praise the Lord'. Following this I was taken by the same undergraduates to a healing rally in Cambridge, and then on to a deliverance rally in Victoria Street, London. Clearly my friends hoped that by this continued exposure to 'the things of the Spirit', as they were then known, I would be worn down by a slow process of attrition. They were nearly right. After some weeks I discovered a pamphlet that suggested that to be baptised with the Spirit one could ask the Lord privately and be blessed in the comfort of your own backyard, so to speak. There was no need to risk embarrassment in front of a crowd of people. Furthermore the booklet said that you could learn to speak in tongues on your own by moving your mouth in faith. This was what I decided to do. If I received something then I would have something to shout about and thus get my Pentecostal friends off my back. If nothing happened then no one would be any the wiser!

I was sitting at my desk in my rooms in Caius College one afternoon, when I became aware of the presence of God in a powerful way. I felt no rushing mighty wind, but God was there in the stillness, and there was a sweetness and love to it as if someone was embracing me. The experience stopped me in my engineering studies that afternoon and I realised that this must have been for me the 'touch' or the anointing or gift of the Holy Spirit or whatever. That sense of presence which I clearly felt that afternoon has remained with me more or less ever since. I did nothing to deserve it. I later found that I could speak in a new language, although it never quite produced for me the euphoria that others have claimed for it. The experience was for me something foundational and has remained. It was just as well, for I had had little interest in reading the Bible and it took several months for me to relate the Scriptures seriously to my life with any enthusiasm. Because of my mindset the Bible belonged to another age, another culture, and I had to achieve a degree in engineering.

By a providential turn of events I found myself spending my third undergraduate year in Tyndale House. Tyndale House was the IVF's further theological studies centre set in a pleasant cul-de-sac near Selwyn College. Around twenty theological students, mainly of a conservative background, lived and studied there. I found myself eavesdropping on endless theological conversations at mealtimes and coffee breaks while I continued to read engineering. I learned a lot; especially that within conservative evangelical circles not everything was as neatly cut and dried as is sometimes supposed. One of the topics that was continuously on the agenda was the relationship between Pentecostal doctrine and traditional evangelical thought on Christian initiation.

Tyndale House was good for me in that being immersed in the midst of theological questions it stimulated my interest in the Bible and doctrinal issues. The house was also the place where I first felt the promptings of the Holy Spirit towards ordination in the Church of England. Although I thought about other denominations, the Church of England seemed the one on my mind and consequently the one I aimed at.

Throughout this time infant baptism had hardly figured in my thinking but I met one or two Christians who understood believers' baptism in water to be a serious part of Christian initiation. The student who had wanted to lay hands on me for the infilling of the Holy Spirit also urged me to be baptised by total immersion. This I declined as much from fear of the unknown as anything else, but baptism in water seemed to me to be of no great consequence in those early days. What mattered was the personal commitment to Christ and the power of the Holy Spirit. I was not, and never have been, a hundred per cent happy with the Pentecostal theology of a two-step initiation, but of the reality of the experience Pentecostals describe I have never been in doubt. I would prefer to couple it more closely with initiation in general, rather than as some kind of optional deluxe version of the Christian life for high fliers. I caricature slightly, but that is how the neo-Pentecostals were coming over in the mid-sixties.

So when did I become a Christian?

Most of my clergy colleagues would reply unhesitatingly: 'At the font'. Others might say at confirmation when my faith was personally professed. Most evangelicals would say at the time of my commitment to Christ seven years later. Many charismatics might agree with the latter but wouldn't count on it for certain until I had been 'baptised' with the Holy Spirit. I was prepared for confirmation in 1956 by a godly old priest whose faith I coveted but whose instruction I did not understand. At the confirmation the then Bishop of Birmingham (Dr Leonard Wilson) asked us to repeat our answers to the renewal of baptismal vows. 'You don't seem very sure,' he said. 'I will ask you that one again.' He was probably right!

My baptism took place in 1943,[13] my confirmation in 1956. A 'penny dropped' in 1963 and in 1964 I could speak in tongues. In 1965 I felt the beginning of a call to ordination. If I had to single out a transition point I would go for the commitment of 1963 when faith became personal, but the touch of the Holy Spirit seemed essential too. The antecedents of infant baptism and confirmation meant little at the time but looking towards ordination meant seriously coming to terms with the rites of baptism, both infant and adult, and confirmation. How would I do that?

I continued to ponder these questions over the next three years. When at the Naval Engineering College in Plymouth I met and discussed ordination with two Christian naval officers, Lieutenant-Commanders John Summers and Richard Dean.[14] The latter took me out one Sunday afternoon for a walk on the cliffs near Wembury. The grandeur of the South Devon coast was an odd background for a discussion on infant baptism. 'Read Bishop Ryle's *Knots Untied*', Richard urged. 'That will help you through these issues.' It did. Bishop Ryle obviously wrote his book for sailors with a title like that![15]

In October 1966 I joined *HMS Fearless* in Aden. She was the Navy's first assault ship and was on her first commission. The morning after I joined the ship I was visited in my cabin by John Venus, the ship's Anglican chaplain. He and I were to become good friends over the next fifteen months, giving me a chance to talk through ordination and baptismal issues. John let me take one

epilogue a week on the ship's internal broadcast system
so that I could get my hand in. John was a product of
King's College, London, and together with Tony Marks
of *HMS Bulwark* and Arthur Nunnerley of *HMS Hermes*
I got to know how Anglo-Catholics viewed the gospel
and the sacraments. John introduced me to daily communion and compline. In turn John joined the Naval
Christian Fellowship, as did several other naval chap-
lains at that time. NCF was a largely evangelical body
embracing everyone from admirals to junior ratings and
divided only about charismatic renewal. All things being
equal we were a well balanced church in *Fearless*. Our
visits to Hong Kong brought us a never-to-be-forgotten
visit from the late Miss Gladys Aylward. She preached
for fifty minutes at one Sunday morning service and held
us all spellbound and in the presence of God.

But baptism was never far away. One infant baptism
actually took place on board the ship using the ship's bell
as a font. It was pretty much a social occasion with drinks
in the wardroom afterwards to 'wet the baby's head'!
Then I attended the baptism and confirmation of one of
our stokers[16] in Hong Kong cathedral. One day when the
ship was in Singapore naval base, some civilian engineers
joined us to spend a few days on board doing trials on
our main boilers. I discovered that one of them from the
Admiralty department in Bath was a Plymouth Brother.
As we chatted at lunch in the wardroom he said, 'Have
you ever been baptised?'

'Oh yes,' I said, 'as an infant of course.'

'No, I mean properly baptised; christening doesn't
mean anything.'

'Not immersed,' I replied.

'I can go down to the shore and baptise you whenever
you want,' replied the engineer.

'Well, is it necessary?' I asked. 'Isn't faith what
counts?'

'Jesus was baptised and so must we be. It's an important witness.' I declined the offer to be dunked and slid out of the conversation, though we remained good friends.

I remember one evening discussing infant baptism with a naval rating as we walked through the naval base in Singapore. Derek Seber was an NCF member and a committed and convinced Anglican to boot. He was also seeking ordination.

'Infant baptism doesn't make you a Christian,' I remember him saying. 'It is a sacrament, an external rite, but in itself it can't do anything without faith.'

The conversation was timely because in the early part of 1967 I was writing to theological colleges to explore my own call to the Anglican ministry. If accepted I too would have to accept the baptising of infants as a normal part of my ministry. Could I cope with that?

The then principal of Ridley Hall, Michael Hennel, wrote me a warm letter explaining the place of infant baptism in the church. Unfortunately I never really understood what he was on about! However, that didn't deter me from going to ACCM to explore my call to the ministry and later to train at Ridley Hall.

In December 1969 I got married and very early on discovered that my wife Avis too had questions about the efficacy of infant baptism. She had been brought up in regular attendance at the Church of Christ, Saffron Lane, Leicester, where believers' baptism was the norm and infants were dedicated. She was approached in her early teens to see if she was interested in total immersion but declined. Her sister, who was later to become a missionary with Sudan Interior Mission and CMS, went ahead with an immersion baptism. My wife wasn't too sure whether she had been christened as a baby, but if she had been it was likely that it was in a Methodist church. When we met she was worshipping in an evangelical Anglican parish church on a large estate in south

Leicester. Infant baptism had been a subject of discussion between my wife and the curate. The curate conducted his share of the many infant baptisms in the parish but privately admitted to my wife that he didn't really believe in it! When she asked him why he continued to baptise babies his reply was predictable: it was expected of him by virtue of being an ordained minister of the established church.

My question on the eve of theological college was very simple: where did baptism—either infant or adult—fit in to Christian initiation? I could read in the Thirty-nine Articles of the Book of Common Prayer that baptism was generally necessary to salvation. I recited in the Nicene Creed that 'I acknowledge one baptism for the remission of sins.' The theological and practical outworking of fitting those pieces together is the fuel for the rest of this book.

Notes

1. Now Admiral Sir Horace Law.
2. The University Church in the heart of Cambridge.
3. There was usually a meeting to interest all new students. It was known as a 'Freshers' Squash'.
4. The Cambridge Inter-Collegiate Christian Union is a trans-university fellowship of evangelical students numbering several hundred. Quite an influential group in vocations to the mission field.
5. Later to become Vicar of Great St Mary's, then Bishop successively of Kingston and Birmingham.
6. The late Basil Clarkson of Public and Preparatory Schools Camps. These camps, known as PPSC, were held for a number of years at Porthdinlaen in North Wales. The Broads cruises came later.
7. Now Captain Ian Brannam, RN.
8. The 'going-down' sermon was one of the high points

of the CICCU programme of outreach. Much prayer went into this event and it was always viewed as the last chance that undergraduates might have to hear a good gospel sermon before launching out into the world!

9. When I was thirteen I decided to try and study the Bible at home to find out what it really said. Unlike most I decided not to start at Genesis or Matthew, but with the Book of Daniel. If only I had known the complexities of that book then!

10. IVF: The Inter Varsity Fellowship; an overarching affiliative body for Christian students nationally. It is now known as the UCCF: Universities and Colleges Christian Fellowship.

11. John R. W. Stott, *The Baptism and Fullness of the Holy Spirit*, IVF (1964).

12. The Fountain Trust closed down a few years ago. Originally it was set up to promote the rediscovery of the charismatic gifts within the historic denominations and to further the renewal in the Holy Spirit. *Renewal* magazine still continues under the editorship of Edward England and is published from Crowborough, Sussex.

13. I recently asked my mother why she had me christened. She replied:

'I was brought up in a Christian family, my parents had me baptised in infancy and when old enough we attended Sunday school and church. Wherever possible we attended the Church of England Day School. In the growing-up stage I believed most sincerely that the path my parents chose for me to start out in life was correct and I have never had cause to doubt their decision. So when I had children I had no hesitation but to start them out on the same path.'

14. John is now Vicar of St Barnabas, Plymouth, and Commander Richard Dean has recently retired from

the Royal Navy having been a trustee of NCF for some years. With his wife, Rosalind, and Ian and Barbara Brannam (see Note 7 above) they have set up marriage growth weekends.

15. Bishop Ryle was the first evangelical Bishop of Liverpool in 1896.

16. The traditional name of 'stoker' from the days of coaling ship has been retained for the mechanical engineering ratings.

Chapter 2

STOWMARKET BY-PASS

In 1973 the Department of Transport commenced work on a major twelve-mile dual carriageway by-pass for the Suffolk towns of Stowmarket and Needham Market. The days of the long queues of traffic in those towns on the major trunk route from the Midlands to the East Coast ports were numbered. The juggernauts would soon leave the town centres.

But there was another phenomenon that I named 'Stowmarket By-pass', and that referred to the large proportion of families that the church had contact with through baptisms, weddings and funerals, but who by-passed the normal worshipping life of the congregation.

Searching for a first curacy was quite a worry for a number of Ridley Hall colleagues. Some of my friends looked at up to six parishes before making an acceptance or being offered a title. We looked at two: the first, St Andrew's, Plymouth, was my first natural choice. I had worshipped there in my naval days, taken hospital ward services from that church and had several friends down there. The church was beautifully situated at the end of the Royal Parade, had a mildly evangelical style of town-centre ministry and was a good curate's training church. However, the weekend we went to visit the parish it seemed that a dark cloud came down over us and we felt from beginning to end of our visit that God was saying 'No, not this one.'

On the other hand when we visited Stowmarket in East Anglia, from the moment the vicar and his wife opened the vicarage door to welcome us we felt that this might be the place. So it turned out to be. On 30th September 1973 I was made a deacon in the parish church of St Peter and St Mary, Stowmarket, and turned my collar round. My vicar, Arthur Muxlow, had been in the parish for some seventeen years and was just entering an encouraging phase there with the introduction of the church's ministry of healing. Two months prior to my ordination, the late Revd George Bennett, then warden of Crowhurst, had conducted a large healing service in Stowmarket parish church attended by some 400 people. This service was somewhat of a contrast to the more charismatic style of healing rallies that I had witnessed, but nevertheless many were healed and helped through that service.

From that beginning, a new wave of spiritual life started to flow gently through the parish church and out into some of the parishes of Stowmarket Deanery. I think it put fresh heart into my vicar, Arthur, who had laboured hard over the previous fifteen years to see some real spiritual growth in the congregation. A prayer group was restarted and a small ministry team formed around the vicar. We were introduced to Mrs Pat Norcock who had been miraculously healed at a Jean Darnall[1] meeting after twenty-five years in a wheelchair. Her presence and ministry gave the Stowmarket prayer group much encouragement.

As a new curate I was gradually eased into the many and varied tasks of the pastoral ministry. I was not expected to run the youth club (we didn't then have one as such) but encouraged to build a youth fellowship. That eventual group of young people, together with the ecumenical work in the town, proved to be my areas of specialisation and delight. But it was not many weeks before the first christenings came along.

'See me do one,' said Arthur, 'and then you have a go.' Actually 'one' meant a batch of anything from two to six! With no further ado I was thrown in if not at the deep end certainly at the sprinkling end.

The first thing I noticed about the administration of infant baptism at Stowmarket was that it involved quite a large number of people. Three infants with their associated entourages of parents, godparents, family and friends would more than outnumber the main morning congregation in size. Sometimes as many as six infants were baptised in the same service, creating the possibility of an even larger gathering. I noticed that many of the families had gone to some lengths to dress for the occasion and the number of cameras indicated that this was an event of some importance, at least in the eyes of the families. On the other hand it was obvious that many families were relatively unfamiliar with the inside of the church building and an act of worship.

The families were welcomed by Arthur and seated in family blocks in the vicinity of the font. The Series 2 baptism[2] booklets were given out and the service proceeded. Arthur began by saying a few words about keeping the promises and reminded the assembled parents and godparents that they had signified their intention to keep the promises by signing the application form. At Stowmarket, baptism parents had to fill in a fairly searching form and sign a declaration at the end that they intended to honour the commitment they were professing on behalf of their children. Some people obviously hadn't read or understood the small print because there were a few blank stares around on the faces of some godparents and parents when Arthur mentioned the form. It was an expression I have gazed on frequently in the last seventeen years!

The next factor I noted was the noise. Oddly, there appeared to be no correlation between the number of babies and the decibel level. Two babies could make on occasions more noise than six. However many there happened to be, it was extremely difficult to sustain a sense of worship. The majority present were spectators in a family ritual. Nevertheless, the families were obviously grateful that their offspring had now received in christening whatever it was they did receive and all that remained was to let them take the photographs and be ushered out into the market place.

The following month it was my turn. My second son, John, had been born some six months before my ordination and Arthur asked if I might like to take the opportunity to make him my first candidate. Whatever I thought of infant baptism theologically it meant that the first baptism I carried out was obviously going to be special. There was one other child to be baptised in the same service that afternoon, Sarah, and I had the job of visiting the parents. Because it was a special occasion for me it became so for them and a good pastoral relationship was established with that other family which lasted throughout my first curacy. That family came very occasionally to the monthly family service and they had had a previously strong connection with their original home church at Attleborough near Norwich.

As the months rolled by I began to take the majority of baptisms and do the home visits beforehand. Arthur would hand me the month's list of infant baptisms and I would visit the families in turn. I saw little evidence that anything I ever said on those visits made much impression on the families concerned. I did the time-honoured things like trying to explain what baptism was, the promises involved, taking them through the service, checking on godparents; informing them of the Sunday school and family service and other useful points of contact with the church. The reactions I got on visiting these families generally ranged from pleasantness to mild disinterest. In a number of cases the television set was not even switched off to enable a conversation to proceed. Some families were mystified why I had visited them at all since they had 'seen the vicar'.

This is all familiar territory to thousands of parochial clergy and I spell it out here for reasons of empathy or sympathy. However, it was good for me to experience at the start of my ministry the most common scenario of administering infant baptisms to be found in the parishes. It was not long before I began to question the wisdom of handling infant baptisms in this way. I talked to Arthur about it. I remember on one occasion being in the vicarage study when a young mum with a baby came to 'book a christening'. She was well known to Arthur. She had been through Sunday school and Girls' Friendly Society[3], confirmation class and wedding. She was thus a regular customer but not a regular communicant. Her child's baptism date was agreed and entered in the vicarage diary without much ado and the baptismal form was handed to her to fill in and return. But there were others who had serious difficulties filling in the form and declaration. Arthur would often spend up to an hour with people who had difficulties.

I use the word 'customer' advisedly because it encapsulated an observation I couldn't help making of something very basic to the whole syndrome of dealing with baptism requests. They are issued from the standpoint of the customer going to the shop to ask as a matter of right for the goods advertised in the window. The customer needs to buy and the vendor glad to dispense. It seemed like that with baptismal requests. Isn't this what we do on our church noticeboards? 'Baptisms, weddings and funerals by arrangement with the vicar.' We do in a very real sense advertise the service we provide and I wondered if the fault actually lay with me in being surprised at the customer's approach. After all we appeared to have set it up. Wesley Carr in his excellent book *Brief Encounters* says: 'One thing is sure. If for centuries the church has insisted on the baptism of infants, actively persued parents to have it done, and urged it as a duty to God and to the child, it is not possible to reverse that teaching by a mere change of doctrinal stance.'[4] Wesley probably overstates it here but I take the point he is making. I doubt however if it would be true to say that the church during the last fifty years has gone out in search of the un-baptised.

Still, at Stowmarket I was concerned. I said to Arthur, 'Could we not invite the baptismal parents to a main service so that they can see a normal act of worship, especially the family service?'

'Ah, no; not really,' he replied. 'If you do that you will decimate your baptisms.' I wondered what he meant by this. Did it matter if baptisms were decimated? He meant of course in numerical terms. Obviously Arthur believed it was important to meet this steady demand for christenings but to what eventual purpose I could not see. With few exceptions I hardly saw anyone added to the ongoing life of the parish church as a direct result of having an infant baptised. All had professed repentance of their sins, turned to Christ and renounced evil but because of some greater inertia which I could not yet discern, any link between their afternoon christening and the morning worship of the faithful simply didn't register in their minds.

The reader will have gleaned that baptisms were administered 'en masse' on a Sunday afternoon (usually the first in the month). A conservative estimate of the numbers resident in the parish and passing through the church from these afternoon christenings alone in any one year might be around 500. The regular congregation from three services on a Sunday would have been around 150; 200 if you were to include the Sunday schools and youth groups. In church growth terms you could look at the fringe of the church, ie, at one of the concentric circles around the regular worshipping core of the congregation, as the most likely source of new regulars. Each year, through baptisms, the ministers of the church were likely to contact a pastoral fringe three times the size of the regular congregation.[5] Purely as mathematical speculation: if we assume 50 baptisms per year and reckon 200 parents and godparents make the promises, then even working on a figure of 5 per cent 'success' rate that would mean 10 new members would start to come into regular worship each year, with the congregation doubling in 10 years.

Is that the growth rate we experienced? I fear it was not. The growth rate from baptism contacts was not an absolute zero. There were tokens of response here and there. However, these were so infrequent as to convince me that we were doing little more than scratching the surface.

These figures did not take into account the numbers passing through the church for weddings and funerals. It was possible to console oneself with the fact that the latter two offices were not ostensibly offering a sacrament of initiation, at least not into the visible church! Yet I felt that the way the occasional offices were handled were bound to have an effect on the general ambience of the church and hence its possibilities of growing. The 'Stowmarket by-pass' was a real phenomenon, and it demanded and received a large slice of pastoral time and energy for a very small return on investment. I am sure the question must have occurred to most clergy at some time in their ministries who recognise the phenomenon I am describing, whether it is right before God and man to allow such a state of affairs to roll on unchallenged.

Baptism is still a technical requirement for at least one of the parties to a wedding in church, and also for a body to be buried in consecrated ground. As long as these requirements exist and clergy feel they must give more than token adherence to extracting them from people, so long will the inertia of ministering to the majority of the population through occasional offices persist in this time-honoured fashion. Mothers probably dream of 'white church weddings' for their offspring and cannot tolerate the thought of granddad missing out in some odd way at his funeral. The departure from established ritual norms is somehow regarded with fear. Those of us who would contemplate reforming infant baptism soon discover that we are not merely making some logical pastoral adjustment to accord more closely with a sharper theology of baptism, but we are trying to pull a rug out from under the essential rituals of life . . . or so it appears.

Meanwhile, I was slowly gaining in confidence in the sheer mechanics of baptising babies. Not under or over-splashing them, learning to rock them gently into quietness if they so much as murmured. I gently filled out the service with my own talk and explanations, left the parents and godparents in no doubt about their responsibilities. At least I thought I had. I carried out one piece of experiment without my vicar's permission: I placed the collection plate at the door as they went out and mentioned it as a free will offering! I invariably found it collected more than when the 'rugby ball into the scrum' approach was used.[6] After a couple of tries at this I reported it to Arthur who invariably asked if I had had a good baptism and what was the size of the collection!

On one liturgical point, Arthur and I were at one. Neither of us was happy to give a newly baptised infant a lighted candle with the words 'To show that you have passed from death unto life.' Our consciences were uneasy at this point and betrayed our deep evangelical convictions that we were unhappy with a simple doctrine of baptismal regeneration. Spiritual regeneration almost invariably came later when the child was of an age to decide for itself. To give lighted candles was a dangerous symbolism which seemed to reinforce in the minds of the families the very notions from which we wanted to prise them away.

But what about the years of discretion? There was always a steady trickle of confirmation candidates coming through the church. I noticed immediately that the majority were linked already to regular worshipping families, and the first group I had were to knit together with other young Christians in the town, especially the Methodists. They organised a number of useful activities, ran youth services and eventually played a major part in the evangelistic musical *Come Together* by Jimmie and Carol Owens. These young people probably didn't realise what encouragement they gave me in my first curacy. To me they proved one basic theory, that if a group of people could be held together of their own free will for long enough in a warm fellowship, with steady Christian influence and teaching, then several would come to a sincere and tangible (to them) faith in Jesus Christ. On the whole, confirmation training suggested itself as a useful training ground, a priority area for development in church growth, but there was another side to it.

I never forgot a story told by the Bishop of St Edmundsbury and Ipswich when he visited our Deanery Chapter one day.[7] He related how he called without warning at a Suffolk country vicarage, and found the vicar in tears.

'I've just been looking through the pages of my confirmation register,' explained the vicar. 'I've been here several years, and confirmed many people, and I cannot think of one person in that confirmation register who is now a regular communicant.' Clearly that man's heart was broken over that particular issue. That account has remained indented upon my memory ever since. I have observed over the years that the situation described by the bishop is perilously close to the truth in a large number of parishes.

Apart from moving the collection plate to the exit door at Sunday afternoon christenings, I took my first faltering step towards baptismal reform at Stowmarket by raising some of the issues at Deanery Chapter. The Deanery Chapter is the gathering of Anglican clergy from about fifteen or so parishes. They normally meet about ten times a year for business, discussion, reflection and to hear outside speakers.

In 1974 the Ely Report on Christian Initiation was being debated by dioceses and deaneries. The clergy chapter decided to give the subject of baptism a 'going over' first, before Stowmarket Deanery Synod did. (The synod includes elected lay members from the various Parochial Church Councils meetings and these meetings normally take place in an evening.) The clergy chapter were an interesting bunch, and I think that I soon discovered why any form of baptismal reform in the Church of England takes an inordinate amount of time! The Ely Report on Christian Initiation had raised a cluster of questions to be sent down to the deaneries. The crucial question at the centre seemed to hinge on the matter of choice and preparation. Should infant baptism continue to be available to all those who requested it or should it be restricted to those parents who in some sense showed evidence that they could keep the promises? (See Chapter 9.)

To me, with all of twelve months experience of baptising babies behind me, the very question raised by the Ely Report appeared as a bright morning star of possible reformation.

'But are we not bidden to seek out the unbaptised?' said one elderly clergyman.[8]

'We ought to have all baptisms in main services,' said another.

'That may be convenient for us, but not for the parents and godparents,' came the retort.

'I think it is wrong to be unwelcoming.'

'They ought to know what they're doing, we must teach them.'

'A seed is sown in baptism and who are we to limit God?'

'I could never refuse a baptism, it would be entirely wrong.'

It was a wide-ranging debate, but I was disappointed by the response in general. I had added my comments on twelve months' experience and suggested that some form of mandatory preparation of a challenging kind should be required of parents. My remarks didn't pass unnoticed, but were probably regarded as a new curate's idealism and were soon sunk by the heavy salvoes of the proven experience of the rest of the chapter. Finally one elderly clergyman of an evangelical persuasion said that the problem wasn't baptism at all; it was nominal Christianity!

'If only we had a few more real Christians about and fewer nominal ones, baptism would sort itself out.' He was to my mind both correct and at the same time missed the whole point. However, the discussion was inconclusive and everyone went home with his status quo intact.

When the issues were debated by the Deanery Synod a few weeks later, the result was the same. The subject had an airing but no changes were made to the existing and time-honoured practice of offering baptism to all who requested. My impression was that the laity were not really aware of the complex issues that the clergy had to handle in pastoring baptismal enquiries. Also there was the feeling that the training and nurture of young people through Sunday school to confirmation was entirely the responsibility of the church. Thus it was largely the fault of the PCC, incumbent and congregation for failing to attract the families of those infants who had been baptised. There is some truth here, but to fail to recognise parental responsibility in the matter is, to my mind, to duck the whole crucial issue at the outset and to spike all possibility of serious baptismal reform.

Throughout my two and three quarter years at Stowmarket, I didn't have to handle the initial enquiry for a baptism. The few I received were passed on to the incumbent without further ado. I was not at liberty to tinker with the system in any way. However, in Post Ordination Training (known also as 'potty training') I had a dry run at handling baptismal enquiries.

POT usually lasts for a curate's first three years and is a continuation of his general training. We looked at a wide range of topics from counselling the bereaved and marriage preparation to personal prayer life and young people's ministry. It was not long before baptism and confirmation had their turn on the agenda.[9] In the baptism session we were asked to indulge in role play for two different situations. In the first situation a baptismal enquirer came to a vicar who was meant to be conscientious about baptism preparation. In the second situation the same enquirer came to a vicar who would baptise anything that moved! I was detailed to act the role of the conscientious vicar. Of course my curate colleague tended to overact, as the temptation is on these occasions, but the roleplay was a harbinger of things to come.

Enquirer: Good morning, vicar. I've called to see you because my wife has just had a new baby and we'd like her christened. When could you do it?
Vicar: Now, wait a moment. Who did you say you were? Have you lived in the parish long? Have you worshipped anywhere regularly before?
E: ...just a minute, vicar. I've come along to ask you to christen our new baby. I don't see what all these questions have got to do with it.

V: Well there's a lot to talk over when we christen a baby, particularly your own understanding of the faith and the promises you will be making. You will of course realise that I would like you to join us particularly at the family services.

E: I'm not a regular churchgoer. I just want my baby christened.

V: Well what do you think christening is?

E: My child is meant to be welcomed by the church and I think you are being unwelcoming.

V: No. I'm not being unwelcoming; you are showing me that you are not really too aware of what the faith is about and you're not very keen on listening. (The atmosphere of confrontation grows.) Before I christen your baby I really would like you to think with me about what it all means.

E: Look, vicar, I don't really want to know what your views are. I've got my own ideas. Now, when can I have my baby christened?

V: Mr Jones, before I arrange the christening I really do want to know that you have grasped something of the Christian faith and the gospel...

E: Are you telling me that unless I spend time in instruction you will not christen my baby?

V: Well...er...in one sense, yes.

E: Right, if you are not willing to christen my baby...(angrily and finally)...then I know a vicar who will. Good day to you!

The enquirer stomps off.

It was only role play but it was very useful. I suppose it represented the worst possible case. In reality I have never quite had to deal with any baptismal enquirer as difficult as my actor fellow curate, though several have run him a close second!

Having left me with egg all over my face, my curate colleague then acted the part of the vicar at the other end of the spectrum and I was the enquirer.

E: (rather gently) Good morning, vicar. My wife's had a new baby; would it be possible to have it christened?

V: Of course my friend. Let them all come!

E: Sorry. I couldn't hear what you said. Could you repeat that.

V: Suffer the little children. We never turn any away!

E: I'm afraid that I don't go to church.

V: Don't let a little thing like that worry you. God's grace is for all! Now when would you like the christening?

E: As soon as possible really. It's really my wife's mother who wants it done. She says the sooner you get them christened the more chance they have of going to heaven if anything happens to them. Is that right?

V: Don't worry about it! We will sprinkle and God will do the rest...

By now the audience was beginning to chuckle and so were we. We called it a day. Everyone seemed to sense that the first role play scenario was closer to reality than the latter.

'The point is,' interjected our POT director, 'you cannot earn baptism. What you have to do is to try and unpack some of the truth for them.'

'Quite,' I thought. 'That was precisely what I was trying to do.'

As my days at Stowmarket drew to a close I was grateful that I had had the chance to work in an interesting and attractive country market town in rural Suffolk. I perceived that the work of the ministry was engaged at several different levels which I thought of as concentric circles. The inner core of the church was beginning to experience the fresh breath of new spiritual life, principally through the healing ministry and its associated prayer group. Then there were the church officers, such as the director of music, churchwardens and deputy wardens. The third circle was the PCC and group leaders. Then outside these was the regular congregation. The occasional worshippers formed the next concentric circle and then right on the edge were the outsiders who only passed through the church for baptisms, weddings and funerals.

A vast amount of pastoral time and energy was put

into this latter group, but for all that, it appeared to remain the 'Stowmarket by-pass'. I would have loved the chance to make some attempts to engage with that group more seriously and to try to win them into closer church membership, but it was not to be. My chance would come when I moved somewhere else.

Notes

1. The Revd Jean Darnall, an American minister and author of some early charismatic books, eg *Heaven Here I Come!*

2. I never encountered a book of Common Prayer baptism until 1990!

3. The GFS was a very influential group in the church. I have not come across it since Stowmarket except when I saw a display stand at the National Christian Resources Exhibition some three years ago, and assume the movement is still going strong.

4. See Wesley Carr's *Brief Encounters* (SPCK: 1985), p 67.

5. The whole church growth movement has taught us to analyse our congregations with reality and has helped us to see that while growth is not an exact science it may be approached in this way with profit. See *What Makes Churches Grow*, by the Bible Society.

6. Our method of taking up the offertory at Stowmarket was to hand the plate into the front row of the family blocks. The first time I did it my vicar asked me to make sure it came out the other end!

7. The Rt Revd Dr Leslie Brown, former Archbishop of Uganda.

8. See the rubrics in the Book of Common Prayer before the baptism service.

9. My original POT Director was the late Jack Church-
   ill, former Dean of Carlisle. Jack always set essays!
   He was succeeded by Canon Denis Pain who insisted
   we tackled the coal face pastoral issues.

Chapter 3

A NEW TOWN

In January 1976 we received a letter from a rector inviting us to look at the possibility of working with him in Bordon, East Hampshire. Bordon was part of the parish of All Saints, Headley, which at the turn of the century was one of the largest parishes in area in England, stretching from Grayshott near Hindhead, Surrey (just off the A3), over to the sandy military heathland, midway between Farnham and Petersfield. The area sounded extremely pleasant and so it looked at first sight. While the area was largely rural, the parish contained a surprisingly large and varied population— 15,000 or so, ranging from admirals to Romanies, the latter category being more numerous than the first! The parish contained the whole spectrum of housing, from the spacious villas in woodland surroundings to the large council estates, and from the modern suburban retired bungalow estates to the shoe-box private dwellings for first-time buyers.

Bordon was situated at the western edge of the parish, separated by the River Wey from Headley to the east. Not only was the river a boundary between communities, but the only way across the river was through a deep ford at Headley Mill and this effectively meant that motor traffic had to take a two-mile detour to reach the centre of the original parish.

But geography wasn't the main separation factor. Sociologically Bordon had an odd feel to it (see Chapter 13 for detailed theories on this). Not only did it have the bulk of the council housing and smaller private housing, but it had a large number of temporary-style dwellings— like corrugated tin shacks. In addition, there were woodland clearings where large caravan and mobile home sites had been.[1] These sites had been the refuge of many families in semi-deprived conditions over the years, and a large number of 'travelling people' had settled there. Unofficially Bordon was recognised as the travellers' home.

The place itself beggared description. It was not a village, not a town. Probably it was best described as a settlement. It nestled under the shadow of the Army Garrison, which was the home of the School of Electrical and Mechanical Engineering. Army artificers came to SEME from the Commonwealth armies. Over the years we were to welcome many Army Christians to worship, particularly from West Africa.

The principal difficulty of Bordon was that it had an identity problem. People were arguing throughout the whole of my thirteen years there over nomenclature. Bordon was originally the Army camps and some said that the old original name of 'Deadwater' should be retained. It lay in the civil parish of Whitehill, and others said that the whole area should be named after Whitehill, which lies about one mile south of Bordon. By whatever name the people who lived in 'Deadwater' wished to call it, this didn't alter the fact that for social life they tended to look to Whitehill, the Army Camp, and turn to Farnham or Headley for community needs. Deadwater itself had a distinct feeling of being a sociological vacuum. That is not a derogatory comment upon the people who lived there—in fact it was to be home for me for thirteen years—but it was a factor which one ignored at one's peril when trying to build a church.

In 1969 Alton Rural District Council[2] decided to draw up and implement what was known as the Bordon Village Plan, which would double or treble the existing population. The Rector of Headley, Derek Head, wisely consulted with the Guildford diocesan pastoral committee about the creation of a new clergyman post in Bordon. This was necessary not only because of the numbers, but because the development brief included diagramatic plans in the new shopping centre for a new church. From the outset it was intended by the rector that, if possible, any new Christian work should be done ecumenically.

It was into this interesting community that my wife and I settled with our boys in July 1976. I was fortunate to have served under Arthur Muxlow at Stowmarket, and equally fortunate now to work with Derek Head in my second curacy at Headley. I learned much from both of them. The regular weekly staff meeting was an important sharing point for the three of us (there was a curate in the centre of Headley parish as well) and the distinctive phrase which stayed in my mind from those early months was 'careful pastoral work'. Indeed 'pastoral evangelism' was the declared and agreed strategy for our work in the parish. In practice, this meant meeting people at their point of need, as well as treating all people equally, whatever their social background, and seeing each pastoral encounter as a possible spiritual step forward for the client. This seemed to apply to all whether in the worshipping congregation or not.

All Saints Parish Church, Headley, in 1976 was a pretty strong church. Although it was rural (so called) it gathered 120 communicants on alternate Sundays and it appeared to me to be one of the best attended churches I had yet seen. Its youth fellowship and Pathfinders group were strong and there was a sizeable core of families in regular worship and in active leadership, with teenagers and a large section of newly retired. On the surface it was a success story, but the population was fairly large, there was no substantial 'competition' from other denominations,[3] and significantly hardly anyone from the council estates came to church.

However, at St Mark's, Bordon, it was a different story. Opened in December 1955 in a wooden dual purpose building on the edge of a new council estate, its congregation had never been large. One Christmas day in the late 1950s only five people attended the Christmas Communion service, and one of those five was the retired Bishop of Peterborough who was leading the service!

For a period after that the congregation had come up to thirty or forty under the dynamic leadership of the Revd Adrian Voysey, when the whole church was propelled into a door-to-door visiting campaign. Out of that effort came a choir and a number of confirmation candidates, but sadly after he left the congregation dwindled. By the 1970s, the congregation was centred upon a faithful core of ten to fifteen people, mainly female, who were totally committed to keeping the church going come what may. When the Bordon Village Plan was published in 1969 and John Weyman became Bordon's first resident priest-in-charge in 1974, new heart and vision started to take root in the remnant congregation. By 1976 when I moved in, the congregation had already risen to around twenty-five. One of the things my predecessor had instituted was baptism in the 'wooden hut'. Previously all baptisms had taken place in the 'proper church' at Headley; so I inherited a brand new baptismal register with the names of seven infants in it.

This was the first point of baptismal policy discussion

in the parish staff meeting, and I was soon to discover how strongly people felt about the importance of the look of the building for the validity of the occasion. (At Stowmarket, of course, it had never been a problem with one town centre church.)

The first christening requests started to trickle in not long after I did and at that stage the requests were treated carefully in accordance with policy with no hint of condition or preparation, other than a home visit. Perhaps because I was a new vicar, and people thought I was a 'soft touch', a number were rather more courageous about asking to have babies baptised at the parish church, rather than in St Mark's. From the first day I always asked if they had considered a christening in the wooden church which was 'the local church that we are trying to build up'. Most said, 'Oh, I didn't know that: yes that's a nice idea, but we really did want the next one christened at Headley because the first one was "done" there and we were married there.' I had to grow accustomed to this over the years. The rector also tried gently to encourage baptism families who lived in Bordon towards worship in St Mark's, but with minimal results. Here and there we did see a trickle of new baptised infants and parents coming to worship at St Mark's, but they rarely stayed with us for long.

I quickly discovered at Bordon that if we are serious about drawing new families into church, the worship needs to have a certain quality which interests and captures the new visitor, not only so that he feels welcomed, but also so that he leaves a service with a conviction that there is a dimension to life that he has been missing and feels sufficiently intrigued to come back.[4] Older members of congregations need to be patient with family services and brighter styles of presentation in order to draw people in. Fortunately at St Mark's most of the original congregation came to everything and so it wasn't a problem. However, it was three or four years before the worship had reached the quality which I knew would communicate something to anyone who walked through the door.

Meanwhile the first three or four years in the parish of Headley and Bordon did little to uproot me from the conviction I had grown at Stowmarket, that the 'by-pass' phenomenon of baptisms and weddings was something that needed attending to. Headley parish was slightly more successful than Stowmarket in seeing people drawn into regular worship, or at least to a monthly family service, but only by a short head.

A few baptisms took place in main services at Headley, especially where a regular church family had a new baby, but the majority took place at 3.30 on the first Sunday afternoon in the month. On some months a second service of baptisms was held at 4.15 pm to accommodate the numbers, as we had decided to limit the number of families to three at any one service. The first baptismal service which I attended with Derek, my rector, in the autumn of 1976 was of the pretty packed, high decibel variety! I remember Derek, who was quite tall, attempting to stand on a pew half way down the church to try and get some sort of order at the beginning of the service, let alone a sense of worship. Indeed that was one skill which seemed to be a *sine qua non* of conducting multiple infant baptisms: class control!

On that first occasion, Derek came back into the vestry at the end of the service remarking with his grand sense of humour: 'I'm no Billy Graham!' Actually he did quite well.

It was the general unawareness of a sense of worship or occasion or more simply the lack of reverence for the house of God which first caused us to share our concern at staff meeting, about how we should conduct infant baptisms. It was obvious that if the service of infant baptism was to be seen for what it was, a sacrament of initiation into the Body of Christ, then more preparation of individual parents would be needed. We gave much care to welcoming the families, pointing out what regular groups and services there were in the parish, but most of it apparently fell on deaf ears.

One thing we were quite strict about was that we rarely administered baptism apart from the advertised times. Occasionally a family would drag its feet at the thought of having to have their infant baptised with other families, but we persisted, mainly out of logistic convenience.[5] We did note one interesting consequence of this however. Certain families were slightly anxious over whom the other families in the baptismal service might be. A couple in charge of the guest list at their child's christening, who chose those who would join them for 'their' occasion, suddenly found themselves thrust into the same service with two other families whom they may not have known or even liked! For this reason and others we made a point of telling a baptism family whom they would be sharing the service with. I always introduced the families to each other at the beginning of the service, stating where they lived, what husbands did for a living (unless one was unemployed, in which case we gave it a miss) and to create an atmosphere of acceptance and oneness. Nevertheless I have to admit that on some occasions we did some social engineering and deliberately grouped certain families together, where we knew they would gell more easily. That was at the parish church.

Meanwhile a steady trickle of baptisms were coming through St Mark's Church (the wooden church in Bordon), and most of these were unforced and nearly always took place in the main service. Many families were pleasantly surprised by the welcome they received and the quality of the worship. Some knew virtually no hymns other than 'Crimond' and 'Abide with me', and were taken aback joyfully by the modern hymns and songs. 'This isn't like any other christening I've been to, but I have enjoyed it' was a frequent remark. Neither had many heard much live Christian preaching before, or heard anyone other than the vicar pray in a service. But even at Bordon, where we have a policy of urging all baptisms into the main services, there were still a few who specifically asked and virtually demanded to have them in the afternoon. Most of the time the request was granted but once that particular mould was broken and a precedent created it became that much harder to enforce. After 1982, when the new church was built and the population of the new town had increased considerably, so naturally did the number of requests for baptism. It then became almost logistically impossible to have all the baptisms in main services and the wheel turned full circle. In fact several of the regular congregation complained that 'whenever it is a family service and you are taking it we get all these baptisms of people we don't know'. Baptism had become in fact something of a bore to the growing congregation. They wanted to be fed and taught. Music groups and Sunday school wanted time and space in the family services to develop their ideas. At almost every service I was bidding for time to do a batch of christenings for strangers they might not see again. The answer was the second service specifically geared to baptism with a short address and hymns, lasting some thirty minutes. We usually held it at 11.30 immediately after the coffee bar time following the main service. It was a solution for the time being.[6]

On the whole baptisms brought expressions of thanks from the next of kin as they left the church, and from time to time letters were received thanking us for the way in which the service had been conducted. Whatever it was these families wanted in bringing their infants to baptism, some were obviously getting it! The feedback was encouraging, and something of what was said in the baptism addresses was getting across because occasionally a family would appear again at a normal service.

From these few we even started to get the first glimmer of interest in confirmation. However, these were the exceptions. On the whole we were dealing with the secular society and we felt that something more was required by way of preparation before the baptism. We pondered in staff meetings about what that something should be, and worried even more as to whether people would comply with any additional demands we might make. We toyed seriously with the idea of requiring families to come once to a main church service, but like a swimmer dithering on the edge of a cold swimming pool, we stepped back from that brink for the time being. We finally settled for the baptism parents' group.

This turned out to be a fairly successful first step. Upon initial enquiry a family would be invited to attend a baptism parents' evening. The key to the operation was not to give them a date for the baptism either over the telephone or at the front door of the rectory. This tended to send slight alarm signals to them, because usually a parent would retort with, 'But can you let us know when the christening will be, because we have got to send out the invitations and some of our folk have to come a long way.' We would reassure them that a date would be fixed at the parents' evening. Often we were asked if it would make any difference to let them have a date on the spot. Quietly but firmly we resisted, explaining that we would make the arrangements at the preparation evening and explain something of the meaning of baptism and the promises they would have to make.

Two important points need to be made here. One is that the decision to try out this new policy was made collectively in staff meeting and agreed unanimously. Secondly, we were more nervous than the families! The PCC were informed as to what we hoped to do and their support was readily given. The groups were intended to last about an hour and be held separately for the opposite ends of the parish. Those families who lived east of the River Wey attended a preparation group at Headley rectory. Those west of the river (ie, in Bordon) attended a group either at my house or, after Christmas 1982, in the new ecumenical church in the shopping centre.

The first thing that surprised me in the Bordon groups was the good attendance. We would invite both parents to attend the group, and over the initial two-year period around 80% attendance was achieved. From time to time only one parent could attend and frequently it was just the father. Now and again my wife would look after the infant in the back room while parents were in the front at the group. I can only think of two families who resisted firmly coming to a group. One was a quiet but firm refusal and I reluctantly gave them a date for the baptism. The other family said, 'What's this group about?' When I had explained, the father replied, 'Oh, if it's RE I don't need to come as I done it all at school'! Reluctantly I gave them a date for the baptism. Derek, my rector, was not too amused by my being weak with these two families because it had the effect of undermining the policy. If exceptions were made, precedents were created and life was made harder all round for the clergy team. But generally speaking the groups got off to a good start.

I would split up the hour into four sections. The first part was a brief introduction, followed by the brainstorm. About twenty minutes were then given to a short Bible study and the last fifteen minutes to making arrangements for the actual baptisms.

The introduction was extremely useful. I would pick on any useful opening gambit: the new church building, how we designed it, the novelty of sharing with other denominations (see Chapter 8), how we intended to build a new vicarage one day, why did I become a vicar, etc. The effect was to put families at ease and open up to them this whole ecclesiastical world of which 95% knew little. Conversely it enabled me to estimate how and where to pitch the rest of the evening. In terms of relationship formation it was good.

The brainstorm usually began with 'What is baptism?' or an equivalent question. As usual the whole gamut of replies came trotting out, but it was interesting how many did realise that in some sense it involved being made a member of the church with consequent responsibilities. They may not have used these terms but this was what was meant. From here one often got on to 'You don't have to go to church to be a Christian' and allied shiboleths! Often (usually a father) would admit that he wasn't a believer, but was going along with it for the wife and child's sake. I then asked them what they thought the gospel was and I received interesting but predictable answers: 'doing good', 'believing in God', 'God loves everybody', 'showing kindness'. I hardly ever pursued these comments to the point of confrontation but made the transition as naturally as I could to stage three: the Bible study.

This was for most a new experience. I would introduce them to the Good News Bible, help them to find certain passages and explain the origin of baptism.[7] Usually the ensuing silence said it all! However, we then finally got down to the making of the arrangements for the great day and everyone went home happy in anticipation.

One other feature we introduced into the groups after a while was either a couple or other lay person from the congregation. This had three beneficial effects. Firstly, it immediately helped to break down for the baptism parents the 'church = vicar syndrome'. Secondly, it strengthened the teaching about baptism being given by adding in the lay person's point of view and perhaps their testimony of faith. Lastly, if the lay person happened to be on the PCC it kept the latter body aware and informed of how the policy was working. Headley were better at including the laity than I was in Bordon.

Lastly, I tried out at Bordon the step of recording my Bible study talk on cassette which I later had copies made of for wider use. I used the recording in the group and on a couple of occasions let the lay pastoral assistant (Gerald Hudson) take the evening on his own if I couldn't be available.

So, how effective were these groups, and how could we measure the result? In an exact sense of course it is difficult, but I think one can tell when one is entering into communication with people and something is registering. Though the vast majority of the families never worshipped regularly, their Christian knowledge and awareness of 'church' wasn't an absolute zero. Derek Head summed it up best with his words: 'The trouble is that these families start so far back.'

That was precisely our problem: how to bring these families to such a starting point that their understanding of the sacrament of baptism and its relationship to the gospel would leave them, and us, with a good chance of spiritual advance after the christening.

Notes

1. My predecessor at Bordon, John Weyman, served his curacy at All Saints, Headley, and then afterwards became Bordon's first resident priest-in-charge. John was instrumental in liaising with the local authorities for the moving of the caravan sites and the rehousing of many of the families into the new homes. John and I first met in *HMS Bulwark* in 1967.
2. Later to be absorbed into the East Hampshire District Council. (Offices at Petersfield.)
3. Stowmarket had six other very strong churches. A

quarter of the town was in some form of regular church membership.
4. See Chapter 15: 'Rural Postscript'.
5. See Wesley Carr, *Brief Encounters* page 70f. Carr brings out the point that the christening is primarily perceived as an event between the church and the family (SPCK: 1985).
6. I obtained the shape of this service from the Revd Michael Sellors of Hale, near Farnham, who held a monthly 'festal' baptism, but in the afternoons. Many other clergy seem to have come back to this form but it is important to have members of the congregation stay on for it.
7. The four passages I used were Matthew 28:16–end (The Great Commission); Acts 2:36–41 (aftermath of Pentecost); Acts 9:17–22 (Paul's baptism); Acts 16:25–34 (the Philippian jailer).

Chapter 4

GETTING THEM TO CHURCH

I remember reading in the newsletter of St Edmundsbury and Ipswich Diocese some words that have
imprinted themselves upon my memory over the years.
The article was about mission and church growth and the
question was put: 'Ought we to continue to go on invest-
ing money and ministry into situations which have a long
tradition of non-response?'.

I was aware that St Mark's, Bordon, was probably just
that kind of situation. It could soak up years of ministry
with not too much to show for it at the end, in terms of a
reasonably sized, spiritually aware congregation; what I
might call a 'live' church. It has to be said that the
original wooden dual-purpose building set on the edge of
Bordon's first small council estate was no architectural
draw! It was functional and regarded primarily by the
locals as a hall rather than a church. Yet when its furni-
ture was re-arranged for Sunday worship and the sanctuary doors were opened, it did make a very pleasant and
conducive atmosphere for worship. Being situated in one
of the play areas of the estate, it meant that during
worship we often had to compete with noisy games being
played just outside the church windows, and worse still

the local lads would practise motor bike scrambling on their untaxed and un-MOTed machines!

It was to this building that we sought to draw people for Christian worship. When the Bordon Village Plan was announced in 1969 and the projected population growth demanded a considered mission response from the parish of Headley, it was realised that any Anglican advance must start from St Mark's. It was also decided that the projected new church in the shopping centre should be an interdenominational project. So it was that the co-operation of other denominations was sought in the venture. It was the United Reformed church and the Methodist church who were eventually to join the project on a formal basis, but there had been for some time a Free Baptist group which shared the wooden church with us. They were eventually to build their own church but for a while a number of projects were undertaken with the Anglicans, such as Sunday school, young people's work and the occasional swapping of preachers. We were sad when they decided that they were unable to come into any joint venture for a Baptist insight would have been a very interesting element to have.

Their presence in the same building meant that there was a certain amount of cross fertilisation between congregations and a number of people would worship at both the morning Anglican/Free Church[1] service and the evening Baptist service. The Baptists did an excellent piece of work with a small group of teenagers. Several young people in Bordon owe their faith to the hard work of the pastor and his wife at that time.[2] However, on the whole numbers were relatively small in the late 70s: twenty to thirty on an average Sunday morning rising to possibly forty for a family service. The first time fifty human beings entered the building for the Mothering Sunday service I realised that the age of miracles wasn't over!

On the whole, however, the gaining of one extra

regular worshipper was a hard won thing. As Bordon grew, most of the people who would have worshipped regularly in their former towns might come looking for the church and stay with us for a couple of weeks before looking for something brighter and more established. We had to elicit a sense of vocation and commitment out of people soon after they arrived, in order to keep them with us, otherwise they would be off. Much of early growth we saw in the late 70s was a kind of 'vocational transfer growth'.[3] There was also, as Mothering Sunday showed, a sign that our baptismal work was not entirely falling on deaf ears.

As we turned into the 1980s, the knowledge that the new church building would soon be ready brought some enthusiasm into the work of St Mark's. Numbers steadily grew and by the time the new church was opened in November 1982 a congregation of some forty or so regulars had established itself. The coming of the new church was one factor, the population growth another. The reality of the ecumenical commitment was an important factor too. In December 1980 a formal Sharing Agreement and Constitution were signed in a special service in the wooden church linking the Anglicans, Methodists and the United Reformed churches in a common mission based on a single new church building. One of the principles we adopted early on was that if the Local Ecumenical Project was to have any value then each denomination must be able to identify its own brand of worship somewhere in the total package of services on offer. Generally speaking it worked.

One morning in my daily prayers I received a 'word from the Lord'. It was simply 'stricter baptismal policy'. I do not want to discuss at length the phenomenon of receiving guidance from God, particularly so called 'words of knowledge' and 'words of wisdom', but suffice it to say that I was fairly sure that God, the Holy Spirit, was leading me to work towards a tightening of the baptismal policy.[4] How precisely I was to do that I wasn't sure.

At about this time I had my first taste of baptismal hostilities, while we were happily working on our preparation group's policy. I now forget the details of how it arose, but one family who had applied for the baptism of their infant was informed that we would include them in one of the parents' groups that we had started and that we would arrange the baptism from there. When told that the group would take place at my house in Bordon there was an insistence that the baby should be baptised in the 'proper' church, by which they meant the parish church at Headley. This we gladly consented to as long as the family attended the local preparation group in Bordon. Once again they objected, so we asked them to attend the group at Headley. I then asked the family to attend a family service in St Mark's wooden church to get a taste of our local worship and I suggested it as an alternative to attending a group. Strictly speaking I was not keeping faith with my clergy colleagues in that I had diverged from our agreed policy. At this stage I was negotiating with the mother of the child, who by now was clearly beginning to dig her heals in. My anger was rising at the increasing resistance of the parent to come to anything. That evening the father telephoned me and the confrontation worsened. He said he had had a previous infant baptised in another parish without 'all this fuss' and that his mother was 'disgusted' at our parish's attitude! When I refused to give him the address of my superior other than my rector, Derek, he hung up.

In the event nothing happened except that a few days later the baby's grandma phoned (the one who was 'disgusted') to put the case for the baby's baptism. It was good that she phoned and I gave myself seven out of ten for the pastoral healing that followed. Effectively I explained what we were trying to do in the parish and why we had instituted our preparation policy. That conversation ended amicably and I hadn't really shifted my position.

The morning after the phone call from the father I felt it important to write to him setting out the position and trying to restore a peaceful relationship. Part of that letter read:

> We welcome all parents to our church and treat each baptism request seriously. The demands we ask of parents before the baptism of children in this parish are quite minimal compared to many parishes: one family preparation group and an act of worship with the local church. The idea of the latter is that families become acquainted with the local worshipping church where they live. We have never insisted that parents become regular weekly worshippers before accepting their children for baptism. Most are not. But we do strongly insist that parents work towards this eventually so that they may truly bring up their children in the Christian Faith...

I felt it imperative that I shared the experience of the clash that I had had on that particular baptism contact as soon as possible with the rector. He decided that the wisest course of action was to go ahead and fix the baptism as they requested at the parish church, but he insisted that they came to a group at Headley first. A date was given to them for the baptism and I was detailed to revisit them and explain!

When I courteously, or so I thought, explained to the mother of the baby that I was there to fix a date for the baptism, she retorted, 'Oh, so you've decided to baptise him after all then.' Eating humble pie I had to say, 'Yes, I'm here to fix the date, but the rector would still like you to attend a preparation group.' They attended! In the event it was the rector who carried out the baptism and as far as I can gather all went off well. It was some time before my relationship was restored with that family, but the mother did eventually start attending the family service in the new church in Bordon. We also just about reached Christian name terms in conversation.

I learned a lot from that brush. Firstly, it was essential to stick carefully to the agreed baptismal policy and not to run ahead of it. The rector's integrity saved the day in that they did come to a preparation group and by the grace of God a relationship was restored.

Secondly, it reminded me that it was important to retain a sense of fair play when things were tending towards confrontation. There was that anxiety that if at the end of the day a family decided to dig its heels in and reject one's preparation there was not a lot one could do. There was also lurking that fear: what if a family felt so aggrieved that they really did take a complaint higher up the ecclesiastical tree? Would archdeacons and bishops support what we were doing? I was in due course to find out the answer!

I hope that it is clear by now to the reader that our efforts to introduce an appropriate baptism policy across the parish didn't arise merely from a whim but emerged over several years. Often when I talked to other clergy about how they felt over trying the kind of thing that we were, they would reply, 'Ah! but it doesn't really matter baptising them all. It is the "follow-up" that you should concentrate on. That is where you should put in the energy.'

We had carried out follow-up over the years; much of it very familiar. We had a baptismal anniversary secretary who would write out and send a card to a family on the anniversary of the baptism. Many times I would do a personal visit with it. Sometimes a birthday card would go out too for the child's birthday. When the child was three years old notification of the Sunday School activities were given. Periodically I would visit and distribute to selected families printed details of family services and other activities. We always tried to capitalise on Mothering Sunday and Christmas services. I believe these efforts were rewarded but only minimally. When we took the step of transferring the playgroup nativity service at Christmas from the hall into the new church and making it part of a larger Christmas act of worship it brought in many outsiders including many baptism parents, but I noticed that as soon as the cameras had clicked recording the nativity scene, the interest shown in the rest of the service declined somewhat!

In 1978, 1979 and 1980 we tried having a Sunday afternoon 'baptism parents tea' and short service. About thirty invitations would be sent out or delivered personally inviting parents to come back to the church for tea and cakes and then to have a short act of worship in which I would remind them of their promises and reassure them of the welcome that the church had for them and hoped that they would come and join us. Were these occasions successful? The attendance was small: usually half a dozen at most, but the atmosphere was good. Nevertheless, I can't think of more than a couple of people who came to worship regularly as a result of these teas and even when they did they didn't stay long.

I don't regret the time and energy we put into our follow-up efforts for the minimal response we saw. One thing however must be said: no one could accuse us of being unwelcoming.

My answer to those who would baptise all and sundry without conditions first and then to try and draw a few into active church membership later is that it is a thoroughly bad return on investment of pastoral time and energy. If the statistics scream at us that only the merest handful of baptismal families are likely to be drawn into worship by normal means of follow-up, then it is in the pre-baptismal slot that we should put in our effort. That was what we were trying to do.

By and large we were relieved that the baptism preparation groups had got off to a good start and were making a mark. They had been well attended and we in the clergy team were feeling good at our newly found confidence. Nevertheless, our concern to see more families drawn into the regular worshipping life of the church still haunted us at staff meetings.

Our continuing discussions led us to seek a way of somehow requiring parents to attend a service of worship as part of baptism preparation. The thought of how we might do this left us a little nervous. After much heart-searching we decided in 1982 to take our baptismal policy up one notch by requiring baptism parents to attend at one of the main morning services on a Sunday. They were asked to attend once and to make their request for the baptism at the end of the service to one of the clergy or lay readers as appropriate. The attendance at the service was in effect a precondition to further consideration of the request. 'We' meant the Anglican team ministry of Headley/Bordon, for the establishing of the Ecumenical Project in Bordon meant that I had to become a team vicar instead of a curate, priest-in-charge. It further meant that because of the new method of governing a shared church from December 1980 onwards, any major pastoral policies worked out at Headley had to further be worked through by the St Mark's executive committee (representing three denominations).

Meanwhile, back at Headley Parochial Church Council, we had to discuss this new step in the baptismal policy. They had without too much difficulty agreed to the establishment of the baptism preparation groups for parents, but requiring them to attend church first set one or two alarm bells ringing. The initial fears were that in making this requirement we might cause people to 'not bother to have them baptised', 'cause them to go elsewhere', 'appear to be unwelcoming', and so on. Gradually, as we explained our theology and thinking to the PCC, these fears gave way to a fairly positive sense of support for us to go on experimenting. The motion to ask families to come to church before baptism of their infants was passed by a good majority, but there were some abstentions. It was the first indication that the PCC covered a spectrum of opinion in the matter.

The key to the operation was the letter. Each family would be sent a letter on applying for baptism and this set out fairly clearly what they were being asked to do and why. The rector and curate at Headley drafted the letter to be sent out to Headley requests and I drafted out a similar letter to be sent out in Bordon. The letter was agreed jointly with my Methodist and URC colleagues and signed by each of us. (The St Mark's executive committee passed the main motion without too much difficulty.)[5]

No publicity was given to the new baptismal policy in the press but it was given clear and careful outline in the parish magazine. The magazine had a good circulation in the more established parts of Headley (ie, in the areas least likely to produce infant baptismal candidates!) but not so good a distribution in the newer and larger estates. This meant that the clergy skills for dealing with the initial request for a baptism had to improve markedly. For now, the average parent would be met with a quite different response from that which they expected. The clergy (and often their wives on doorstep or telephone) would have to manage this gap in expectation with the utmost pastoral care. For the first time the offer of the alternative service for the thanksgiving for the birth of a child was included in the letter.

The decision to notch up the baptismal policy came at an interesting time. During the early part of 1982 Derek Head, who had been rector for nine years, was invited to move on to the parish of Chertsey where another Local Ecumenical Project had been started. Derek left us in October 1982 not many months after we had decided on the baptismal change. This meant that the policy would largely be left to the curate (Revd Harry Dickens)[6] and myself to implement over the months of the interregnum and hopefully into the time of the new incumbent, whoever that might be. There is an unwritten rule in Anglican parishes that when an interregnum occurs no new policy decisons can be taken during that time. The parish is run largely along the lines agreed by the previous incumbent and PCC. Headley was no exception, and here we were with a new policy to work out! It was an interesting time indeed.

The new policy got off to a good start. We soon got into the habit of handling the initial baptism enquiries with care and concern. With few exceptions people received what we had to say with a sense of acceptance, but nevertheless it was possible to begin to detect signs of slight annoyance, inconvenience and indeed mild shock. Without exception the pastoral explanatory letter would be sent out to the enquirer and then we would wait. For the first months we waited with a measure of anxiety. The majority did turn up for their one service in church and give their names to one of the clergy or church leaders. They were immediately given a date for a preparation group and the procedure continued as it had done previously via the baptism parents groups.

There were a minority who would turn up at the end of the main morning service rather than attend it! When questioned about this we were often told 'Well, your letter told us to ask at the end of a service.' In such cases grace prevailed but it was obvious that wherever we started to make rules there would be those who would try to find a way around them. The real difficulty was not simply the lack of understanding the words of the letter, but the obvious cultural gap that existed between the applicant and the social centre of gravity of the regular congregation. 'Going to church' for many of these families was something that didn't happen, except for baptisms, weddings and funerals. All our baptism policy did was to expose this cultural habit. However, we didn't abandon or modify our agreed policy. Once families in which there had been no tradition of Christian worship did take the plunge, they were pleasantly surprised. The conversations at the parents' groups would quite regularly throw up comments like, 'We never realised that church could be so enjoyable.' This was particularly said after family services.

A baptismal visit to one family in Bordon made me question what we were doing. It was the third child that we were being asked to christen. The previous two had been baptised in Surrey, where the incumbent had asked them to go to church for three Sundays before they 'could have him christened'. They had never attended regularly since. Here was I explaining that we wished baptismal families to attend church once, and talking to someone to whom a requirement of three Sundays had not made the slightest bit of difference! There was little or no understanding of what baptism was and the message came home to me loud and clear that simply having 'hoops' for people to jump through wouldn't in itself steer baptismal parents towards spiritual understanding. Nevertheless, we pressed on and our efforts didn't go unrewarded.

I used to find at Bordon that if a baptism family turned up to attend its regulation one service on a good day they would be so touched by the ethos and ambience of the place (especially the new church) that they might well come again. As the congregation grew the chances increased that they might know another family in the church and get invited along to the midweek Mothers' and Toddlers' group. Not long after the new church opened in 1982 I decided to make a first effort to mobilise this growing congregation to do some follow-up visiting. I had always had the niggling suspicion that if I raised the idea of a visiting team in the wooden church they would have thought that the vicar wasn't doing his job properly and 'we pay him to do it'. But by mid-1983 with a large proportion of Free Church members in the church keen for us to grow, the climate was very receptive to the idea of training some lay visitors.

I went back to the baptismal registers and wedding lists and other casual pastoral contacts we had had, and drew up a long list of visits. We had five purposes to the exercise:

1. To begin to make the congregation aware of the pastoral/outreach dimension.
2. To help people going on the visits to discover individual ministries.
3. To reach outsiders.
4. To increase sales of *The Marksman*—our new magazine.
5. To build up housegroups.

In the event goals one and two were achieved somewhat, but the surface was only scratched in the case of three, four and five.

The statistics I drew up for the baptismal contacts made interesting reflection. These represented not all of the baptisms in Bordon, but the sixty-two baptism family contacts made between July 1976 when I started in Bordon and the end of 1982 (all before the new church).

Nine were *regular* in worship (at least monthly).
Three were *infrequent* in attendance.
Eleven came *occasionally* to church.
Two were *lapsed* (came regularly but dropped out entirely).
Thirty-seven had *never really been* in the worshipping life in the church.

This means that around 60% of baptism families make no contact with the church after the baptism of their infants. Note that these figures don't take into account all baptisms of Bordon families, or several of those who went up to the parish church for their baptisms.[7] Thus the figure is closer to 70% or even higher.

Nevertheless, we did succeed in that some families made a sincere effort to join us. Again it has to be pointed out that a number of our regular worshippers were regular before they came to Bordon and simply transferred their regular membership. One of the nine families in regular worship mentioned above was ourselves. Our daughter Kathryn was baptised in the new St Mark's and so part of the statistics.

On the whole it wasn't a too encouraging picture. But we had only in the previous four years started out tentatively to pursue a baptismal policy. More time was needed to see whether the policies would have any long-lasting effect on the general picture.

We did start to notice that now and again a family would not appear after the letter was sent out to them. We deliberately did nothing at this stage; partly not to disturb the experimental conditions but also not to risk possible conflict. Occasionally we would hear on the grape-vine that a baptismal family had gone to another parish for the baptism of their infant. We hardly ever heard from the incumbents of those parishes, although according to Canon Law a clergyman is supposed to seek the 'goodwill' of the parish from where the baby comes before proceeding to baptise it (Canon B22.5). I hardly ever found that this rule was honoured. Conversely, we always informed other ministers in other parishes if a family openly asked to go there. Furthermore, we asked that minister if he wanted to do the baptismal preparation, or leave it to us. Frequently we would receive requests from couples who had been married, usually at the parish church, to baptise infants after they had moved away to their new home around the country. This is a common request and we had to tackle it with integrity towards our new policy. I would ask the couples if they had made contact with the church where they were now resident, and if not would they like to as a first step. I sent them a copy of the letter that they would have received if they had been living in our parish so that they could see what we had in mind. In all such cases we asked for the permission of their home vicar and this was usually in writing. It was never refused. Such baptisms of babies where one had married their parents were nearly always occasions of joyful reunion and served well to edge them in the direction of regular worship in their home parishes. It also became obvious that the time to begin baptism preparation was in the wedding preparation!

When Harry Dickens and I set out on the interregnum in October 1982, we expected to have about six months to wait before a new rector was appointed. In the event it was to prove much longer. By the spring of 1983 no new rector had been found and it was obvious that we were going to need some additional ordained help to cope with all the services, pastoral work and to have space for a holiday. We had been given marvellous assistance from two retired priests who were living in the parish, but with their existing family commitments they could not undertake the main duties we were looking for. After much prayer I felt particularly led to ask a neighbouring incumbent, Richard Inkpen, Vicar of Blackmoor, if we might borrow his non-stipendiary minister for some Easter services and a couple of weddings. Richard gladly consented and so for a few weeks we had the services of the Revd John Cherrill. The coming of John to Headley parish was to be of much more significance for baptismal reform that I could have imagined at the time.

John was just turned fifty years of age and an architect by profession. For some years he had been lecturing in architecture at the Portsmouth Polytechnic and lived in Whitehill at the southern end of Bordon New Town. He had been churchwarden at St Matthew's, Blackmoor, and a churchgoer for most of his life. In his own words he would have regarded himself as a rather nominal catholic

Anglican—at least until he came into contact with the charismatic renewal. This he did via Catholics in Basingstoke and later at Alton 'Days of Renewal'. At one point in his pilgrimage he had a special spiritual experience which must remain private, but it was certainly foundational for his faith. Ordination had been in his mind for some time, but his discovery of renewal added impetus to it. I found out very quickly that he had grave doubts about the way infant baptism was administered in the Church of England! Added to all of this John had what I describe as a 'short-fused' conscience! This meant that he could not live for too long with a course of action that disturbed him. He had to be involved with reform. Finally John's love for evangelism and the desire to see people come into a deep personal faith in Jesus Christ led him to minister with the Full Gospel Businessman's Fellowship International (FGBMFI for short). You would think from this description that he was someone to avoid lest you be buttonholed. In practice he was one of the steadiest and gentlest persons with whom it has been my privilege to minister.

John, while continuing his lecturing duties in Portsmouth, was to stay with us for the whole of the Headley interregnum and on into the time of the next rector.

In January 1984 Michael Powell joined the Headley/ Bordon team as team rector. Michael was an Anglo-Catholic by background, a keen cricketer, and still owned his Welsh roots. He put great stress on the enthusiastic leading of worship in contrast to the more measured, wordy tones of we evangelicals! Not long after Michael came, Harry Dickens, who was originally an NSM of the parish, was ready to move off to his own living within Farnham Deanery and that left Michael, myself and John Cherrill as an honorary curate on a week-end assistant basis. Within a short while John was invited to become a full-time stipendiary curate of the parish, and so took early retirement from his lecturing.

Thus a new team was in place: two Anglo-Catholics, of whom one was used to the charismatic circles of the FGBMFI, and myself. Michael Powell very quickly shared his concern that he too believed that infant baptism should be ministered with much more care than hitherto, and so there was no problem with continuing our baptismal policy. It had been agreed by the PCC just before the interregnum and had been faithfully adhered to throughout it. Now, with two new staff members both keen to further our thinking and practice on baptismal reform, we could consolidate our thinking. Would the existing baptismal policy prove to be merely cosmetic, or would it eventually require even more strengthening?

Notes

1. Once a month a Methodist service was included as the main morning act of worship, and we introduced a quarterly Methodist Communion service whilst the congregation remained unchanged.
2. Ken and Verna Susans. The Free Baptist Congregation though small in number still exists and met latterly in the old wooden church of St Mark's (1989).
3. In so many words we were trying to build a team of front line missionaries!
4. There are numerous books which refer to this phenomenon. A good one to start with is *Come Holy Spirit* by David Pytches (Hodder and Stoughton: 1985), especially Chapter 12.
5. The Executive Committee functioned as the local church council for St Mark's. It worked under the authority of a Joint Church Council which was legally specified in the Ecumenical Sharing Agreement.

6. Harry was the great-grandson of the author Charles Dickens.
7. (Two footnotes) I found that if a baptism family got up to Headley without coming to St Mark's first for a service or preparation then there was slim chance they would come to worship afterwards. Many Bordon baptisms also went elsewhere for the usual reason of wanting to go back to the place where the parents were married.

Chapter 5

FRUIT FOR LABOUR

One of the central challenges of the church growth movement is the sobering analysis of our congregations. A minister may bask quietly in the vague notion that 'we had a good number in church last Sunday', but it is quite another thing to look at that round number and ask some awkward questions. Are we declining or growing? How fast? What age ranges are in the congregation? Where do new people come from? Do they stay? Some of the answers can hurt when we face reality.

My wife used to talk of the 'good old days' when her church in Leicester was well attended. In practice it was a well known preacher who drew a middle class congregation from the University environs, an 'electric' congregation, although the church also had some impact on the council estate in which it was situated.[1]

So too at Bordon. What looked like success, or the first scent of it, had to be carefully considered. Much of the growth came from transfer growth—already established Christians moving in to the new town. The challenge was to hold onto them. This was slightly easier in the early days when we were small than in the new church when numbers were growing. It seemed that

when the congregation was in a formative stage, new-
comers could see immediately what the needs were.
They either committed themselves or backed off. Those
who stayed found they were working in a team where
morale was reasonable and were encouraged by it. In the
new church when the numbers went over fifty, people
came and went with much more of a consumer mentality. If the church was too Free Church, too charismatic, too Anglican, too many children, too noisy or
whatever, they quietly moved off to look for something
more to their taste. There was a period when growth
became too fast for our own good. More people came
through the congregation than we could cope with in
terms of integration. Perhaps our pastoral ministry was
not sufficiently developed to carefully meet and integrate
new families.[2]

That was in the mid 80s. What about the late 70s?

From the beginning I tried to emphasise to baptism
families the importance of confirmation. The baptismal
liturgies made explicit and unambiguous reference to
adult commitment in confirmation. Each year, as a direct
result of my pushing confirmation, we would group
together eight or so confirmation candidates. The course
lasted ten weeks and covered what I call the Christian
basics. After the Ecumenical Project was signed in 1980
the groups were led jointly by the three denominational
ministers. Quite a number of these confirmation candidates 'stuck'—something like 80% of them. I noticed in
Colin Urquhart's church in Luton, the important part
the 'Know Jesus' groups played.[3] I tried to allow that
same atmosphere and style to develop in our confirmation groups, and each year it definitely brought one or
two people through to a commitment to Christ. Those
groups were some of the most rewarding times I had in
the church. The relationships forged there lasted. It
showed that where you have someone who is open to
God and who is prepared to sit in a teaching and faith-

sharing situation for a few weeks, then the spiritual step forward is likely to be significant.

One day in 1977 Irene walked down the path of the curate's home, her child in a pushchair. I said that I would be pleased to arrange for the baptism, but first I talked about it with her and her husband, and I stressed confirmation. She had often wondered about confirmation but had thought it was for teenagers. The baptism was duly arranged and carried out (this was before the days of the preparation groups) and to my surprise she was genuinely interested to pursue the matter of confirmation preparation after the baby's baptism. She had also brought along her younger sister who was equally interested. The confirmation was duly arranged, and Irene continued to worship regularly afterwards. I was aware of a genuine spiritual response in her case. Sometimes God brings these cases before us to give encouragement in the whole process of trying to lead people into authentic Christian faith.

In 1980 I had a phone call from the secretary to the Parish Council who wanted to make an appointment to see me about a rather confidential matter. Wondering what on earth it could be I waited for two or three days in some anticipation before she finally walked into my study.

'I am rather concerned,' she said, 'because I have never been christened.'

'Oh yes,' I replied, 'what is it that you are concerned about?'

Her reply focused on her concern about being buried in the churchyard, coupled to a sense that she had missed out on something. This was the first time in my ministry that an adult had requested baptism. I was actually unprepared for such a situation. I explained quickly that baptism wasn't merely a rite that was thrust upon people, but was linked to a decision about the gospel. If she was interested in baptism then I had to explain the gospel to her. Would she like to make a further appointment for an hour and I would explain further?

A few days later I took her through what evangelicals would recognise as the basic steps of Christian commitment. Having explained these I deliberately sent her away to think about what I had said. If after that she wanted to make a sincere Christian commitment, then I would arrange the baptism. I further suggested that she should proceed on to confirmation in accordance with Diocesan regulations. Jenny gave 'green lights' all the way through. This worried me. I thought she might just be saying 'yes' to the Christian faith merely to please me. Her baptism was arranged for Christmas Day in the morning service, and was a lovely occasion—a double joy for her and the congregation. Some of her family were slightly mystified at this rather odd use of a Christmas morning, but there was no doubt that Jenny had taken a spiritual step forward. She was with us very regularly until soon afterwards her family decided to move to Alton and apparently found some difficulty finding a suitable church there. (I will return to this in Chapter 13.)

But Irene and Jenny were exceptions. Interestingly, I had another enquiry about adult baptism shortly afterwards. A woman whom I knew at a distance enquired if she could be baptised, largely because she hadn't been 'done' as a child. Once again I took her along the same basic steps of Christian commitment as with Jenny, but this time when I invited her to go away and think about it, she never came back. I had particularly hoped that she would make a sincere commitment, because this could have opened an important spiritual door for her whole family and several other families on that estate.[4] However, it was not to be. Such cases as this left me with slight questions of conscience: Had I been too heavy handed? Had I overstressed her role—commitment, decision, discipleship—and played down God's undeserved grace? If she wanted to proceed with her baptism she could quite easily have done so by returning and it would have been arranged. Had I made this clear? It was her decision and I had to leave it. If I had followed her up she may have consented to be baptised as a formality and then not come into the worshipping life of the church.

Then there were two teenage girls who wanted to be baptised under pressure from their parents. I gave them some preparation, which they duly attended, and made it clear that I expected confirmation to follow within a few months, but after their baptisms I never saw them again in church, despite trying to draw them into youth group and other activities. They remained friendly, however, and always waved in the street.

The folklore belief behind these last few requests does not lie too far below the surface. There still is a sense of fear or mere irregularity at not having been christened. It often presents as a fear that not to be baptised in infancy might disqualify from being able to marry in church or to be buried in consecrated ground, but generally there is a pressure to conform. My two sons who passed through the local schools reported on more than one occasion that if it were discovered that a child had not been christened he would have a finger pointed at him by his friends. Parents sometimes said that if one of their children were not christened they might be thought odd. It is an interesting notion, but surely not new; that it is odd to be unbaptised, yet equally odd to see that baptism as implying anything about being connected to a local church.

In the case of the two adults above, the routine request to clear up an omission in the routine of childhood led on to adult Christian commitment. But this was rare. In general I found that adult commitment came as the result of a complex of factors and rarely showed any consistent pattern. There was, however, from 1983 onwards a greater exposure to a variety of other churches and Christian groups. At one point we had a fairly thriving 'Pathfinder' group of thirteen- to fifteen-year-olds, mainly girls. Their leaders worked hard with them and occasionally the young people took part in family services. There were youth services with visiting speakers of an evangelical nature and a number of youngsters showed interest. However, with two exceptions, most of them eventually drifted from the life of the church. On some occasions the two leaders took them to the Millmead Centre in Guildford (the Baptist church) so that they could see a 'real live church'. Once I went with them, but the visits didn't make too much impression. The two leaders spoke to me about getting baptised as adults by immersion. We had had a few similar requests at Headley over the years, but these were the first ones put to me personally. My reply was probably predictable. I advised them not to do so as they had both been baptised in infancy, they had both come to a sincere Christian faith, they had tasted in no small measure the work of the Holy Spirit, so what more could baptism as an adult in a tank of water add?

We entered into an amicable discussion about the validity of infant baptism, at the end of which the Pathfinder leaders decided that they ought to proceed with their immersions as they felt that God had brought them to this point. In the event I attended their immersions at the Guildford Baptist Church, and was quite moved by the occasion. It was the first time I had attended an adult baptism by immersion and I hadn't realised what a powerful symbolic witness it was. Both the leaders continued in our church in Bordon and remained quite loyal and hardworking. I think that if I had adopted a harsh or critical attitude towards them over this question of a 'second baptism' I might have lost them. I had heard of several cases where loyal members of Anglican churches had gone to house churches for a baptism and stayed to join the new congregation. On the other hand I felt that every little bit of spiritual input into an individual's Christian life would in the longer term help to build up our own church.

By the middle of 1987 the baptism policy requiring parents to attend a service in church once, as a first step, had been running for five years. It was time to see how it was going. I did a fairly careful check on a twelve-month sample from July 1986 to July 1987. The results showed the following:

Enquiries requesting infant baptism—52 (one per week)
   17 of these 'backed off' after receiving the letter (29%).
   32 were baptised in the parish (28 in St Mark's, 4 at the parish church.
   3 were baptised in neighbouring parishes (for genuine reasons).
   of the 32 baptised in the parish, 8 (25%) had continuing links with St Mark's.

The first thing I noticed was the high proportion who were deterred by the letter. I do not in any way believe the letter was at fault. It was well written and agreed by the church committee and ministry. Its fault probably lay in the fact that it made no mistake about what was intended in baptism. If a family did not respond by attending church, we didn't follow it up. The letter made it clear that the next move and the choice was theirs and we respected that. I have no doubt that several of these families had baptisms arranged in other churches. I never heard officially about any of them.

The three who were baptised in neighbouring parishes came clean with us and asked if they could go back to the place where they grew up or were married. We encouraged them as explained in the previous chapter to do our preparation or that of the other parish.

After the enquiry had come in and the letter had been sent out, I waited for the family to appear in church.

When they did there was a good chance that I might not be taking the service that morning, so the system was geared for the family to approach one of the other ministers or elders. I would normally visit the family during the next week. That would be the point when I would start to discuss what baptism meant and the nature of the promises. I would then leave with them a copy of my baptism teaching cassette tape and asked them to listen to it at their convenience. In only one or two cases was it not listened to. On one occasion the tape was accidentally half wound when I handed it over, and I noticed it was in precisely the same position when they handed it back! The baptism went ahead in a routine manner. I never saw the family in church again. Sometimes in operating the baptism policy I suffered from emotional exhaustion trying to handle everything with kid gloves.[5]

But the overwhelming response to the teaching tape was favourable. Even the rank outsiders appreciated the teaching material that was on it. For the most part, at least.

One of our congregation called Leslie, a member of our Liturgical Dance Group and a bright Christian, had been approached by a friend who wasn't a regular churchgoer about having her baby baptised. This friend went through the system of receiving the letter and attending a service, but had an argument with my tape. Wishing to discuss the matter further she did so with her friend Leslie (with my consent). After some days she rang up saying that she didn't agree with the tape or Leslie and would go elsewhere for the baptism.

Even with a new church building there were still those who objected to it on architectural grounds. One family phoned asking for the baby to be baptised at Headley because they wanted the church to look like a church 'and not a house'. Another family asked for Headley initially, but changed their minds after attending a service in St Mark's.

I had another taste of hostility with a mother over precisely this issue. She received the baptismal letter and was very irate when she phoned some days later to say that she would in no way enter St Mark's as she wanted her child baptised in the parish church. I explained that this was fine provided she attended one service at St Mark's as the letter had requested so that she would be aware of and acquainted with the local worshipping body. She replied by saying that she never intended to come near the church, if she came at all it would be to Headley. We began to discuss the matter over the telephone, but her emotional temperature rose rapidly and she put the receiver down on me. I didn't ring back immediately, but next day composed a letter. Part of it read:

Naturally I am upset by your architectural comments on St Mark's, but never let it be said that it is not a 'real' church in any respect. It is, in fact, the first completed brick worship centre properly dedicated that Bordon has ever had. It has been planned for twenty years as part of a comprehensive village centre. We built up to a standard rather than down to a price (otherwise you would have had a second-rate hall). I think by a short head I would prefer the new Bordon Library for our building, but am quite satisfied with what we have, and as I say there is a very 'real presence' within it.

By such means I sought to win friends and influence people. The rest of the letter was concerned with explaining the baptismal policy. I heard no more from this particular lady for several weeks, but one morning I was taking the main Eucharist at the parish church and to my surprise she turned up. All went according to routine after that. She heard my tape, and the baptism was duly arranged for the parish church one Sunday afternoon. I don't think she ever came regularly to worship after that, but I remember her turning up once later on at a family service in St Mark's. My labour was not altogether in vain, perhaps.

But there was also encouragement. Just once in a while everything went smoothly as the system intended. I often used to surmise that if all godparents and parents did their stuff impeccably as the Prayer Book assumes they will, then England should be the most Christian nation on the planet. The situation is self-evidently otherwise.

One couple whom I shall call James and Mary requested a baptism. They had moved to Bordon for the husband's job. They rang to ask for the baptism of their second child and went through the process of the pastoral letter, the visit to the church, and my home visit. The baptism was performed and the family started coming regularly to church. Shortly afterwards they reminded me that they had expressed an interest in confirmation. James and Mary were duly confirmed and remained regular communicants thereafter. They became involved in several jobs in the church, went to a house group, and James joined the men's prayer breakfast on a Saturday morning. All they did was to request an infant baptism and the rest went like clockwork. I treated them with no more or less pressure than anyone else and somehow it went along naturally. 'If only they were all like that' I would say to myself.

Sometimes it was at the baptism of the second or even the third child that a meaningful contact was made. Two confirmation candidates came this way. After the baptism of her third child, one mother was taken to the FGBMFI meetings, developed a keen interest in spiritual gifts and clearly began to exercise the gift of prophecy. We weren't quite sure how to handle it but it was there nevertheless. I mention this because the wife in question told me that when she had asked for her first baby to be baptised, my attitude was depressive and harsh! Perhaps she was right! Nevertheless, she turned in the end to an authentic faith.

Then there was Lorna. Hers was a request for baptism for her infant and for herself. I concentrated on preparing her for baptism and confirmation and told her that the child's baptism would then fall into place. Things did fall into place for her. She grew in the faith in which she had been baptised. The confirmation group was held in her home and she took an active part in the life of the church. However, within a few months she had moved house to Aldershot and we lost touch with her.

But top of the bill came Sally and Steve Puddick. In December 1986 they telephoned requesting a christening for their second child. I went round to deliver the baptismal letter and some days later they asked if they could see me. They were a quiet and basically friendly couple, but it was obvious that they were slightly annoyed that we had asked them to come to a church service first. This led on naturally to a conversation and providentially not a confrontation. I began by asking the question 'What do you think baptism really is?' I spent about half an hour with them and left my cassette tape with them. The opening part of the cassette tape was an interview with two women on their experiences of baptism of their children. I asked them what led them to ask for baptism, when did they come to a mature faith and such questions and recorded their answers.

Both of these wives were acquaintances of Sally and so she listened to the tape with some interest. This happened before she attended a service in church. I would have expected at this stage to have been arranging a date for the baptism. However, for some reason I received a message that Sally and Steve had decided to wait and think things over. About a month went by and we were into the new year before John Cherrill said to me one day at our staff meeting that a Bordon family called Puddick had approached him about baptism.

'That's interesting,' I said, 'perhaps you had better go and see them.'

We knew that families would often shop around churches until they found one that was more amenable than another, but obviously Sally and Steve didn't realise that Headley parish church was all part of the same team ministry with the same baptismal policy! They later told me that after I had visited them they did decide to look around somewhere else and decided to start at Headley and took pot luck on the names on the clergy noticeboard. We did always work consistently as a clergy team, so that parishioners from whichever end of the parish they came would not try to manipulate the clergy one against another. It is, I suppose, a fairly human instinct to try and get hold of the person who is thought to be an easier touch than others. Pupils say such things of teachers, drivers about driving testers and the clergy are as fair game as anyone else. In the event John Cherrill went to spend an evening with Sally and Steve, and they agreed to go with him to an FGBMFI meeting.

'That will really cap it,' I thought to myself. 'They will not want to speak to any of us again after that.' What little faith I had.

A few weeks later my telephone rang.

'Hello, it's Mrs Puddick here!'

'Oh no,' I thought, 'here we go again.'

'I just wanted to ring you up and say that I have now come to understand what being a Christian is all about and I have decided to become one sincerely.' 'Oh yes,' I replied, looking at the telephone receiver to check whether I was hearing correctly. 'That's good news, how did it come about?' Then she related the whole story of how after they had seen me they went off to John Cherrill. He asked them exactly the same questions that I had asked and they began to wonder if there wasn't something in what we were trying to say. This led to the

FGBMFI meeting and an encounter with Christian testimony of the sharper kind. After I had got over my shock I immediately set about building a positive relationship with Sally and Steve and the baptism of their second child came out almost as a matter of course. In fact it was me who suggested it. 'This means,' I said, 'that we can go ahead and arrange the baptism of your son without any problems at all.'

I must make it clear that the baptism of their baby would have proceeded as a matter of course anyway, had they requested it earlier. However, it was important to positively support the new step in faith that Sally had taken and to be seen to be consistent with what I had said to her and her husband on the first evening.

This was, however, only the first part of the story. Sally joined the congregation and started to take a full part in its life. She, in fact, had been a lapsed Roman Catholic and something of that catholic background was stirred into life through her newly found faith. Like St Paul she wanted to work everything through again in her own mind, after coming to terms with a new revelation. She then renewed her baptismal vows in the evening service according to the ASB rite as a mark of her commitment. This led her to ask formally to join the congregation on the Anglican Electoral Roll. At a suitable confirmation service she was received into Anglican membership from the Roman Catholic Church according to a form of words agreed by the Dioceses. She steadily gained height spiritually and joined in prayer groups and shared her faith within the church and outside it with others. Then came a shock. She asked if she could be baptised by total immersion. It was the first of a number requested at this time and I decided to handle it by declaring that as she had been baptised in infancy she no longer needed to be baptised again. She had come to a living faith. She had expressed that by making a renewal of her baptismal vows in church, she was as far as I was concerned, perfectly in order. I was prepared to say that if she renewed her vows in water then that would be acceptable, but I hoped she wouldn't ask me to do it! In the event Sally proceeded with an immersion baptism arranged through what might be called 'extra-church' circles.

Sally's testimony

I have been a Christian for nearly four years now—four wonderful years. The happiest years of my life. I'd like to tell you a bit about where it all began.

I have a Roman Catholic background. Memories of my school life include numerous Religious Knowledge lessons, and forever standing in the school hall for Mass, but no one ever really told me about Jesus, as a personal Saviour and Friend; about living your life for him.

I rebelled against 'religion' after I left school and trod a path which for me went slowly downhill. I suffered depression; only on odd occasions at first, then as the sickness took hold with more frequency and for longer periods, during which I did a lot of things that I am not proud of. I was seeking some form of excitement in my life, but always coming up against a brick wall—finding nothing but pain, misery and hurt; hurt for myself and for others.

When my second child came along, I approached the church for him to be christened. The Reverend Clifford Owen came to see me, but asked a lot of questions which at first made me indignant. 'Did I understand what being a Christian really meant?' 'Did I understand what I was doing having my baby baptised?'

Of course, with my Roman Catholic background, and a very large chip on my shoulder, these were not questions to be posed! I approached another church (not realising it was the same parish) and this time I was visited by a Reverend John Cherrill (now here was a sensible looking chap!). If I had expected him to reach for his diary and arrange for a nice little christening—my son in a pretty white gown, lovely family gathering with celebration afterwards on the lawn—I was wrong! The same hard-hitting questions were posed.

'Tell me,' he asked, 'Do you understand baptism?' I tried to answer; I know now that I did not. We spent many hours talking—I believe that God lifted the barrier of my mind during that time. John talked of his personal relationship with God, about how he had given his life to him. I didn't know what was happening to me then, but I had a deep yearning inside to know more.

A few days later at a FGBMFI dinner I gave my life to Jesus Christ; I felt as if he had given me a new beginning. Everything felt new, different, exciting. I knew he had changed me. My life had purpose, direction. He taught me how to love my husband and family in a way I never thought possible.

I have recently had another child, but instead of baptism, I chose a blessing and thanksgiving service instead. I feel that baptism is a *personal* declaration of faith. You declare your belief and trust in Jesus Christ, you promise to follow him and live your life for him, and you are completely immersed to wash away your old life in readiness for the new.'

Several others followed Sally in this immersion because it seemed that once one person had done it then others felt that somehow they didn't want to miss out.

Two people who were being prepared for confirmation hadn't been baptised in infancy. They were asked if they would like to consider immersion as the mode of their baptism, which was now, of course, quite legal. I attended a service of immersion for these two at the Garrison swimming pool, which had been hired for the evening. The ASB baptism service was used and accompanied by a short address and the singing of some popular hymns and choruses. It was a most moving occasion full of joy and power. It made me think seriously whether by challenging our baptismal families a little harder on the meaning of baptism, we might allow their offspring to experience the joy of having a 'conscious' baptism in riper years when they are ready for it. Families who press hard to have their infant baptised in case 'he misses out' in one sense ensure that he does miss out on the joy of a 'conscious' baptism later on.

On two or three occasions I had conditional baptisms, where the adult candidates were genuinely not sure whether they had been baptised in infancy and there was no documentary evidence or witnesses living. I baptised them at the new font in St Mark's, but they could have been legitimately offered immersion. With another candidate for baptism before confirmation, I did offer immersion, but it was declined. He was baptised by the bishop at the confirmation service and looking at the amount of water the bishop used, the candidate might just as well have been immersed!

The experience of Sally and several others meant that we had in the local church not only an influential core congregation with a growing faith, but a group who were prepared to challenge current pastoral practice over baptism. At times it took some handling.

Meanwhile back at the baptism policy, one could not ignore the fact that although there was definite fruit for five years of its implementation, three quarters of those who had infants baptised under the scheme never darkened the doors again.

Notes

1. The church is St Christophers, South Wigston, Leicester. I have since been corrected by my sister-in-law! The church always did make a meaningful

impact on its surrounding council estate; the constituency for which the church was built.

2. This is an aspect of ministry which deserves fuller treatment. It was partly a problem of sharing vision within the leadership team; partly a problem of communication within the complexities of a Local Ecumenical Project, and the range of pastoral approaches that found themselves under one roof.

3. Colin describes these groups in his first book on the account of the growth of St Hugh's, Luton. (*When the Spirit Comes*: Hodder and Stoughton.)

4. This particular lady might have been the key to reaching a group of people whom I might refer to as the 'original Bordonians'. They were on the fringe of the travelling families and had been in the locality virtually all their lives. I knew from the outset that the distance spiritually, sociologically and in other ways between that group and many of the congregation was large, but God is a God of miracles and she had after all asked for baptism!

5. This point is important. Emotional exhaustion could tip one either into a harsh rigorism on one hand or a lethargic defeat on the other. Either way would be counter-productive.

Chapter 6

HURDLES AND HOSTILITIES

If you were reading this book as a war story, then I
suppose you could say that the shooting starts here! Five
years of a modest baptismal policy had shown some fruit,
but with the majority of families still making only a 'brief
encounter'[1] with the church we wondered what we would
have to do next in order to tighten the whole system up.
If our modest policy caused about 30% of people to look
elsewhere with some flak and some fruit, a quick extrap-
olation would suggest that an even harder policy might
increase the fall off, the flak and the fruit. It did!

John Cherrill, Michael Powell and I had worked
together for some four years implementing the baptismal
policy. As I had been the longest on the team I was
probably the most satisfied with the system, but had to
admit that for much of the time I administered it with a
heavy heart. I told myself that it would be a long time
before any noticeable change would come over the community in its expectation of a christening as a birthright
on demand. I had, in other words, to content myself with
seed sowing. John and Michael were more radical. Baptism frequently came up for discussion in staff meetings
and the question was put 'Do we have to go on doing this

in this way?' If families really were not yet ready for baptism of their infants, then we must have the right and the time to prepare them to something approaching our priestly satisfaction. The seeds were sown for the introduction of a fairly demanding policy. We decided to stay with the existing style, but with three important changes.

A. We would seek the goodwill of higher authority before starting.
B. The main test would be a requirement to attend church for three months, not one service.
C. There would be a 'hard sell' for all families for the Alternative Service of the 'Thanksgiving for the Birth of a Child'.

To move to the scenario outlined above meant that we would be somehow 'into a new ball game'. It meant effectively that in addition to some annoying delay at having to attend a service in church and a preparation group, a baptism family would now have to sit down and seriously consider whether they wanted to proceed to a baptism or a service of blessing and thanksgiving. If they opted for the latter then they would still be visited and arrangements made for the service, but no further demands were put upon them.

I suppose John was the most skilled of all of us at marketing the service of thanksgiving. From the beginning the three of us felt that somehow the service of thanksgiving for the birth of a child in the ASB was a bit thin in terms of content. We wanted it to be a positive, clear and joyful service and a real family event, rather than a consolation prize for those who didn't qualify. John added in an address, an optional annointing signing the sign of the cross, the giving of a certificate and the starting of a new register for all such services.[2] At first some families were slightly confused, but when the occasions were over most people appeared satisfied with what they had experienced. We included the provision of godparents where desired and the 'christening cake' was still made and the family went back to the house afterwards for the party and presents. These services were included in main acts of worship, usually a suitable family service, though some were done as separate services and very occasionally as a private event in a home. It meant that there was something for everybody when they enquired about baptism.

Of course, with this new baptismal policy we were technically moving closer to 'discriminate' infant baptism, though it is important to note that the discrimination was done by the parents not by the clergy. We gave them the option; they made the choice. If they wanted to go on to baptism of their infant then a rephrased pastoral letter explained what they had to do. After setting out the meaning of baptism simply the letter read as follows:

1. If you wish to proceed further to the baptism of your child, we ask you to attend church regularly over the next three months. The reason for this is so that you can meet a local Christian congregation in the weekly act of worship, and have an experience of what the regular commitment is like. Baptism means becoming a member of the local body of Christians. We realise that for many people a regular life of worshipping in church on a Sunday morning (or evening) may be quite a jolt to a life style. However, for many people the effort involved has been repaid many times over, not just in discovering a whole lot of new friends, but above all in finding a new and vital faith to sustain them through life.

2. During the time of three months worship you will be asked to join a baptism preparation course. In it you will receive basic instruction in the Christian faith leading, we hope, to a clearer understanding of the responsibilities of bringing up a child in the Christian faith.

   It could be that as a result of being part of such a course you may want to do a full confirmation preparation.

3. After the three month period you will be in a position to make up your mind about baptism, or not, for your child.

    If you decide 'no', then please take up the offer of the service of thanksgiving.
4. There will be cases where either the husband or wife is not keen to comply. It is acceptable for one parent only to be prepared for the baptism, but the other partner shoud not make the promises or profession of faith in the baptismal service.

    The Church has given years of careful thought to this question of the best way to prepare people for the baptism of their children that is appropriate in the late twentieth century. Nearly all churches now have some sort of preparation such as we have outlined above.

    It should be realised that in the end the object is not to qualify for baptism by completing an obstacle course, but to bring parents and ultimately their children to a living faith in Christ.

    Yours sincerely,

I can see looking back after three years what a shock such a letter must have been to families right outside the church. In trying to come clean and invite families to see precisely what we meant by a serious keeping of the baptismal promises we were facing them with a challenge which we knew many of them would not take up.

We had much discussion on the clergy team before launching. A period of six months was suggested as a 'qualifying time' of worship before asking for baptism, but I felt that that would be too long. Looking back now I would have opted for a month, but we settled for three. We then qualified it by saying that we wouldn't expect them to come every week and that we wouldn't be monitoring their attendance! We would simply suggest that they make themselves familiar with the local church over a three-month period if they were not already in regular attendance. I felt that for our Bordon congregation and our communities on the big estates, we needed to be more specific about what was being asked and so I produced a tick-off chart for each family, which effectively asked them to come to church five times. I suggested attendance at one family service, one Communion service, one Songs of Praise, one Methodist preaching service and one other. Quite a number of families did just that and a handful stayed on in the church after their baptisms.

I succeeded in 'selling' a thanksgiving to a couple of families. One or two went away to think about it and came back having made a choice, some for it, others for baptism. They then faithfully attended their five services, and the baptisms were duly carried out.

I found it was necessary to change the way of doing things in marketing this tougher policy. I felt that now it wasn't sufficient to briefly inform the families about coming to a main service and approaching the clergy at the end, but that I had to explain the policy fully from the outset, and then to take or post the letter afterwards. On a couple of occasions I established a good pastoral relationship in this way which helped them to accept the message of the letter when it came. On other occasions the letter turned an initial relationship into mild hostility. Some families had checked up with other vicars who had obviously supported a case against us; so that when a family contacted us again they were forearmed.

It was obvious that we were making great demands upon ourselves as ministers. On occasions I felt emotionally exhausted trying to administer the first baptismal policy with kid gloves, and now the tension was even more keenly felt. We were with a good conscience, administering a shock to baptismal enquirers and then having to pastor it afterwards. Because of this I took to leaving my teaching cassette tape with a family on initial enquiry. By this stage I had four copies of it, which was just as well as on two occasions I never saw it again. But there was fruit here and there. I received the following letter:

Dear Revd Owen,
    Thank you for your visit last Monday. It was much

appreciated. Unfortunately this weekend my mother-in-law was taken ill with a heart attack and we were unable to attend the service on Sunday. However, depending on her condition we hope to attend next Sunday. We have listened to the cassette and return it to you, together with the thanksgiving sheet. We will leave making the decision until we have attended some services.

Many thanks once again.

Yours sincerely,

Mrs J. M. Chant

Where was our authority for what we did? Michael, our rector, informed the bishop what we were doing and we presumed we had his consent to attempt the policy, but we detected 'anxious vibes'. The PCC were also informed of what we were about to do, but we didn't debate the issue. Looking back this was a mistake, though we would probably have pressed ahead even if general assent was not forthcoming. But the real can-opener was the press. In our discussions in staff meetings we wondered whether in making such a leap forward in our baptismal policy we should put something in the press. On balance we decided not to. In retrospect perhaps we ought to have done so and given three or even six months warning of impending change. In the event we did a series of articles in the parish magazine. The clergy team did one each and these were laid alongside each other and the parish was informed of our new policy. The three articles are included as Appendix 1 on page 267. This was in October 1988.

A few days later I was wandering past the newsagents in the new shopping centre in Bordon. Something told me to go inside. As I did so I caught a glimpse of the headline of the week's edition of the *Petersfield Post*. 'SUPERSTITION IS NOT THE ANSWER—Parents must attend course before baptism carried out.' There it was. We had made the front page! The press had got hold of the parish magazine and raised the subject of baptism for us. The report was straightforward and basically a compendium of extracts from our magazine articles.

The following week the *Petersfield Post* sent a reporter down to the shopping precinct to question young mums about our baptismal policy. The result was a short feature article in the next week's edition which was extremely revealing, or should I say confirming. (The article is set out together with the remainder of the newspaper extracts in Appendix 2.)

Certain obvious comments come from a reading of the feature:

1. Nobody agreed with what we were doing, but the reporter did discover that a similar baptismal policy was in operation in a neighbouring parish. (See next chapter.)
2. It is as clear as crystal that the population at large feel they have an outright unconditional right to infant baptism, regardless of whether the parents go to church.
3. Several parents said they had been refused baptism. Strictly speaking this was not true. I think I have 'refused' about two baptisms in seventeen years, using 'refused' in the sense of 'declined on initial enquiry, when it was a clear case where one could not in all conscience proceed'. The parents in the feature article meant that they had been refused *on their terms*.
4. The idea that the church is trying to 'shut people out' was expressed. I only wish many families had shown more evidence that they actually wanted to come in.

The following week carried a block of letters on the subject of baptism. It was clear that baptism is an extremely emotive subject if you press hard enough. Most of the controversial areas of discussion in and around the congregations and parish—such as the ordination of women, speaking in tongues, healing the sick, ecumenism—all of these took second place to baptism.

After the letters, the *Petersfield Post* let the issue drop and apart from a brief column in the *Farnham Herald* no other newspaper took up the issue. In one sense I was glad that it had cooled off a little. Oddly nothing was said on the PCC, or in the St Mark's, Bordon, executive committee. There were odd mutterings in the background, but no one tried to raise the issue within the congregations to review the baptismal policy or to check on the wisdom of our procedures. Neither did anything come down from 'above'. We pressed on quietly with our new policy.

Just before the new policy came into operation I had what was arguably the most difficult encounter with a family that I have ever had over baptism. Note that this encounter took place under our former policy, when we were only asking families to attend one service and come to the preparation group.

The phone rang one day for a baptismal request which my wife took down. There was the name and address, which I did not recognise. I sent out the letter. A few days later Mrs Burdett phoned. (The name and some of the details have been disguised for obvious reasons.) She thanked me for delivering the letter and asked me to explain it in more detail. She claimed not to have understood it, but the subsequent conversation suggested that she had understood quite well what we had said on the first reading. It was immediately obvious that she had a fundamental difference of opinion with us and was committed to challenging the baptismal policy. I recognised immediately I had to make a decision. If I backed down from our agreed baptismal policy, it would create a precedent for others to follow and it would undo months, possibly years of work. Thus I pressed on. I sensed we were committed to conflict. My instinct was confirmed by the succinct way in which Mrs Burdett put the 64,000 dollar question to me.

'Are you telling me that if I do not attend a service of worship you will not baptise my baby?' Summoning the last grains of diplomacy I said, 'If you phrase the question in those terms, then regretfully I have to say yes.'

'Thank you,' said Mrs Burdett, 'that is all I wanted to know.'

During the conversation it was made clear that her baby wasn't going to be allowed near St Mark's for all the usual architectural reasons, neither would Mrs Burdett attend any classes, services or groups at Headley. All they wanted was a Sunday afternoon private christening with no strings attached.

There are some situations which have a sense of inevitability about them...almost 'meant to be' as test cases.

Half way through the telephone discussion Mrs Burdett reminded me that I had taken her wedding just two years before. Had I forgotten? I had indeed, but my non-realisation of the fact stemmed from my wife's misspelling of the name when first given over the telephone. I hadn't recognised that particular surname. However, even if I had, I doubt whether it would have made much difference to the situation. I then remembered that this particular couple were rather annoyed that they were asked to attend some wedding preparation. In other words my previous pastoral relationship with this family wasn't sufficient to save the day.

I expected to hear no more about it, but three weeks later a letter arrived from our archdeacon, Paul Barber, Archdeacon of Surrey.[3] The family had complained to the bishop, who had asked Paul to investigate. I wrote back to Paul setting out the facts as I understood them on two and a half sides of A4 paper. My first sentence read: 'This is the first baptismal complaint we have had in Bordon in eleven years. Is that par for the course?' I remembered my naval training injunction to keep a sense of humour in all circumstances.

He replied with a phone call, asking me if I felt I could go and visit the family and try to establish a relationship with them and see what their difficulties really were.

Around that time Headley was experimenting with the baptismal preparation by offering the now well-known course in Christian basics *Good News Down the Street*.[4] Carol Snipe, who had recently moved into the parish from a parish in Essex where the course had been tried was very keen to have a go with it, particularly with baptismal families. Michael, the team rector, gave her permission to try it out in one or two hand-picked cases. This course requires a team of people familiar with and trained to use the course, and so one or two people were trained, including Sally from the last chapter. It was suggested to me that as I returned to visit Mrs Burdett I might offer her this course. So one fine morning I set out to visit Mrs Burdett on a prearranged appointment determined to exercise my pastoral and diplomatic gifts. I was not too hopeful.

Archdeacon Paul had previously sent a letter to Mrs Burdett supporting the 'thorough' baptismal preparation which we had offered, and informing her that I was coming to talk matters through. Paul was being over generous as I thought our preparation was pretty minimal. However, Mrs Burdett was expecting me. What was meant to be a healing meeting turned out to widen the gulf still more. My letter to the archdeacon afterwards said it all:

> I visited Mrs Burdett this morning, but I have to say regretfully that it turned out to be a quiet but sustained confrontation on virtually every point of discussion. I have never quite had an assize like it and I hope not to again. Normally I manage to establish a pastoral relationship, but this time I failed... I sense that she is challenging me not only on her own behalf but half of the post natal class in Bordon as well. It was clear from my visit that Mrs Burdett represented the 'baptism as of right, on demand with no preparation or commitment school' and in defending that position she prevented us from getting down to the heart of Christianity and the theology of baptism.

We did not fall out in any abusive way, but I spent a

whole hour with her and left by stating that I couldn't see any mileage in my trying to proceed as we would only run into confrontation. Instead I suggested that one of my colleagues (or one of our lay people) could visit to talk further. She was not keen and suggested that if any visitors were going to take my point of view then there would be no point. They said that they would either come back to yourself or the bishop or find a 'willing parish'. Where do we go from here?

In the event Mrs Burdett agreed to accept a visit from Sally and from Carol Snipe. They went to try and bridge a gap and to talk about 'Good News Down the Street'. After their visit I received a sad phone call from Carol explaining that Mrs Burdett had ended the meeting in tears. Within a few days I received a letter from Archdeacon Paul confirming the failure of the last meeting and he took action to have Mrs Burdett's infant's baptism carried out at another church in Farnham Deanery. The relevant part of his letter to me read:

So, the impasse would seem to be worse than ever and the baptism in terms of Canon B22 (2)[5]—subject to undue delay—and I have therefore, with Bishop Michael's consent, approached the Revd X and have put Mrs Burdett in touch with him.

I well appreciate your motives in taking the line that you do, but I have the strong impression that you are asking folk to jump through spiritual hoops that many, though not all, find beyond them. If those many, as a result, are made resentful and alienated by your Baptism Policy what does this do to help the Gospel?

Kindest wishes,
Yours ever,
Paul

I have to say that I admired the most gracious way in which Archdeacon (now Bishop) Paul handled all of us in the matter. He knew that for years I had been keen to see infant baptismal discipline and preparation made clearer. He had been Rural Dean of Farnham when I had introduced a discussion on it some years earlier in the chapter meeting. He had also presented a programme on baptism on County Sound at Guildford which included a recorded piece by myself on the formation of MORIB.[6] He was no stranger to my concern in the matter. Now we found ourselves out of the studio and the relaxed atmosphere of the chapter meeting and in the pastoral reality of the parish. Were we on opposite sides? Paul was carrying out his pastoral duty with the authority with which he was invested and so was I. We were probably on a mild collision course, but commonsense said 'enough is enough'. After Paul's letter came I left the matter there; gladly I might add. There were two or three points I wanted to take up but felt that pastorally we were looking for the 'referee' to give a verdict.[7]

In case the reader is mistaken, I have to state clearly that I did not enjoy this conflict. But bearing in mind that this was not the policy we moved to in the autumn of 1988 I could not quite agree with Paul's assertion that the spiritual hoops were too much in this case. As for the relationship between baptism and gospel, I will discuss that in Chapter 11.

But there was one more case to come. It was similar to the Burdett case in many respects, but over more quickly and I was able to close the matter with the couple concerned at the friendly end of the scale.

We had moved to the stricter policy in the autumn of 1988 as outlined above. A baptism request came in from a couple I knew well, had seen at a couple of family funerals and whose wedding I had taken. I had also previously baptised their first child under the previous policy, so there was no possibility of mistaken identity here. They had insisted in the case of the first child that the baby be baptised at Headley and the wish was granted. This particular request put to the test a decision we had taken in our staff meeting about what to do if, in implementing the new policy, we found couples requesting baptism for a second and third child who had been prepared under the first policy, especially if they had made no obvious attempt to build a worshipping link with the church. We thought long and hard about this one. I harked back to some of my training weekends at St Paul's, Harlow New Town in Essex, where Canon Donald Knight had built up a lively town centre congregation through a baptismal policy which was fairly demanding on the instructional content. I particularly remember what he said about second and third child baptisms if the parents hadn't come into church life after the baptism of the first child. All subsequent baptisms were subject to delay until the parents gave evidence that they were going to make good their promises.

There was an interesting suggestion put forward as early as 1940 that if a family have children of five years of age not yet attending Sunday School, then the baptism of further children in that family should be delayed until the over fives have joined the Sunday School.[8]

The decision we came to was commonsense given the parameters we were working to. We did not want to impose penalty clauses on subsequent infants because of the parents tardiness to attend church. We had no right to refuse baptism, but power to delay it for instructional purposes. Thus, given that the policy had its own delay built into it (at the parent's choice) we would ask all families to come through the same policy regardless of whatever policy previous infants had been baptised under. After all, the parents should have been in church anyway. We were asking no more than they themselves had promised on the occasion of their first infant's baptism.

In the case of this family whom I will call the Hardakers, the policy letter was sent to them, and I waited with some anxiety because we had only just got going with the new policy. Nothing happened for a while and then one morning the mail dropped through my letter-box and I recognised Archdeacon Paul's handwriting on the outside of the envelope. It read:

> Following a telephone call I have now received a letter from Mr and Mrs Hardaker of Whitehill. They find the pre-baptism discipline outlined in your baptism policy letter beyond them. They quote particularly the section of the letter dealing with a considerable change in lifestyle which they feel you have no right to demand! (The letter didn't actually say this. It said effectively that regular Sunday worship where one hasn't been in the habit can be 'quite a jolt to a lifestyle'—see above.) Paul continued:
>
> They are particularly annoyed because you took their wedding and baptised an earlier child as well as two nephews without the present stipulations. I have to say that you are, whether you wish to or not, creating an atmosphere of some hostility to the church in Bordon by possibly demanding that people should run before they walk. Unless you have a particular reason why I should not I will refer the Hardakers to the Revd X who is in the picture.
>
> I am sorry that these things keep on happening as I am certainly no believer in indiscriminate baptism and appreciate what you are trying to achieve, but I do begin to question the pastoral wisdom of the way you are going about it.
>
> With my best wishes,
> Yours sincerely,
> Paul.

What makes a valid sacrament? Archdeacon Paul said that he was no believer in indiscriminate baptism, though it is not clear exactly what he meant by that. It did come up for discussion in the County Sound radio programme where I remember Paul saying that indiscriminate baptism was to him the carrying out of a baptism without any real attempt to try and explain to parents and godparents what was actually involved in the sacrament. In a sense that was all we were trying to do, but in a more clearly defined way.

The decision to direct the Hardakers to another parish at a time shortly after the introduction of the new policy, marked as it was by the press debate, effectively meant that we had reached a point beyond which we could not go. Without clear support from above we could never enforce this policy with any long-term understanding by the community. The families who had finally had their offspring baptised elsewhere, having 'toppled' our policy in their particular cases, obviously saw their achievement as a victory for human rights. Very recently a close friend of mine from Headley went into her village shop and overheard the following:

'I thought everybody had three rights in life in this country—to have your baby christened, to get married in your local church and to be buried in the churchyard.'

Those casual remarks underline the clear assumption running through English folklore: baptism of an infant is a right, and it is a sore grievance to refuse or to appear to refuse anyone their right.

Despite archdeacons letters and occasional mutterings of discontent we carried on with the baptismal policy. We knew that had we asked the PCC to debate it and make a decision it might not have got through, but the consulting of the PCC was an act of pastoral wisdom not a legal requirement. The three Anglican clergy felt that we were the ones who, by our ordination, had the responsibility for administering Word and Sacrament and that at the end of the day would have to give an account for our ministries. It was our conviction that the Sacrament of Holy Baptism ought not to be administered without due preparation, and this is what motivated our actions. We were prepared to run with our convictions. There was a cost for doing this, but it was a cost which, at the time, we were prepared to pay.

I said at the beginning of this chapter that by moving to the new policy we would find ourselves playing a new ball game. We most certainly were. The pace was moving faster than I was happy with at the time, but the policy had my support. I had a hunch that there was a sliding scale of ascending criteria in baptismal policies, and I had been thinking for a number of years about how those criteria might be defined. I listened to clergy on their differing baptismal policies around the country and I gleaned from books and magazines that there were parishes who operated much tougher standards over infant baptism than we could get away with. How did they get there? I wondered. My first sabbatical leave and a meeting with an old friend gave me the chance to find out.

Notes

1. I borrow the phrase from the title of Wesley Carr's book on the occasional offices, *Brief Encounters* (SPCK: 1985).
2. At the time of writing the Chairman of MORIB has been in communication with the Church Commissioners about including the number of infants undergoing a service of thanksgiving and blessing in their annual returns. It is likely that Chester Diocese could be the first to experiment with this (see next chapter).
3. Now Bishop Paul Barber of Brixworth in the Diocese of Peterborough.
4. See Michael Wooderson *The Church Down our Street* (MARC: Eastbourne, 1989).
5. See my Chapter 12 on the Canons.
6. The local radio programme was initially set up by the late Gerry Dunkley, the religious programmes producer of County Sound. He telephoned me to ask for suggestions for the programme. I was invited to participate but for family reasons was unable to do so. In

the event David Pawson took part. The programme was lively!

7. It would have been destructive all round to have pursued this further with Paul and the Diocesan Bishop. Conflict might well have undone years of previous work, but it makes the point that those in higher authority must take responsibility for intervention and its consequences.

8. See *Reforming Infant Baptism* by Buchanan, Wright and Owen (Hodder and Stoughton, 1990), page 72.

Chapter 7

THE BAPTISMAL RICHTER SCALE

When the driver of an electric train starts it from rest, he does not immediately put the control handle to full power, otherwise he might burn out the traction motors. The train has to gather some speed first to create a back voltage in the motors and so limit the amount of current passing through the windings. The driver therefore accelerates the train through a series of notches.

I had been eleven years in the parish of Headley/ Bordon. During that time we had 'notched up' the baptismal policy three times. We felt after October 1988 that we were close to burning out our baptismal traction motors! I wondered how far it was possible to go in a parish without running into serious trouble 'from above'. If those in ecclesiastical authority were to support strict baptismal policies, then the church as a whole might be ill thought of by the populace (cf the marriage revision proposals) but the clergy would have support and would feel supported. Hostility could be lived with from 'below'. If those in authority feel in all good conscience that they can not support a baptismal policy, then that effectively limits how far one can go. We had found that limit in our particular case.

But where is the limit?

In the spring of 1987 I took five weeks' sabbatical leave, two of which I spent in the splendid Gladstone Library at St Denial's, Hawarden, near Chester. St Denial's was bliss. For two weeks undisturbed by parish business I buried myself in books on baptism and attempts at reform. Almost as an aside from my main study I doodled on a piece of paper with a Richter scale of baptismal policies. Starting from what I had known at Stowmarket, I pencilled in a series of clearly defined notches up to a last sector, which I called the 'red zone', where an incumbent does not baptise babies at all. (It has been done!) I came up with six categories which I labelled: All comers, Open, Hurdles, Communicant status, Rigorist, and Red zone.

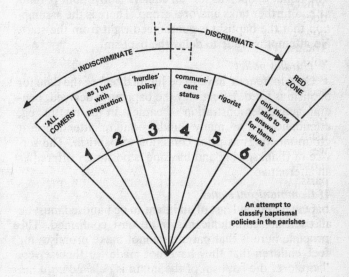

An attempt to
classify baptismal
policies in the parishes

I defined them more closely as follows:

1. *All comers*

An open policy which is indiscriminate. Baptism is never refused to any who request it. Minimal Canon Law conditions are met (sometimes not even these!), for example, all sponsors are baptised, though none may be confirmed. No preparation offered, other than vicar's visit and form filling. No requirements to have worshipped regularly insisted upon or required afterwards. This position is assumed by the majority to be the traditional baptismal policy of the Church of England.

2. *Open policy*

There is some form of firmer pressure for preparation. The policy is open as for 'all comers' above, but parents attend further talks and/or a group. There is the assumption that the baptism is guaranteed right from the start. No attempt is made to delay the baptism.

3. *Hurdles policy*

Certain 'fences' have to be jumped before the date for baptism is fixed. Effectively the baptism is delayed, pending active demonstration of earnest in the matter, eg, attendance for so many Sundays and/or attendance at group meetings as prior condition to baptism. The service of thanksgiving and blessing is positively offered as an alternative.

4. *Communicant status*

One parent at least of an infant to be baptised must be a practising communicant, or at least confirmed. The principle here is that parents cannot make promises for their children that they have not made for themselves. Therefore, the baptism of the infant is delayed until the condition is met; normally through the confirmation of one of the parents. If they are already confirmed, but lapsed communicants, they should 'return to the fold'.

5. *Rigorist*

Only children of established church families baptised. They will have been in the life of the church for a period, well prior to the baptism of the infant. Normally clear evidence of authentic Christian faith is sufficient.

6. *Red zone*

Only those able to answer for themselves are baptised. This should work within the conscience clause of Canon B22, the bishop being informed that the incumbent does not wish to baptise babies.

These divisions on the scale were arbitrary in one sense, but matched what I had either experienced or read of in other parishes. Every parish in the country is somewhere on the scale. The nation's expectancy is still at stage 1, but more and more people will have had experience of some form of firmer preparation, as envisaged in stage 2.

I used to question families when they approached me for the baptism of the second child whether they had experienced the kind of preparation we were doing in other parishes. It was still quite rare. The vast majority had usually been prepared by the vicar on one visit to the home or at the parsonage study.

In stage 2 I had in mind particularly the kind of filmstrip or video evening which more and more parishes are using for preparation in groups. At stage 2 I am assuming that there is still no requirement to attend church beforehand. In Headley/Bordon we moved from stage 1 to 2 when we first introduced the preparation group meetings.

At stage 3 things are starting to be 'felt' by the families. They will realise that the baptism appears to have become conditional on clearing the fences and they may want to consider the alternative. At stage 2 they will have been encouraged to reflect on the Sacrament. In stage 3 they are sensing that decisions need to be made.

Stage 4. 'Communicant status' represents a minority of parishes who take the very logical step of asking for the confirmation of one parent. Canon Law requires godparents to be confirmed, but parishes which insist on this are rare. Throughout the time at Headley/Bordon, I worked to a 'one out of three' godparent requirement and obtained it in 90% of the cases. Most applicants were a little fogged as to what confirmation was in the first place!

The Alternative Services place greater emphasis on the role and commitment of the parents in the services of initiation. This means that the law (ie, canon law) now lags behind liturgical expressions. The baptismal policy at 4 tries to bridge the gap.

Stage 5. The 'rigorist' parishes represent those where there is a genuine observable faith and commitment on the part of the applicant for the baptism of the infant. Those will be the people who are well 'inside' the congregation already. We had a number of these at Bordon and the baptisms were always congregational occasions of joy and thanksgiving. This is precisely what is envisaged as the norm in the Prayer Book: all citizens are part of a Christianised, confirmed, believing country. The reality of the situation, to borrow Colin Buchanan's phrase, is 'self-evidently otherwise'.

A rigorist parish isn't necessarily an evangelical one. Catholic parishes whose doctrine of the sacraments is high would naturally want to ascertain the right intention of a request for baptism. But there certainly will tend to be a majority of evangelical 'Bible-belt' parishes in the rigorist camp. They will be looking for evidence of serious intention and genuine faith before agreeing to baptise a baby. These parishes do exist!

So do parishes in the 'red zone', stage 6. I called it the 'red zone' because on an engine temperature gauge when the needle is in the red something is likely to go wrong. In theory it is not quite possible to have a Church of England parish where only those able to answer for themselves are baptised. In practice certain clergy have come to a point in all good conscience where they feel they cannot baptise babies any longer on theological grounds. In such cases the Diocesan Bishop appears to have made an alternative arrangement where another clergyman or reader does what infant baptisms there are. The precedent for this was set, as far as I am aware, by the Revd Christopher Wansey at Roydon in Essex. His case appeared to be a 'one-off' at the time, but I have since heard of other clergy and parishes in his situation.

Thus far my baptismal Richter scale was doodling on a piece of paper. I wondered what the real picture was out in the parishes. Here was I having experienced some minor flak down at stages 2 and 3 of my scale. How did parishes who worked higher up the scale live with it?

There followed one of those God-incidences that we experience from time to time. While at St Denial's I went over to visit my old friend from Ridley Hall days, Raymond Dent. Raymond was vicar of Emmanuel's, New Brighton at the top end of the Wirral peninsula, and his rectory garden runs down to the banks of the Mersey. Lunch at his parsonage is an entertainment, watching a never-ending stream of vessels ply down the estuary of the great river, with the sky line of Liverpool in the background.

Raymond had spent all of his ministry in Chester Diocese, at Hyde, Eastham and Runcorn before moving to New Brighton and so he knew the diocese pretty well!

At the time of my visit he was just drawing up a questionnaire on baptismal policies for the Board of Mission and Unity of the diocese. To my surprise and delight he agreed to use my Richter scale for the diocesan wide survey. From this I would get a picture of a diocese.

The questionnaire sent out to the parishes contained thirteen questions and three sliding scales on which to mark where parishes thought they were on the policy spectrum. There was also a space for comment.

The whole survey went off extremely well and the information returned quite valuable. I am indebted to Raymond for all that follows.

The questions covered population and the number of baptisms per year in three categories: Adult (over 13), Child (4 to 12), and Infant (0 to 3). It then enquired whether there was a recognised baptismal policy and how many years it had been in operation. The remainder of the questionnaire went as follows:

5. Was the policy initiated: by the incumbent alone?
                                by the incumbent and staff?
                                by the incumbent and PCC?
                                by the PCC alone?

6. Was there any conflict in establishing the policy from:
    Parishioners   a lot/some/very little/none
    PCC   a lot/some/very little/none
    Clergy   a lot/some/very little/none

7. How well is the policy running?
    very well/moderately well/acceptable/badly/atrocious!

8. After how many years do you expect to review the policy?

9. Do you positively suggest a 'blessing' as an alternative in your literature or verbally?

10. If you have a hurdles policy (see spectrum):
    How many times do they have to come to church?
    How many times do they attend groups or other meetings?

11. Do other denominations acknowledge the policy?
    Yes/Indifferent/No.

12. Is there a follow-up programme?

13. Are lay church people involved in any follow-up?

The questionnaire was sent out on 20th October 1988

to the clergy of the Diocese of Chester including 244 incumbents, 15 to bishops, archdeacons and others as well as 33 to assistant clergy. From these, 148 were returned by the 28th November 1988 showing a 53% response. This indicated a great interest in the subject. Apparently a 30% response to a questionnaire is considered good and clergy are no better than other groups when returning surveys. A few more forms came in after the November 28th deadline.

The principal findings were as follows:

The average parish size (parishioners per incumbent) was 8,100.

The population size covered by the returned questionnaires was 120,000.

Average number of baptisms per parish per year was 44, of which 5% were adults, 9% were children, and the remaining 86% infants. A majority of parishes had at least one adult baptism each year.

73% of parishes had a recognisable baptism policy.

40% of these policies had been started by the incumbent alone.
20% by the incumbent and staff.
40% by the incumbent and PCC.

Controversy experienced in starting the policies was minimal.

Similarly most policies seemed to be running moderately well.

One third of parishes offered an alternative series of blessing.

The policy spectrum was of course the part I was longing to see. The questionnaire had asked three questions of which the answer was to be a mark on the sliding scale of policies:

1. Where is the parish policy now?
2. Where would the incumbent (with proper backing) like to be?
3. Where would the people of the church like to be?

The results were placed on a bar chart as below:

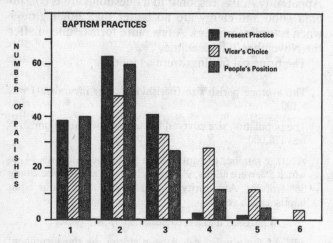

BAPTISM PRACTICES

- ■ Present Practice
- ▨ Vicar's Choice
- ▦ People's Position

N U M B E R OF P A R I S H E S

1) **ALL COMERS:** Baptism is never refused. Minimal canon law conditions are met and no preparation is offered other than Vicars talk/visit and form filling.
2) **OPEN POLICY:** As for ALL COMERS but parents attend further talks/course with perhaps written material or film strip.
3) **HURDLES POLICY:** The Baptism is delayed pending active demonstration of earnest in the matter, eg attendance at church as a prior condition to Baptism. A Blessing is offered as an alternative.
4) **COMMUNICANT STATUS:** One parent must be a practising communicant.
5) **RIGORIST:** Only children of established church families baptised.
6) **RED ZONE:** Only those able to 'answer for themselves' baptised. (Within conscience clause of Canon B22.)

One might have expected that with a Richter scale of ascending difficulty the numbers operating the various policies in the different categories would be highest on the left and showing a slow decline to the right. In fact the most used category was number 2: The 'Open policy with preparation'. However, if the other 47% of the diocese had returned their forms and those results added in, the picture may have been just that. Nevertheless from the sample received it showed a significant proportion who were in favour of the kind of policies we were operating down in Hampshire. Only a minority of parishes were into zones 4 and 5 with none in the red zone. But note that four clergy wished to operate in the red zone and still more would have liked to operate a communicant parent status policy. The people were not far behind the clergy in desiring to work a tighter policy. To me this is the significant factor. It showed that there is a groundswell of support for making infant baptism more of a challenge and offering it at a level which requires people to face the spiritual issues involved more clearly.

It is possible to prove any point one wants using statistics in the way politicians do after a general election, but it is the comments received from the clergy which are perhaps the truest indicator to the state of baptism in the parishes of Chester Diocese. They are now appended without further comment in the order received.

Other parishes don't acknowledge my policy.

Thanksgiving service obligatory for all. I would be very enthusiastic about a Diocesan policy.

Note local church 'model'—community church or gathered church. Difficult implications in rural parishes.

'Open policy' tried. Uncomprehending parents in rural area can make results of firmness disastrous and far-reaching.

Keep in mind the difference between a descriptive and prescriptive report. If you want the latter join the Baptists.

Baptism seen as opportunity for mission, a way of keeping 'open-door' access. Bad experience as layman of rigorist vicar in country area.

Numbers are very important. With population of 20,000 and 70 baptisms a year any other difficult to administer. Lay people unwilling to be involved in preparation.

CPAS video used with explanation, not judgement. With

crèche, mums and toddlers and evangelistic outlook, policy is producing new members.

Thanksgiving offered to all enquiries. Three training sessions to go on to baptism. Policy only just started.

The major hurdle is at Confirmation and the increasingly specific teaching on Christian responsibility.

Major review in progress. Policy likely to be 'Hurdles' from 1989.

Minimum of one confirmed godparent or parent to make response 'I am willing' with integrity. Caused great gulf between church and unchurched parents.

Thanksgiving first, then attendance, 'Stairway' video, home visit followed by baptism if required.

Parents and one godparent must be confirmed.

Only been running one month. Confirmation offered to church-going parents. Preparation leaflets available. PCC disillusioned with hundreds of baptisms and no new members.

'Hurdles' refers to discussion/understanding groups, *not* making them come to church for so many weeks!

Would love to be stricter. Cheap grace is worthless (Bonhoeffer). Neighbour baptises all-comers. Need/want a thorough Diocesan policy to represent church.

My 'open policy' veers to 'all-comers'. I do not like to ignore rules and to lower standards, but I do wish to 'suffer little children to come unto him'.

A continual problem. People generally promise anything to get the baby done. The grapevine always tells them which parish will 'do' it, with no questions asked.

Need for a firm Diocesan policy recognised and practised by nonconformist churches also.

With two small-numbered parishes I know all the people— fortunate. Helpful attitude encourages worship, the reverse antagonises.

In a small village with generations of residents all with strong, close loyalty to church, anything other than 'all comers' would cause hurt and dismay.

Nothing short of a 'Rigorist' Diocesan policy would give the climate for a similar one in parish—that's the aim. Problems with neighbouring parishes.

Aware of internal tension between conservative theology and 'graced response' and psychological motivation. I am being pushed reluctantly towards 'Hurdles' policy.

Treated as a 'public relations' exercise with as few obstacles as possible. Strict about permission if from outside the parish.

Although our theology is somewhat mixed, many are coming to faith in Christ as part of our follow-up programme.

Lay people deliver MU anniversary cards. Baptism cards distributed at Family Service. Pram Service fills gap between baptism and Sunday School.

Parishioners only. No child refused baptism if parents resident or on electoral roll. Otherwise not spiritual refugees.

I find the categories unhelpful, since our open policy is not indiscriminate. It is the policy we believe is right.

Churchwarden answered (interregnum). Committed core/younger members would prefer 'Rigorist'. Older generation can't understand this.

A few would ideally like 'Red Zone' but without 'conflict'.

Baptism used as an evangelistic tool—follow-up brought 45% of couples to faith and commitment. Hurdles can sound disapproving, but follow-up is effective.

Not easy to analyse. Some possibly don't apply because they know they would not come to church. What good is the rite without the right attitude and faith?

Great variety of opinion in the congregation. Younger, keener more to right. Aim is to get lay involvement, care and responsibility.

Used to refuse to children of unmarried parents, now regret this. I regard all baptisms as a privilege to undertake. Deplore restrictions.

When Inducted I promised, as all incumbents do, to seek out and baptise the unbaptised. THAT I DO.

I am founder/committee member of MORIB and am always happy to speak for them whenever possible.

Not entirely satisfied with 'all comers' but any alternative would have to be followed by every parish in the diocese.

Controversy for clergy—inside or outside the parish? Congregation covers the whole spectrum.

'Rigorist' is great theologically, but 'Red Zone' is the only one sensible in 1988. Confirmation should be commissioning occasions only.

'Do you have...policy?' prejudges the whole issue as to what is meant by 'policy'.

The majority baptised are those of regular/fairly regular members plus those married in the church. Some non-attenders come regularly after.

Slight follow-up: magazine and cards with Mother and Toddler and Sunday School.

Feel strongly that imposing 'Hurdles' is counter-productive. Parents will not understand the substitution of a blessing and go down the road to next church.

Not really 'all comers'—there is a lengthy home visit using the service as a teaching vehicle. I respond to requests rather than seeking out unbaptised.

Insisting on service at Morning Prayer, first Sunday in the month is quite a 'Hurdle'—out here anyway! Half go off next door for Sunday afternoon do's.

We are finding that church families prefer a service of blessing and it is the non-church members who actually want baptism.

All applicant families receive instruction. But in the last resort all presented for baptism are baptised. God acts in baptism—we must not hinder his action.

Inherited an indiscriminate policy with no visit made, so some ill-will ensued when minimal preparation required. Child of co-habiting couples not baptised while parents unmarried.

Newly inducted so cannot be certain about parish position, but use my own feelings at this stage.

'Hurdles' or more is contrary to church and Christ's teaching. Rather grab the opportunity. This is the official Church of England position.

I would welcome believers' baptism. Failing this would welcome 'no cheap grace' and even a loose Diocesan policy.

Parents must be believers (of any denomination). Would like to discuss baptism with the PCC and ask where they think the emphasis should be.

Incentive for this exercise is that results will be published. Number of requests for baptism outside parish: 24. Reason for low number is not the policy.

Would like to tighten policy up but only with agreement/ cooperation from neighbouring churches.

New incumbent, adapted existing policy. To be reviewed shortly with staff for recommendation to PCC.

Our task is to encourage and nourish faith and not to put hurdles in the way, nor can we sit in judgement on the faith of others.

The problem in introducing a firmer policy is the prevalence of neighbouring clergy who accept all-comers. Some firm Diocesan guidelines would help.

Use made of video presentations.

We have an open policy, but we do not assume that the baptism will take place until after preparation completed.

Follow-up through Pastoral Link Scheme.

Unease felt with policy where 90% are never seen again. Could only support more rigorist policy with uniform policy abided by in Diocese and Deanery.

'Thanksgiving' Service is a condition of coming to baptism.

Visitation and anniversary cards used. Mothering Sunday and Family Service.

Policy involves meeting with vicar and, if baptism is private, parents come to following family service for welcome and to receive a card. Pram Service encouraged.

Although I think there is quite a lot of dishonesty in the matter as it stands, in practice the present system has brought some adult communicants into church.

I have tried a policy and have found it not to work. I visit and there is a genuine concern to maintain proper principles, not allow church to become a sect.

I feel that Canon Law is perfectly adequate.

I would be unhappy to turn people away unless they were blatantly unwilling to consider seriously what we're about. Inclusive rather than exclusive.

Easier if PCC see need for new birth and saving faith. Publicising policy necessary so that PCC members can answer questions.

Difficulty of bringing in a policy where none has existed. Especially dealing with flak. Difference between urban/country.

We involve 'Hurdles' with the hope that this will mean parents seek God deeply and we give them the opportunity to attend new Christians courses as follow-up.

I am interested in researching the connection between Baptism and Christian instruction. Dr D. McGavea said post-baptismal teaching is more valuable than any done before.

I would support an open policy that included the option of thanksgiving if after reflection parents request it. Responsibility for choice is theirs.

Not only politics is the 'art of the possible'. All baptisms at public service—trims the number of requests.

The 'old brigade' were brought up on open policy, uneasy about its passing. The newer folk are uneasy that we are not at least clearly Communicant level.

Follow-up in encouraging to come to Pram Service, etc. I am open to suggestions as to baptism preparation material.

Policy is under review at present.

I do not like the wording of Question 3. Those who operate an open policy (your category) ARE 'pursuing a deliberate pastoral policy of help and encouragement.'

We prepare parents and some godparents. Baptisms only during a regular Sunday service—currently 3rd Sunday, 10am, 11.15 and 6.30pm.

'Open' policy for parishioners with letter and visits for parents/ godparents. Follow-up via Mother and Baby Groups (3) and lay visiting. Sunday kindergarten for 3 years upwards.

Nearly all parents have a fringe affinity. Group preparation not possible. Church of England baptism policy is a chaotic mess—theologically and pastorally.

Conscientious position for me. I feel I cannot condone the perjury involved in other positions. But alternatives and follow-up could be more pursued.

Each baptism is an individual case and has to be ministered differently in village situation. A hard line with one family could turn the whole village.

Promises are to be kept. But when this is pointed out some parents object to basic honesty! 1970 Diocesan Form quoted Series II Introduction—it was withdrawn!

A new scheme is at present under consideration by PCC and should be implemented in the New Year.

I feel absolutely bound by the promises made at my institution, 1958. I emphasise this *is* a policy with theological understanding, *not* laissez faire!

Chapter 8

DIFFERING NEIGHBOURS?

For many years we have prepared our own cars for their annual MOT tests. Most of the time they fail on one or two minor points, which we can put right. We are tempted to look around to find one garage which is easier than another. Certain garages have reputations for being stricter than others, but in theory there should be a uniform standard for passing and failing a vehicle as the regulations are centrally laid down. In practice one garage will fail a component, whilst another will overlook it.

Operating a baptismal policy can at times feel like running a garage. If the hurdles seem too high to jump, the word soon passes around that ours is a church worth avoiding. The list of those that will 'do it' gets around the community grapevine.

From the beginning of our excursions into the realms of tighter policies, we became aware that neighbours with differing standards could upset the whole strategy. It wasn't simply a case that a family might find that a neighbouring parish would baptise their infant, but the fact that it did so left the local church with a black mark over it. People would be confused by greatly varying standards and their already negative opinions about us would be reinforced in a counter-productive way.

'Why is it that the Revd Bloggs is normal over christenings and our local vicar is so awkward?' we could imagine them saying.

There were at least four sets of neighbours who were relevant in the case of Headley/Bordon where baptismal practice was concerned—the Anglican deanery, St Matthews, Blackmoor, those who differed from us within our parish boundaries and congregations and in the case of St Mark's the position of the Methodist and United Reformed Church members.

Farnham Anglican Deanery

Quite early on in my time in the parish, I raised the matter of baptism in Deanery Chapter meeting and I discovered that there were as many opinions in the matter as there were parishes. Any thoughts that we could move towards a common policy as a deanery in the matter were totally unrealisable. Over the course of ten years in the deanery a large number of parishes had changed incumbents and discussions we had ten years before needed to be replayed. Baptism was never again discussed in Deanery Chapter in an open way during the rest of my time at Bordon, though I raised the matter again in 1989, a few months before I came to leave the area. It was mentioned as a possible topic for a meeting, but never got onto the agenda. When we moved to the three month attendance rule in October 1988 we had mentioned this to the Chapter meeting and expressed the wish that parishes would support what we were doing, at least in the matter of informing us if droves of parishioners were moving towards a 'softer' parish. The response was muted (the attendance was small at the meeting) and I had the distinct feeling of déjà-vu from the desultory conversation. We were pretty much out on our own in Farnham Deanery, but in a sense it didn't matter too much. Headley and Bordon were at the southern end of the deanery and six miles of open country formed a barrier between us and the urban end of the deanery around Farnham and Aldershot. There were two more supportive parishes.

One parish in the northern end of the deanery had an incumbent who operated a fairly 'clean lines' policy on infant baptism, to the extent of not baptising babies whose parents lived outside the parish.[1] In a couple of cases this worked in our favour. Where parishioners asked to go to another parish for baptism with good reason (such as their home or where they were married) the request was never refused, provided the other parish would take it on and liaise with us over preparation. A couple from my parish had approached the incumbant of the parish concerned and had been referred back to us. The incumbent told them quite simply and sincerely that they should approach their own parish for baptism (us) as that was where they should worship. The interesting thing is that there appeared to be no resentment on the part of the applicant at this response, and they were perfectly level-headed and accepting about it. I had previously made it clear in asking this couple to approach Revd Z that it wasn't automatic that he would accept their request, but they could ask him. Care taken setting up this sort of approach in this situation pays dividends for all concerned. The Revd Z's position is accepted with respect, as is ours, and the couple approach the whole matter with serious consideration. The church as a totality also presents a face of integrity of practice to the outside world. Incidentally, the parish to which I refer was not of evangelical churchmanship, but at the higher end of the scale—it is not only evangelicals who are interested in stricter baptismal policies. Another Bordon couple had approached this parish first, and had been subsequently referred to me. They were honest about it. Both this couple and the previous one above went through our procedures to get their infant baptised, but I can't remember seeing them again.

To the east the parish of Grayshott bordered ours. Grayshott is one of those desirable, mostly middle-class villages set in the pleasant Surrey/Hampshire border country. Many of the properties in the area appear from time to time in *Field* and *Country Life* magazines. At first sight such a parish would have little in common with the large estates of Headley/Bordon, but it was within walking distance of Headley Down and baptism requests were an ever present phenomenon. For some years in the mid 80s the youngish incumbent of Grayshott discussed the matter of baptism and baptismal reform quite seriously with me. It wasn't a matter of we in Headley/Bordon seeking to win other clergy to our parish policy, but there was a sincere interest to find out what had led us to introduce our patterns of baptismal preparation.

I have found that there are many clergy around who are seriously interested to follow up baptismal reform when a lead is given. Many older clergy have also shown an interest. In former years they may have made identical suggestions to the ones we were now trying to implement, but found as we all do that baptismal reform in the Church of England is a very large mountain to chip away at.

I don't think there was ever any formal arrangement made between us and Grayshott over baptism. Our policy as already outlined was to allow all who wanted to to go elsewhere, subject to certain courtesies. This might be viewed by some as abdicating our pastoral responsibilities and by others as forcing people to look elsewhere. I maintain that it wasn't quite the case. If numbers drifting to Grayshott had been large then some formal arrangement might have been needed to cope with the refugee problem, but numbers weren't large and Grayshott and other parishes gladly did the baptisms that were requested (with the exception of the parish above).

One night I had a vicar from Chichester telephone me to say that a parent from his parish was probably going to approach me over the baptism of their child, because they were trying to get around *his* baptismal policy! Their plan was to join in with another related family, who did live in Bordon, and book in for what is known in folk religion as a 'double christening'. It was a good job that the vicar tipped me off, for not only was I able to explain our policy to him, but also I could lend support to his. The relation did indeed approach me and mention the double christening and I explained very carefully our policy and our policy towards non-residents. I was able to do this without mentioning that I had been tipped off and so I made it quite clear to the person who was resident in Bordon that I could not arrange a double christening including their other relation without the written consent of the vicar concerned. I knew that in this particular case this would not be given. I don't think that the 'local' christening went ahead either. Neither do I know if they tried another parish somewhere and were taken on there.

St Matthew's, Blackmoor

There was one parish that simply could not be ignored, if any tighter baptismal policy in Headley/Bordon was to work and that was St Matthew's, Blackmoor. Blackmoor church is a fine Victorian building, set in the orchards of the Selborne estate and bordering on its famous neighbour parish of Selborne, from where the Revd Gilbert White wrote *The Natural History of Selborne*. To the east of Blackmoor church lie the dark military training ranges of Longmoor Camp, but to the north lies Whitehill, a community of some eight thousand people at the southern end of Bordon/Whitehill new town. (I apologise to the residents at my deliberate confusion of nomenclature. I assume at the time of writing that this problem of one name for the one town has still not been resolved.)

Not only was Blackmoor responsible pastorally for one third of the town, it was also in the Diocese of Portsmouth. Some discussion of the diocesan boundaries took place in the late 1970s, but in those days there was green space between the dioceses; now it is completely built over. One street makes all the difference. Given the way things are, several folk who were resident in Bordon would worship at St Matthew's and vice versa. It was essential that clear co-ordination over baptismal policy should be established. Not only did this apply to baptisms; weddings and funerals had to be co-ordinated too. We always kept strict faith with regard to roads for weddings residence qualification and Christian Aid collecting, but not for funerals. Sadly, through no fault of the clergy concerned, but largely from pressure of certain families and undertakers, I ended up taking a slightly greater number of funerals than I should have done. For folk religion reasons (and because Blackmoor churchyard was nearly full!) many Whitehill families insisted on coming to Headley. Given that a large proportion of these families were from the 'travellers' groups, off the former caravan sites, they were hard to resist. Precedents created here in the matter of funerals could have long term consequences.

Fortunately there was only one incumbent at Blackmoor throughout the whole of my time in Bordon. That was the Revd Richard Inkpen, former Rural Dean of Petersfield and one of the early leaders who sparked off an interest in charismatic renewal in the late 1970s. Richard and I and our wives soon got to know each other. We discussed everything from prayer groups to ley lines, from theology of mission to lobbing funerals at each other. We talked about setting up a proper council of churches for Whitehill and Bordon, about relations with the Garrison church and how to cope with a growing exodus from our churches of many charismatics to surrounding house churches. We didn't see eye to eye on the beneficial effects or otherwise of the 'Full Gospel Business Mens Fellowship International'. He was from a strongly Anglo-Catholic background and at the end of a thirteen year friendship he had to confess that he was still none the wiser in understanding how evangelicals ticked than when he first met me!

However, we were at one over our concern for a co-ordinated baptism policy over the new town, indeed the whole area. The population of Bordon and Whitehill was approaching 15,000 and it was highly likely that the young growing mobile population would approach our two churches for the majority of their infants to be baptised.

From the beginning of my time there we liaised strictly about baptising across the parish and diocesan boundary. In the early days when I tried to encourage families to have baptisms in the 'wooden' church, a fair number would want to go to Blackmoor. Richard gave me good support in those days and would only accept baptisms from Bordon where there was a genuine Whitehill and Blackmoor connection. When the new church was opened in 1982 and our congregation was growing, the trend reversed itself. The new building attracted a lot of people (and repelled others—see previous chapters!), but where an applicant was resident in Richard's parish I always stalled such requests and referred them to him.

After 1982, when we introduced the 'attendance at one service' rule, we liaised carefully and Richard watched with interest to see how things would go. After discussion with his Parochial Church Council, he introduced a series of teaching sessions for baptism applicants (I think it was three in number) and baptisms usually went ahead after that.

When in 1988 we moved to the three-month rule, Richard and Blackmoor PCC took a parallel step forward and instituted something similar.

Like us a letter was sent out to families, the text of which (in full) read as follows:

Dear

Thank you for your enquiry about baptism. This letter is to let you know about our policy for infant baptism in this parish.

What is baptism?

It is called a 'sacrament'. This means that as we experience some visible or audible act, so God gives a special blessing represented by that act. We pour blessed water over the head of the infant (or, of course, adult) and claim those inner spiritual gifts that Jesus teaches us about. Just as water is used for cleansing and for reviving, so the water of baptism represents what God is offering to those being baptised—a cleansing from the taint of sin (our tendency to disobey God), and a re-vitalising. In fact Jesus talks of 'being born again', making a completely fresh start in life.

Through baptism we become part of God's church, members of his family, the representatives of Jesus, to whom we belong, and whom we are to follow and obey.

Infant baptism

The church has always been prepared to baptise infants and children on the understanding that they belong to God through their parents provided, of course, that their parents are themselves fully practising Christians. Infant baptism also involves godparents.

What is expected of parents and godparents? Going to church?

Going to church is not enough in itself. In the Baptism Service you would be expected to say (among other things) 'I turn to Christ', which means you accept Jesus Christ as your Lord and Saviour, and you belong to him as part of his church. This will have involved your being confirmed by the Bishop, and your regular receiving of the Holy Communion, as Jesus instructed us to do, and a seeking after what

God wants you to be doing for him, day by day, as his servant.

This doesn't fit our situation—so what do we do?

If you are not confirmed, or don't go regularly to church, you are one of many who ask for baptism. Most are themselves baptised, usually as infants, but have never accepted this wonderful relationship God offers us. If this is YOU, please read on—

Step One:

As a gesture of thanks to God for the gift of your infant, we ask you to come to church for a short service of thanksgiving, during Evensong, on the first Sunday of the month, at 4.00 pm. The only preparation you need for this is to let the Vicar know you are coming. You may bring a few family, etc if you wish, but the only people who are needed for this are the parents and the baby!

Step Two:

If you wish to go on from there to baptism for your infant (some people feel this thanksgiving is enough) we will then ask you to attend church regularly, either at the main 9.45 am service, or at Evensong (4.00 pm) for a period of three months. This will help people to discover what the church really is, and also give you the chance to offer worship to God with his church.

Step Three:

During this time you will be asked to join a series of 'teachings' on the Christian faith and life. This will help you to know just what you are asking for in baptism.

Step Four:

If, after all this, you are not happy about the commitment parents are asked to make in baptism, then you back out, at least until you feel ready to ask for more help and guidance.

If you are happy about it all, then we can make the necessary preparations for the baptism of your infant.

It may be that one of you is happy, the other not—at this stage parents are welcome to go ahead, on the understanding that the one who cannot accept the teaching should not make any promises or declaration at the baptism.

Step Five:

You may at this stage conclude that you should start preparing for confirmation. This is the way in which we, as adults, openly accept Jesus, and his spiritual gifts, and prepare for God's special blessing, after which we can go on, as regular receivers of Jesus, in the sacrament of bread and wine, the Holy Communion, to live as part of God's family.

To sum up

Arrange for the thanksgiving; come regularly to church; attend the teachings; bring the infant to baptism; prepare to go ahead yourself to confirmation and regular Holy Communion.

Richard Inkpen,
Vicar.

The letter represented a baptismal policy, which I considered to be tougher than the 'Hurdles' policy we had instituted. Richard's text was clearer and bolder than ours, and perhaps because of his clarity, he earned more respect! There was an integrity to the letter as a whole and he was honest about confirmation. It was challenging and yet, if we are honest in our understanding of what the Prayer Book and ASB require of parents and godparents, there is little that could be contested, apart from the courage Richard had in daring to send it out. It based itself on covenant theology in terms of 'they (the infants) belong to God through their parents provided, of course, that their parents are themselves fully practising Christians.' He also said something about godparents which we in Bordon and Headley largely ignored.

This policy also placed a further first hurdle. The service of thanksgiving was the first hurdle, not an alternative option, as we tried in Bordon. Richard also made the point that we made about one parent only being willing to make the promises. What was the result?

After a few weeks I asked him, 'How is the baptism policy going?'

'Badly,' he replied in his inimitable way.

'How badly?' I asked.

'Well, a couple of families have made a start. Some are going to look elsewhere and another family have challenged me openly.' In short he was getting precisely the same reaction that we got. He was considering how he might soften it up a little, but I suggested that perhaps he stay with it for a while to give it a real run. As far as I know, he did. I received one or two phone calls over the next few months from Whitehill families wanting to come into Bordon and Headley but I carefully explained that the baptismal policy at Blackmoor was precisely the same with us. Usually hearts sank at the news! However, some were caused to think quite deeply in the matter and the fact that we ran in parallel gave us much mutual support.

One telephone call was from an irate father who wanted my support over a grievance that Blackmoor parish would not christen his children. Towards the end of the conversation I felt his anger being turned towards me, especially when I would not collude by giving the bishop's and archdeacon's addresses. I suppose strictly speaking I was working against the letter of the law of Canon B 22.2, which allows parents to refer the matter to the bishop, but these were not my parishioners and I think Canon Law is something of an ass in the matter anyway. After all that is one of the reasons why I am writing this book in the first place! In any case none of us were technically refusing baptism.

If I had any criticism to make of the Blackmoor policy, and it is really a piece of hindsight wisdom rather than criticism, it would be that to suddenly jump to a three-month attendance rule from cold is asking for trouble. In Headley/Bordon I would have tended to make a similar criticism, except that we had run with a one-service attendance for six years and so the word was around that 'you had to go to church'.

As time went by Blackmoor modified slightly and it is interesting that more reliance for establishing the initial pastoral encounter has been placed on the first visit or phone call, and slightly less on the letter of explanation. This was something I discovered quite early on: the letter delivered cold when the family were unprepared for it could arouse hostility, however right we may have been!

In recent correspondence with Richard, I am pleased to see that he has persisted with baptismal experimentation and has stuck to his guns. Part of a recent letter read:

> It is interesting to see how situations develop over the months and years. I have not used one of those papers for enquirers for several months. I suppose the main change in approach is that when people inquire we first ask them if they are confirmed, and if not, why not. I regard this approach as necessary if we are seriously to help people to mean their promises at infant baptism. You will notice that this inquiry was explicit in the paper you refer to. In this decade of evangelism surely it would be contrary to our purposes *not* to challenge people about their own faith before discussing the baptism of their infants. Maybe God is directing things more than we realise, but the principal effect of this policy has been to bring a number of young couples into the worshipping community, and some of them already to be confirmed. We have stuck to the policy of inviting couples to make their thanksgiving—not in any sense as a possible alternative to baptism, but as an important first step—of accepting their relationship with their Maker, and starting their desire to co-operate with him over the spiritual development of their infant. None have refused the thanksgiving. No doubt some people are by-passing us, without our knowledge.

I hope that this parish of Blackmoor will stay with this policy for the whole of the decade of evangelism and carefully monitor and document it. One of the main recommendations I want to make in this book is that by seeing confirmation of at least one parent as the general qualification for the baptism of an infant, we are making sound sense of our doctrine and liturgy, and being evangelistic in the best Anglican tradition. Also, if we are skilled marketeers, the public will acknowledge that what is being asked is fair and sensible. Anything less may miss the goal. Well done, Blackmoor!

Other neighbouring parishes

To the south of Bordon lies the parish of Greatham. I discussed the Bordon policy with the incumbent there in the mid 80s and also with the Vicar of Liphook, to the south east of us. Bordon's main link with Liphook was the Social Security office! I frequently gave lifts on a Thursday morning to people who were unemployed and hitching lifts to Liphook in order to 'sign on'. But as far as baptism was concerned, there was little overlap.

At Greatham there was some. A number of families from Whitehill/Bordon tried to gain their children places in the crèche or play school in order to get them into Greatham Primary School. From here they would have an odds on chance of getting along the Longmoor Straight into the new comprehensive school at Liphook. Frequently a family would ask to have a baby baptised at Greatham as a first rung on the educational ladder! Such situations were carefully and sensitively handled. If I am to be honest, there were times when I would feel quite angry over this educational manipulation that went on. Blackmoor, as well as having a bold baptismal policy, also had an attractively situated Church of England Primary School. The admissions policy required that parents outside the catchment area should furnish evidence that they were regular worshippers before applying for their child to be entered on the school roll. This meant that I frequently had to sign letters for the Chairman of the Governors (Richard Inkpen above), that so and so had attended St Mark's regularly. At first I used to rejoice when a new family would turn up for worship. Ostensibly it was to accord with our policy, and thus get the child baptised, but there was also the motive of qualifying for admission to Blackmoor School. Some parents regularly joined the congregation as a result of this legal requirement, but there were others who disappeared promptly as soon as the school had agreed to take their offspring. Part of me laughed at their cunning, but mainly I was angry.

To the west of our parish lay a string of extremely thinly populated rural parishes in Alton Deanery and the Diocese of Winchester. A number of our families had strong links with Alton, but our baptismal and other pastoral links were minimal. I sensed from the vibes off various grapevines that there was little sympathy there to our policy, although we sought over the course of several years to relate what we were doing to our neighbouring Anglican parishes.

There were also dissenting voices within. Some members of the church committees, including the PCC, were far from happy with a strict baptismal policy. If one had to wait for everybody to be unanimous one would wait for ever, but I think it sound to say that if a baptismal policy is to work in a parish, then it needs a fair measure of support from the PCC.

The baptismal policy in our mixed congregation

At St Mark's we were a Local Ecumenical Project, a shared church with Methodists and United Reformed Church members. We operated under a Joint Church Council and an executive committee, which was effectively our PCC. A decision to work a baptismal policy could not be undertaken by one denomination alone.

What did the Methodists and the United Reformed Church feel about it all?

Local Ecumenical Projects stand or fall by the trust and relationships between their ordained ministers. My colleagues were Tony Bullock, Methodist superintendent minister of Petersfield, and Paul Dean, United Reformed minister for Farnham and Bordon. We enjoyed an excellent working relationship and on the whole we shared everything that mattered for the running of the church. I used to joke that between us we commanded a 20-mile length of the A325.

We spent a long time discussing baptismal practice. In short the Methodists and the United Reformed Church operate within a different set of co-ordinates when it comes to infant baptism. A Free Church minister may refuse to baptise any particular adult or infant if he so thinks fit, and he is quite within his rights so to do as a minister of Word and Sacrament. In practice few Free Church ministers refuse individuals and most would work within a policy agreed by the elders (in the case of the URC), or the stewards (in the case of Methodists). Not far from Bordon were two quite small Methodist churches in the same circuit as St Mark's, at Lindford and Standford. Couples who wanted to be remarried in church usually went there after being unable to be married in the local Anglican churches.[2] Several baptismal refugees took their infants to these Methodist churches too. They were all baptised with little fuss, which was good for the chapel funds if a family stayed, which some did. But it again left us in a bad light at Bordon and Headley.

I was once asked to go and lead a debate on the subject of baptism at Standford Methodist midweek fellowship. An animated discussion ensued and I sensed that, on the whole, the Methodists were more indiscriminate than the Anglicans. John Warren, one of the stalwart pillars of Standford Methodist church, whose family had been influential in building the church in the previous century, wrote an interesting letter to the paper on the matter of baptising infants. This letter is printed in Appendix 2. John's wife, Marion, a teacher, was an outstanding local preacher on the circuit and was always in demand for special occasions at St Mark's. Despite baptismal differences here and there, our fellowship remained good across the denominations.

With the URC's the issue of baptism was raised at an interesting time as it was a hot topic of debate within Guildford United Reformed Church district. One church in the district had a strong charismatic style, and tended to adopt a policy of baptism for believers only. While it was possible for an individual URC minister to take this position, individual churches could not as a matter of policy. The knock-on effect from this meant that the theology of baptism was very much under discussion in the URC circles. As far as St Mark's was concerned, the Methodists and URC representatives agreed with our experimenting with stricter baptismal policies, provided we weren't reckless or insensitive in our handling of requests.

The Free Church christenings were quite small in number by comparison with the Anglican ones. Requests for a Methodist christening were infrequent and usually meant that a family had a previous Methodist connection. Usually Methodist and URC baptisms came from those Free Church families who were already in the congregation, and like all such baptisms 'from within' they were truly family occasions. Nevertheless, there were Free Church lapsed members for whom christenings were no different in ethos from the majority of Anglicans. On one point of policy we had to agree ecumenically and that was that if families simply went down the list of ministers on the church noticeboard to find out who would do it, then they would find we had closed ranks. In practice this hardly ever happened, because the initial baptismal letter which we sent out was on church headed notepaper with all the denominational names on, and all of us had agreed the letter.

Last but by no means least we had dissenting voices of another sort. The significant band of lively believers who had come to faith through FGBMFI and house church circles didn't believe in infant baptism at all. They were represented on committees and voiced their opinion. They went along with our strict baptismal policies as a matter of solidarity with us, but in practice they didn't request baptism for their own offspring. They preferred, for genuine theological reasons, the service of thanksgiving. On several occasions I conceded to the use of rites of 'other churches' for the dedication of an infant and also some home grown services.[3] Strictly speaking I might just have been outside the law in doing so, but our Shared church constitution did allow us to experiment and from time to time use the rites of other churches.

These thanksgivings were a sight to behold. Several of them completely eclipsed the usual christening services for sheer sense of occasion. There were special songs written for the infant, special dances danced, extempore prayers prayed around the cot, the whole atmosphere was a kind of Graham Kendrick celebration. I think even the infants must have noticed that something was happening!

Why not? I think that if churches are to grow and we are to have a hope of penetrating this highly resistant nation of ours with the gospel of Jesus, then we have got to be prepared to take risks. The sure way to eventual demise is to take none.

I have come to the end of the account at the coal face. In July 1989 my family and I moved to a new ministry in Worcester Diocese and I write about that in Chapter 15. My work of over a decade in Bordon and Headley has to be left in the hands of successors, who will make of it what they will. I have talked about differing neighbours in a geographical sense and in a denominational sense, but there are also neighbours in a time sense—one's predecessors and successors. I have always found that going into a new pastoral situation it was wise to relate as far as one could to the work done by one's predecessors. It is rare that one could totally identify with all that had gone before, but if one's predecessors were seeking to follow the guidance of God and we were trying to do the same, then one might expect a clear sense of continuity.

Notes

1. The parish of St John's, Hale. It was this parish that informed me of its monthly special 'festal baptism' service.
2. This was at the time of the major debate on remarriage. The clergy and PCCs were considering the implications very carefully and Michael Powell, John Cherrill and I found ourselves in unanimous agreement that we did not wish to proceed to remarriages. This left an interesting situation in the Local Ecumenical Project at Bordon where the Methodist and URCs already did second marriages. After much discussion (totally amicable) among the three ecumenical ministers we decided that each tradition would follow its own discipline, with the condition that my Free Church colleagues would not automatically take on any wedding couples I wouldn't do. There had to be a genuine Methodist or URC connection first.
3. One member of St Mark's came from an apostolic pattern church in South London and we used their form of service for the dedication of the infant.

Chapter 9

DO WE REALLY REFUSE?

A few months ago I asked a question of the candidates who were standing in the elections to General Synod from the clergy of Worcester Diocese. I simply asked if the candidates felt they would support any moves in General Synod to make clearer the conditions upon which infants were admitted for baptism.

In their replies the seven candidates covered the whole range. One candidate admitted that he had problems with infant baptism as such, but was happy to continue working the church's rules. Another said that in his parish they operated a strict policy of welcoming everybody.

It is possible to find across any fair sample of Church of England clergy the whole range of baptismal policies that I outlined in Chapter 7. The comments from the clergy of Chester Diocese bear this out, but the time has come to ask some important questions.

Is there any dividing line between what has come to be called indiscriminate infant baptism and discriminate infant baptism? Is one welcoming and the other unwelcoming? Is one legal and the other illegal? Has one theological justification and the other not? Have both or neither any basis in Scripture?

These questions and the associated issues take us into a large area of pastoral and theological discussion and a fair slice of synodical history. I will start by asking the question 'Do we really refuse baptism to certain families who ask us for it?'

I often reply that I have 'refused' about three families in total since I began my ordained ministry seventeen years ago. Even then I would be reluctant to say that I listened to the request over the telephone or on the doorstep and gave a simple refusal: 'No, I am very sorry I cannot baptise your infant.' I virtually said that on only one occasion that I can remember. The whole attitude and approach of the person concerned was so negative, so cynical, so provocative and almost mocking of the Church that it would have been virtually casting pearls before swine to have gone ahead in that particular case. It happened at Bordon quite early on in my time there, before we had a baptismal policy of any kind in place.

Another case happened around the same time. I said 'no' in terms of an indefinite delay until the person concerned really showed that she was serious about the whole matter.

The third case of my saying 'no' was outlined in detail in Chapter 6, the case that was taken to the Bishop. Thus I have to say that I have never made a habit of saying 'no' to families who have requested baptism for their offspring, but I would want to say that I believe baptismal reform should include the giving of this right to the individual clergyman. Technically he does not at present have it.

It is interesting that my first vicar, Arthur Muxlow at Stowmarket, was asked by one of our youth fellowship there whether he had ever refused to baptise a baby. He replied that he had refused just once in his ministry for precisely the same reasons that I had mentioned above.

Nevertheless a large number of families would have said that they were 'refused' baptism under our tighter policies at Bordon. (See the newspaper cuttings in Appendix 2.) Strictly speaking and legally speaking they were not refused. They were merely being asked to join a process of preparation which would render them in a position to be able to take a meaningful part in the baptism of their infant. In saying this I have made value judgements and used language which will require unpacking and examination.

It is clear that where families felt they had been refused, what they meant was that they had been refused *on their terms*. But who makes the terms for baptism? Who lays down the conditions for baptism to be a valid sacrament?

Many times I tried to put myself in the position of the families. It's their first infant. They have been married in church by a vicar who 'did a good service' and it seems a matter of delightful routine for them to approach him to carry out the christening. In nine cases out of ten they are met by a smiling face at the vicarage door and in the opening sentences of the conversation the vicar gives the impression that he is only too delighted to carry out the request, whatever internal misgivings he might have. One couple in ten comes across someone like me, and are perplexed to be stalled a little in a routine matter which they have regarded hitherto as a human right. In the place of a simple uncomplicated routine they find themselves entering an unfamiliar world of attendance at services and preparation. They have not met it beforehand, neither have any of their friends and relations. They start to ask questions. 'Has the church the right to ask these things?' If the hurdles are jumpable then they may well do what is asked and suffer it. If not they may look elsewhere.

In one of the most useful books I have read on this area, the Dean of Bristol, Wesley Carr, puts it thus:

'One thing is sure. If for centuries the church has insisted on the baptism of infants, actively persued parents to have it done, and urged it as a duty to God and to the child, it is not possible to reverse that teaching by a mere change of doctrinal stance.'[1] My experience suggests that it will take much more than a change of doctrinal stance to reverse anything in baptismal practice!

The expectation of the population at large is of an all comers baptismal policy on the part of the whole church. They are confused and hurt when they find some odd person asking for more in the way of conditions, which they judge to be offside. The Chester Diocesan survey revealed that parishes are very much towards step 2 on the Richter scale and that preparation of some kind as a preliminary to baptism is steadily becoming the norm. This means that over the course of, say, a couple of generations it may be possible to get across to a large slice of the population that baptism is a holy sacrament that must be approached after proper consideration. The fact that the number of infant baptisms has shown a gentle decline over the last twenty years may be due to increasing secularisation; it may also be due to the effect of tighter baptismal policies.[2]

The case is being quietly built that it isn't sufficient for a parish here and there to be stricter. It needs a fairly broad-front agreement on policy across the face of the church. Until we have that and the public is aware of what that stance is, we are likely to continue to get annoyance and resentment from families over difficult baptism policies.

The fact is that many generations of parents, grand-parents and great-grandparents have passed through the occasional office of baptism and taken it for granted that the christening of their babies was a right with no strings attached, particularly of regular worship. In the main the populace has remained immune to the best efforts of the church to draw them into the worshipping body later on.

The by-pass phenomenon has rooted itself deep into English social rituals and there is still a profound surprise when vicars question it.

But the tide is turning. It is fair to say that the last thirty years have seen a quietly gathering momentum for a change in initiation procedures.

Wesley Carr informs us, for example, of an important conference of clergy held back in 1963 in the Diocese of Chelmsford (which has always been an interesting diocese for baptismal reform). At that residential gathering the clergy were almost unanimous in asking the bishop to devise and promulgate a policy for the administration of infant baptism in the diocese. After a later synod on the theology of baptism, the Chelmsford clergy voted on seven propositions. They were as follows.

	FOR	AGAINST
1. Holy baptism is rightly administered to children.	94%	6%
2. Christian parents may rightly postpone the baptism of their children until the years of discretion.	51.5%	48.5%
3. The church should provide a service of thanksgiving for and blessing of a child.	53.6%	46.4%
4. In present circumstances this service should be offered for all children, including those looking forward to baptism.	36.6%	63.4%
5. Baptism should not, save in an emergency, be administered without preparation of those concerned.	98.5%	1.7%

6. No child may be baptised elsewhere than in the parish in which the parents live, or are qualified as electors on the Electoral Roll, save with the consent and co-operation of the minister of that parish.   87.3%   12.7%

7. Baptism should normally be administered in the presence of a congregation of regular worshippers.   89.4%   10.6%

Had these recommendations become Canon Law and pastoral practice immediately following this vote, the Church of England would have been different today and I would not be writing this book!

The figure I want to focus on here is the 98% who voted that preparation of those concerned was important for the administration of the sacrament. Baptismal preparation does seem to have established itself firmly on the agenda.

In the General Synod debates of 1974, following the Ely Report of 1971, the members of Synod had the guidance of an important working paper by the Revd P. R. Cornwell.[3] That paper in my view first started to clear a way through the jungle. Cornwell focused up the key issues. In particular he separated out two possible directions ahead for administration of infant baptism: one, that it be administered subject to certain conditions and two, that it should continue to be at the request of the parents, who are willing to make the promises. This contrast should be taken as broadly defining what is meant by discriminate/indiscriminate infant baptism. Given this definition of this important boundary I would suggest that with reference to the Richter scale outline earlier, it is wrong to suppose that the policy steps we took in Headley/Bordon were discriminating or that we were operating a 'rigorous' baptismal policy. We were close to the boundary of rigorism, but it is arguable that we weren't quite there.

At a MORIB Conference in Shrewsbury in 1988, Bishop Colin Buchanan talked about boundaries in the matter of discrimination in baptism. He believed that a parish could operate quite demanding baptismal preparation policies within the scope of present Canon laws, but added that if one was over rigorous 'you might be pushing against the laws a bit'. 'It all depends,' he went on 'on what you mean by preparation.' This is indeed a key issue focusing on this boundary in the Cornwell discussion paper. What were we supposed to be preparing parents for?

The Ely Report in a footnote had first tried to define preparation of baptismal parents. It was as a test of 'sincere desire'. If baptism was to be continued to be administered to all parents who sincerely desired it, how would we know what sincere desire was? Virtually all the baptism parents I have had to deal with would have said that they sincerely desired it and would have wondered what the point of the question was. But the footnote said that sincere desire would be demonstrated where such parents were willing to receive such instruction as would allow them to take a meaningful part in the service of baptism.

This is excellent as far as it goes. It makes legitimate the necessity and duty of a minister to prepare parents for the service and it has the support of Canon Law (B 22.3) which makes it clear that parents have the same responsibilities as the godparents.

The choice of goals in preparation basically boils down to two: One, you prepare parents to take a meaningful part in the actual service of baptism. Two, you give the preparation necessary for parents to become full committed Christians, having made an adult profession of faith and being regular communicants. In the first case we are probably going not much further than the preparational goal that has been the vogue for a long time in the parishes of the Church of England. Most priests would try to attempt this kind of preparation. How effective is this? Is it even legitimate to have a form of preparation which is no more than a conscience quietener? Can parents and godparents take a meaningful part in any baptismal service if they profess the Christian faith, promise to encourage the child to be regular in public worship and private prayer (Alternative Service Book), to live by trust in God and to come to confirmation, yet have no real intention of fulfilling their commitment?

Is there some kind of 'half-way house' which allows parents and godparents to do this, as opposed to those who really intend to try and fulfil, because they have themselves come to a point of adult commitment to the faith?

The second goal in fact is really asking for conversion of one parent in order to proceed to a baptism and this immediately brings us into the related topics of baptism and evangelism, which I discuss in Chapter 14.

The General Synod at the time of the discussion following the Ely Report obviously began to home in on the fine distinctions to be drawn out from this crucial area of discussion. The discussion document circulated to the parishes spelled out both points of view.[4]

Infant baptism, except where the parents (or one parent) are members of the Church, practising, believing and worshipping' was seen as unscriptural. The practice of "baptism on request" or, as its critics described it, "indiscriminate infant baptism" devalued the sacrament in the eyes both of those within the church and those who are outside it, and the taking of promises in some cases at least had elements about it of the hypocritical and the blasphemous.

On the other hand, those who supported the traditional open baptismal policy on request saw that in discriminating between cases the clergy were putting themselves in the position of likely unjust judges. One clerical member of the General Synod put it thus:

> Rather than asking the parish clergy to make judgements upon people, we should be asking them to make quite sure that they explain as best they may the meaning of the requisite promises. We must do our best to help people understand what they are doing when they bring their children for baptism, but then we must leave the decision to them and the issue to God.

If this quotation sums up the argument to maintain the present system, then I have to say that that position covers the operating of a rather strict policy, such as we operated in Bordon.

I have always maintained that an essential part of baptismal preparation must be to introduce parents to the worshipping life of the church. In the majority of cases they were barely aware of its existence. I frequently used to receive enquiries from within the parish to speak to the vicar on a Sunday, and the enquirer was frequently nonplussed to be told that I was in church! There was no awareness that there existed a group of people who went to worship God one day a week, in this special building which they would enter only for a wedding, funeral, or of course the christening when their turn came. I maintain that it is not being unwelcoming to require such people to be made aware of the life of the local Christian community, as an essential component of any course of baptismal preparation. Of course preparation is crucial if we want to get this point across, otherwise it will merely be interpreted as a tiresome hurdle to be got over. It is easy to give the impression that a certain number of attendances qualifies for baptism, but this is not the point one is trying to make. In school, time is taken out for work experience. Visits are made to places of educational importance. Any apprenticeship requiring practical skills means time spent having a try and learning on the job. Baptism preparation should include a face to face encounter with the main weekly act of worship. We should then be able to say, 'How did you find the Sunday service? Have you ever been to a family service before? This is the community we hope you are going to start relating to after your baby's baptism.'

When we moved into the curate's houses at Stowmarket and then at Bordon, in both cases we had to contend with overgrown gardens. Previous curates had not exactly obeyed the Genesis injunction to till and keep the garden. Our first few weeks saw us mowing, cutting, digging and discovering. At first sight both gardens looked like continuous overgrown lawns, but slowly they were worked on, and boundaries became discernible where vegetable plots and flower beds had once been. Eventually the original shape of the garden emerged. Until the cutting and weeding had begun, no boundaries were assumed. Now they stood out.

Something like this has been emerging in baptismal reform. The digging and working in the garden of baptismal reform has thrown into relief some very clear boundaries. Some parents who have had some baptismal instruction, know what is involved, and accept in good faith the nature of the commitment and try to keep it. These must be distinguished from those who have similarly understood the nature of the undertaking and covertly have little serious intention of making any commitment, but still insist on the baptism of their offspring. One school of thought in the church says we must prepare them so that the onus is on them and we must leave the outcome to God and in each case baptise the baby. The other school of thought, the reformist, believes that the parent(s) should demonstrate a visible faith and seriousness of intention first before the baptism can be proceeded with.

No less a person than our excellent archbishop

appears to confuse the boundary here. Or at least he is not clear enough! In a short piece written on the 'Grapevine' (the diocesan newspaper of the Diocese of Bath and Wells), Bishop George takes the line that the Christian church has boundaries, but they should be open to all.

Christ may be the centre of our faith, but who belongs to him and his church? Is it open to all? In a real sense the answer is yes. Our church is the established church and all in our parishes have a right to avail themselves of our ministrations. It is not our practice to exclude anybody on grounds of class, creed or colour.

Of course, this 'right' doesn't imply unrestricted access to the Sacraments and ordinances, any more than a citizen who has the right to use public transport, but expects to have it free of charge! A simple test of this will result in a speedy exit from a bus or train.

And that may not be a bad analogy of the church. On the one hand, everyone has a right. Let us take baptism—the sacrament of initiation as an example. I hope that we encourage the baptism of young children, because that is central to our doctrine.

We should never set up such barriers and hoops that we actually discourage people from presenting their infants for baptism. I have not known rigorist baptismal practices to work. They usually result in the alienation of families from the church for generations to come.

On the other hand this does not mean we resort to indiscriminate baptism. Of course not. The caring church will want to be assured that the parents are serious in their desire for their child to be baptised. Do the parents understand what it entails? Are they willing for their child, as it grows up, to go to Sunday School and enter into church life?

Nurture and loving pastoral care will be central to our baptismal policies, but they will be built upon a foundation of genuine welcome and delight, because Christ himself set no limits to the children he welcomed. 'Let the children come to me. Do not forbid them.'

Are there boundaries? There is only one definite one that I can think of and that is the fixed boundary that each of us will face when we meet our God as Lord and Judge. Until that day the church sets boundaries at its peril.

A cross which bids all come to its welcoming embrace cannot give birth to a church which sets rigid boundaries that keep people out. This surely, has implication for our Decade of Evangelism.

When I first read this article my reaction was that it was a curate's egg. Good in parts. There is much in it that I can buy, but it still contains this odd Anglican cocktail which sugars the pill to such an extent that the consumer is not even aware of the pill at all. Bishop George's stance here will ensure indiscriminate infant baptism stays the norm for generations to come.[5]

First of all it makes the assumption that all who would seek to tighten up baptismal policies are unwelcoming individuals who are doing damage to families in an irrevocable manner. There is some truth here, as my experiences related in earlier chapters bear witness, but it need not be so. We are, it seems, encouraged to be assured that families mean what they will say, but are somehow left powerless to obtain that assurance. Then there is the assumption that the Lord's welcome of young children is in an infant baptismal context, which is clearly not so. Using the transport analogy, what is the cost for the baptism family? The assurance of sincerity?

Bishop George believes it is wrong to set up hoops to discourage families from bringing their babies for baptism, but is that why hoops are placed there? I confess that my baser motives in providing a stricter policy occasionally included the hope of sorting out the sincere from the insincere, but I maintain that the steps we set before people were quite reasonable and not unfair. I have heard families say, 'We can't come on Sundays, because we have to work.' This was true in several cases but they would move heaven and earth to be there on the christening day. In other cases I have heard '10 o'clock is too early. We have a lie-in on Sundays,' but on summer mornings families would be waiting at a bus stop at 7 am to go on special trips to the seaside. Those addicted to fishing could be at their riverside by 5 am, but asking families to church for five weeks over the course of three months was somehow judged to be breaking the rules. I have to ask what game are the parochial clergy of England being asked to play where they have to prepare families for baptism, but are frustrated by obscure conventions from making the preparation much more than a charade?

In the end I have serious questions as to whether it is possible to prepare families to take a meaningful part in the christening service, apart from preparing them for adult discipleship. Is there not an element of fiction involved in not so doing? Is it being unwelcoming to want to take people on in the faith, to lead them to a serious and loving commitment to Christ while delaying the baptism of their infant? In the very simplest terms, it may be that the practice of indiscriminate baptism which has largely been the norm in the Church of England until recently is simply putting the cart before the horse. We produce a statistic of nominal Christian adherence, which remains largely a notional thing, within the population, but in practice has little to do with real church membership. The sacrament of baptism is the sacrament of initiation into Christ's church and I would maintain that this must be a meaningful boundary in an absolute sense. When faith is largely absent from the participants I would say that the efficacy of the sacrament is called into question. I could wax eloquent and angry about this, but we are unable to extract ourselves until we have the courage to own the situation as it really is. Such courage is hard to come by.

If we are to talk of boundaries and discrimination, the Lord invites those who follow him to follow without compulsion, but not without cost; with the call of a loving Father where none who come sincerely are turned away. What we appear to have in indiscriminate baptism is no more than a notional adherence to Jesus Christ, coupled to an extreme reluctance to be associated with the rest of his body, the church. Perhaps there is more of an unwelcoming attitude on the part of those who would nominally express good will towards the institutional church, but who are generally unwelcoming to any serious demand in discipleship. The parish priest is expected as a religious functionary to collude with this notional discipleship by delivering the sacramental rites on demand. He is effectively barred from making clearer the real nature of being a member of Christ's Church by a pastoral practice long overdue for revision.

The boundary between discriminate and indiscriminate infant baptism was further confused in the 1974 debates in General Synod by the use of the words 'willing and able' in the motions. What does it mean to say that infant baptism ought to continue to be available to all who were 'willing and able'? Officially parishes could now claim that they were entitled to baptise babies where the parents are willing and able to make the promises, and to delay baptism to those who are not so 'willing and able'.

But what do these words actually mean? Bishop (then Canon) Colin Buchanan made probably an historical remark by saying that willing and able might mean no more than 'having the power of speech'. The Revd Christopher Wansey clearly meant the words to exclude infant baptism completely, since no infant candidate is able to make the promises! Confusion still reigns in this area. The phrase 'willing and able' did not find its way into Canon Law amendment, and has now come up again in General Synod for further debate.

I entitled this chapter 'Do we really refuse?' and I would technically maintain that in the parishes in which I have worked, the answer was 'No'. When hoops or hurdles are part of a baptismal policy it is still not the intention of the policy maker to raise those hurdles so high that they dissuade people from seeking baptism, or to construct hurdles with the deliberate intention of there being 'fallers' on the course. Examination papers are deliberately designed to give a spread of questions over the whole ability range of a particular academic course. They are designed to discern the brightest from the less bright, with some kind of theoretical threshold marking the crucial boundary between passing and failing. Not so, I would maintain, with baptismal policies. It is perfectly possible in baptismal preparation to cater for everyone from the *Sun* reader to the *Times* reader (and some people read both) with hurdles that are appropriate. Perhaps 'steps' or 'stages' might be a better word. Whether it is a video, private interview, discussion group, attendance at certain church services, or elements of all, it is quite possible to draw up a basically fair baptismal policy for instruction which commends the consent and respect of all in the parish, or the vast majority. The way baptismal policies are set up and marketed is crucial for their 'success' or acceptance within a community.

This raises another important question. Should acceptance by the community be the criterion of success? I would answer 'no', but it is not irrelevant. Some families might be alienated from the church by a tough baptismal policy, but their hostility may be nothing more or less than a rejection of the demands of the gospel. However, there is a measure of friendliness or goodwill still residual in most of our communities which most clergy (including me) are reluctant to dispense with at a stroke. One bad incident can do the church such harm in its public relations in a community, which might take years to live down or heal. This unseen goodwill is an unquantifiable amount in the pastoral bank with which any parish priest starts to minister. Jesus even seems to have had it in no small measure with the common people. Goodwill means that a community, congregation and individuals are at least willing to give free passage and a fair hearing to the Christian ministry in a parish. But if the gospel is denuded of its essential challenge, or the preaching of truth is so measured and cautious that we distort the truth out of fear, then it is too high a price to pay for some of the friendliness and goodwill that we all secretly desire.

Many times I have remarked to clergy colleagues that life would be so much smoother if we just administered the rites that people want on their terms and smile at them. I doubt whether my conscience would be so easily quietened in the process.

There must be an element of challenge in baptismal preparation. It must be a challenge which is seem to be reasonable and realistic, given the starting conditions of most twentieth-century secular men and women. It must be administered with welcoming and joyful spirit by the ministerial teams in a parish, but it must include facing up to the demands that Christ makes of all who would seriously follow him. If this is to happen, then the Church of England must cross over an invisible boundary and remarket infant baptism under clearer conditions that the population are aware of in advance.

Notes

1. Wesley Carr, *Brief Encounters*, p 87.
2. Prebendary Michael Saward has recently produced the results of a survey he did in London Diocese showing a figure of around 10% of live births who actually come to baptism. The highest percentage of live births brought to Anglican fonts is in Carlisle Diocese. The figure in the latter case is around 60% (my memory!).
3. See *Reforming Infant Baptism* for the details and

context of this (Buchanan, Owen and Wright; Hodder and Stoughton, 1990).

4. *Christian Initiation*: a Discussion Paper produced by the General Synod, circa 1975.

5. Archbishop Runcie, in his address to the November 1990 General Synod talked of the special gifts which the Church of England would bring to the Decade of Evangelism: including its 'thoughtful holiness', and its ministry to the wistful, the half believing and the seeking. 'We are not a church of hard edges,' he said. 'God has worked to keep our borders open' (*Church Times* 23rd November 1990).

This evokes in me the 'Hallelujah...Oh no!' response!

I am delighted with the sound pastoral instinct to want to minister to the wistful and meet the half believing but I am not sure God *has* worked to keep our borders open in quite the way described. Loose phraseology leaves the way open for anyone to pour into the mould whatever meaning they choose.

Chapter 10

THE MYSTERY OF FAITH

What happens in baptism? That was a question which had been in my subconscious mind for years. After my commitment to Christ at university it was easy to make the assumption that nothing of interest happened in the waters of baptism. In my case I was 'done' as a matter of routine while semi-conscious in 1943. I was unaware of the date until my baptismal certificate had to be chased for the purposes of my ordination years later. No one had ever talked to me about my christening other than that it had happened and that was sufficient to enable me to be confirmed at the age of fourteen.

I can still remember the day the church organist approached me, a choir boy, about confirmation. She had been sent as a piece of pastoral good sense as an emissary of the vicar. I remember thinking that this was important and I felt a sense of privilege to be asked about confirmation. It seemed like a mark of social approval within the church congregation! Theologically I was totally inarticulate then of course, but the actual preparation meant a lot to me and so did the rite when it was performed.

I do not undervalue the importance of confirmation,

167

but as far as baptism was concerned I found it difficult for many years to say precisely what happened in the waters. What spiritual transaction took place? Was my name mysteriously transferred in some heavenly ledger? During the late 1960s I had puzzled for a long time how to reconcile evangelical commitment as the starting point for the Christian life with the Pentecostals' teaching about being filled with the Holy Spirit. The place of water baptism remained insignificant in my thinking.

However, when I got to Ridley Hall Theological College and began my training in January 1971 I could no longer postpone the attempt to find a rationale for the practice of infant baptism. The pieces had to be fitted together into some coherent theological system. I was given an essay title to write as part of the worship course.

'The Baptism of young children is in any wise to be retained in the Church, as most agreeable with the institution of Christ.' Article 27 from The Thirty-nine Articles. Discuss.

The question was taken straight from a General Ordination examination paper and I was thrilled by that word 'discuss'. At least the issue of infant baptism may still be open for discussion, I thought with some relief!

As I read the essay again now after a lapse of some years I am intrigued to find out how much my subconscious mind had been working away at the problem throughout the late 60s.

I seemed to have come to the conclusion in 1971 that baptism, whether infant or adult, was *instrumental* provided it was received rightly. It was the means of grafting into the church. The Holy Spirit was given in regeneration or new birth provided there was faith present on the part of the recipient. I then had the problem of trying to state in the essay how infants could have the kind of faith that would appropriate the baptismal promises. I turned to Luther and Calvin to rescue me. I wrote:

Both Luther and Calvin accepted baptismal regeneration of infants, but would qualify what they meant by regeneration. To them it was not an instantaneous change, but the sowing of the seed of spiritual life which is merely the beginning of a process which is life-long and not complete even in this life. Hence they would mean by regeneration what nowadays might be meant by regeneration and sanctification taken together. They stressed the importance of faith to bring the sacrament to life, to make it work. The sacrament without faith is reduced to superstition.

Thus I wrote in 1971. I do not think I have actually shifted much from this view since. I personally think that whatever is given in baptism objectively through the grace of God (in older scholastic language ex opere operato) must to a certain extent lie dormant if the personal response element of faith is not there. Whenever I have baptised babies over the years I have always tried to point out that it is the infant's own response in due course that will 'activate' his baptismal grace. I recognise in passing, in a way that I didn't in 1971, that this is a powerful argument for postponing baptism in any case until the years of discretion. If a right reception depends upon an 'awareness factor' (Karl Barth calls it a 'cognitio' element) then there is a real sense in which any infant baptism conveys little until the awareness of the candidate has developed. It is a matter of debate at what age this should be. It could be as early as four or five years.

Set against this, I put forward in my essay the view that perhaps somehow baptismal regeneration gave an infant a propensity for faith which he might not otherwise have had. I went on to say:

As the child receives the grace of God which ought to be mediated through the Christian home (I ought to have added 'and the worshipping body as well') he progresses in the way of faith, and theoretically if the child were to pass on to adulthood without deviating from the path of faith, there would be no need for later "conversion" or ratification of promises made on his behalf. We have all met Christians with a very authentic Christian faith who cannot put a date or time on anything we evangelicals might want to call "conversion". They have developed slowly and surely over the years and must not be unchurched by those of us whose Christian progress has been more jerky.

It is interesting that the judgement of the Gorham case in 1850 stated

> that baptism is a sacrament generally necessary to salvation, but that the grace of regeneration does not so necessarily accompany the act of baptism that regeneration invariably takes place in baptism. The grace may be granted before, in or after baptism. Baptism is an effectual sign of grace, by which God works invisibly in us, but only in such as worthily receive it—in them alone it has a wholesome effect...in no case is baptism unconditional.[1]

The question of the relation of the sacraments to grace has been under discussion in some sense throughout the period since the Reformation. Gorham focused the issue of regeneration and baptism. A very interesting appendix on the subject was written in the 1922 Doctrine Report. The opening paragraph is a good summary of the problem:

> Anglican theology, following the formularies of the Anglican Church, has in general consistently affirmed that the sacraments are "effectual signs"—that is to say, that they do not merely symbolise the reception of grace, but are means by which grace is received. On the other hand, there has been in Anglican Theology comparatively little exact discussion of the manner in which the sacraments *are* (italics mine) means of grace and can therefore be said to cause grace. In part this has been due to the extent to which the question has been confused by controversies and in particular, by exaggerated fears, in some quarters, lest any allowance of a real sacramental causality should involve the

admission of magical conceptions and, in other quarters, lest any rationalising of such causality should minimise its reality.[2]

I think this opening paragraph is saying that because of the highly emotive nature of the debate (the discussion is about sacraments in general including of course the Eucharist, not only about baptism) each opposite pole of the discussion fights its corner so hard that it obscures the truth that the opposite corner is trying to safeguard. The real 'mechanism' of reception of grace in the sacraments, I believe lies somewhere between the two poles of thought. How may we define those two poles of thought?

One pole as far as baptism is concerned is the 'hosepipe' mentality. If baptism in the name of the Trinity is effective, irrespective of the condition of the recipients, then one might just as well tour the streets with a hosepipe proclaiming the baptismal formulas effective over anyone on whom the droplets happen to fall. Such a bizarre postulation should serve to illustrate the point. At the other pole there lies the view that the sacraments are no more than 'acted sermons' (as the Doctrine Report called them) or as I prefer to label them 'wet visual aids'. I think in all honesty many of we older evangelicals have tended to the latter. We have not seen baptism as effecting *anything* instrumentally. Nothing is given, nothing is lost, and therefore we may administer the sacrament to anybody who asks for it with a clear conscience. This is frequently the undeclared rationale for indiscriminate infant baptism on the part of many evangelical clergymen.

How can we hazard the attempt to explain how grace is received through the sacraments, excluding magic at one pole and visual aids at the other?

It is not my purpose here to attempt an exposition of faith and grace from the Scriptures in anything approaching a proper measure. That has been done by far better men and women than me in countless commentaries. I just offer the starting point that in seeking a 'mechanism' of sacramental efficacy, Ephesians chapter 2 verses 8 and 9 give us a clue: 'For it is by grace you are saved, through trusting him (through faith); it is not your own doing. It is God's gift, not a reward for work done. There is nothing for anyone to boast of.'

Romans chapter 6 and following identifies baptism with the individual dying and rising with Christ and uses instrumental language.

Faith somehow is the mystery quality that unlocks the instrumental door to the grace of the sacraments. I believe that it is not simply a case of chance, as if the sacrament of initiation can be dispensed to a random group of people and that in one case it 'takes' and in another it does not. That reduces baptismal efficacy to the status of luck. No, every serious rightfully intended administration of the sacrament has within it the sure promise of grace, but only as it is unlocked, received, 'accessed to' by the faith of the recipient. In saying that I have probably drawn a big question mark over infant baptism *per se*!

In touching on faith as a mystery quality, I think it is worth making the observation that one of the effects of the last thirty years of Charismatic renewal has been to make charismatics themselves more sacramentally conscious. We are taught by the theologians that experience is primary and the theology is secondary as it seeks to relate, understand and analyse new experiences of God in relation to all that has gone before and work it into a coherent system of thought and doctrine (if possible!). As an aside, I think that much liberal theology and the almost obsessive desire among theologians to accommodate to prevailing humanistic and secular philosophy has been because there has been so little first-hand experience of God to work on. Charismatics on the other hand have majored on the primacy of experience, at times excessively so and to the consternation of many older evangelicals. The latter group have at times needed to recall charismatics back to the 'Word'.

However, charismatics have brought new insights about sacraments through the experience and observation of healing, specific prayers with the laying on of hands, deliverance prayers, the move towards urging believer's baptism on previously christened individuals (I am ambivalent about this), anointing with oil for healing, and the claiming of God's authority over areas and buildings. All of these things taken together lead me to suggest that charismatics have discovered afresh a sacramental dimension to Christian experience which the older evangelicals were unaware of or nervous of. Anointing with oil in *faith* does something. Taking bread and wine according to the Lord's command does something for those who receive in *faith*. Baptising in water effects something where it is done for the right reasons and received by *faith*.

The concept of vicarious faith raises its head here. Jesus healed a paralytic through the faith of his friends who let him down through the roof. Prayer at a distance prayed in faith works. It affects and changes events. I would not suggest that we drag the vicarious faith concept immediately over to infant baptism as a justification, but covenant theology does invoke this concept.

On the occasions when I have witnessed adults being immersed, I have observed something happening, as though the passing through the waters actually effected something. Individuals have testified to feeling released, and come up glowing. They seem to look back on these immersions with such joy and with more importance than when we older evangelicals would have recalled the day when we first made a commitment to Christ.

But what is faith?

Faith is spiritual receptivity. It has an element of straight-forward instruction in it. Faith is that which effects; that which makes spiritual facts real. The Epistle to the Hebrews answers the question this way: 'Faith gives substance to our hopes and makes us certain of realities we cannot see' (Hebrews 11:1). Faith is a cluster of things which function together to link heaven and earth. Faith itself seems to be a gift of God, inspired by the Holy Spirit, and yet though a gift it seems to have a human response in it. It has an air of certainty about it, of unshakeable conviction. In a real sense, faith can be caught from, and also recognised in, others. An atmosphere of faith can be detected in a church, a group or in given situations that require it.

When in 1965 I attended a healing and deliverance rally to hear the evangelist Peter Scothern, I was interested to hear him say about faith: 'Faith is a strange thing. You either have it or not. You can say a lot about it, but you can never quite define it.' His lack of definition didn't stop him healing the sick and sending a few cripples home carrying their crutches under their arms!

When people come to baptism with faith of this kind, especially if they are making their own profession of faith, then the occasion can be truly wonderful. I have to ask—not in judgement, but simply in a cold admission of stark reality—'Is this the kind of faith I find when the average christening group gathers together to sprinkle the latest offspring?' Oh that it were true!

How does one get this kind of faith? Basically St Paul says, by hearing the Word of God, by being in or near situations where people have faith. There is no limit to the ways that people can discover faith and get drawn to Christ. But it underlines the case for good baptismal preparation. In Bordon we tried to do more than merely prepare people to understand more of what they were promising. We wanted to sow the seeds of faith in their hearts that would in due time grow into real responses towards Christ.

I had the pleasure a few years ago of an afternoon's

conversation with David Pawson at his home near Basingstoke. It was a most instructive occasion for me. I had been interested in an article he had written some while previously in *Renewal* magazine on baptism. In it he seemed to come close to proposing an instrumental view of baptismal grace. This seemed confirmed in our conversation. David was as critical of some Baptists who held a too low view of the sacraments as he was of Anglicans who bothered to baptise babies at all!! In many cases, Baptists see baptism as a 'wet witness', he said 'when to me the scriptural language is instrumental.' He believed that baptism effects what it symbolises, but only where faith is present. This for him ruled out infant baptism. He also went on to outline the process element of initiation. Is a baby born when it is conceived? After a few weeks of embryonic development? When the cord is cut? When the infant starts to breathe? Surely natural birth is a process. Spiritual birth similarly has this cluster of elements about it. You have baptism as the sacramental washing, the profession of faith, the repentance from sin, the necessity of faith. In what order should they come?[3]

I do not want to labour unduly this question of faith, but I do certainly ask for this discussion of the nature of receptivity (or my word 'mechanism') for the efficacy of the sacraments to be put back on the discussion table. If infant baptism continues to be practised as in any sense a norm of the major denominations, then our theology of infant baptism must be credible. It must hold water!

If I am close to the truth with my theory of faith as the key to the instrumentality of the baptismal sacrament, then the sacrament can only be valid if the candidate can in some sense exercise and be seen to exercise faith for himself or herself. I know I am straying close to the judgemental here. What about the disabled? What about the young children who die before the age of understanding? What about the mentally subnormal?

There can be no absolute answer to these imponderables, as only God would have the answers. However, I would suggest one avenue of approach would be that beneath the age of understanding or apart from the reasonable moral sense of accountability which might be annulled through disability, then God is unlikely to hold such a child or person morally answerable for his or her sin. On that basis baptism is not yet necessary as the instrument of remission of those sins. Maybe, the propensity for faith goes hand in hand with a moral accountability. The *Alternative Service Book* puts our minds at rest here. Under 'Emergency Baptism' the rubrics ask the minister to assure parents of a dangerously sick child that they should be assured that questions of ultimate salvation for an infant do not depend upon whether or not he has been baptised (paragraph 106). This says a lot about the theology (or theologies) of baptism lying behind the *Alternative Service Book*. John Calvin would generally agree (see *Institutes*).[4] The age of discretion or answerability, in relation to baptismal vows must be open to debate. But if baptism is carried out before this age, then the 'faith' element must inevitably remain a dormant thing or at least be regarded as on a slow-burning fuse.

This brings me to what is broadly termed covenant theology. Calvin states boldly that 'From this sacrament, as from all others, we obtain nothing except what we receive by faith' (*Institutes* p 193), but he goes on to declare infants of believers already accepted (and thus included in the covenant).

Most evangelicals in the Church of England probably justify the practice of infant baptism on the grounds of covenant theology. Put at its simplest this means that the efficacy of a particular baby's baptism is tied to the authenticity of the parent's faith.

The idea of covenant and its implications for the practice of baptising the infants of believing parents is dealt with at some depth in an excellent book by Archdeacon Gordon Kuhrt.[5] He goes at some length into the nature of the covenant-forming God and the implications of this. Michael Green also mentions the covenant nature of God in *Baptism: Its Purpose, Practice and Power*.[6]

> God is a covenant-making God. He binds himself by a physical token, as if he could not be trusted! The token to Noah was the rainbow (Genesis 9:8f). The token to Moses was the Passover (Exodus 12) and the token to Abraham, the supreme mark of belonging, which continues among Jews to this day, was circumcision.

Michael Green then goes on to justify the practice of baptising the infants of believing parents by use of a seven-stranded argument. I append my comments after each one.

1. Children were admitted into the Old Testament church.

Yes, they were. But we need to look at Abraham's natural descendents and the covenant promise to a race rather than to those of faith.

2. The whole family was baptised when proselytes came over into Judaism.

Yes, but this is still the same as above. They were being admitted into a covenant with an ethnic group. My children are English, whether they are aware of it or not. Their Englishness doesn't depend upon their awareness of it.

3. Whole families were baptised in New Testament days.

Yes, and they may have included children and babies. I wonder whether we place too much weight here, though.

4. Jesus accepted and blessed children too young to respond.

Yes, but too much has been made of this passage and the context is certainly not baptism.

5. The church down its history has baptised children.

Yes, rightly or wrongly! It depends what weight you give to tradition.

6. *Infant baptism stresses the objectivity of the gospel.*
   Yes, but so does preaching! There is the danger that it is used here as a visual aid.

7. *Infant baptism stresses the initiative of God in salvation.*
   Yes, but there are two sides to a sacrament.

None of these reasons taken by themselves seem to provide a conclusive 'knockdown' argument for baptising infants. I would say that only 1,2,3 and 5 taken together give some strength of support. But the reader must look at Green and Kuhrt for himself!

My task in this book is to be pragmatic, and to bring baptismal preparation in the parishes into the late twentieth century. This necessitates an awareness of the secular reality of the age.

I am making out a case for what has unfortunately, but probably accurately, been called discriminate infant baptism. For example, if covenant theology is sound and I am not altogether convinced that it is as cast iron as it has been claimed, then we should with joy and a clear conscience baptise the infants of believers. These Christians are already in the church congregation (I assume) and we may count their offspring in. What if the parents are not believers? Is it sufficient to have a believing godparent, or midwife, or a believing, but non-attending grandparent? Is it sufficient to have had a saint in the family three generations back in order to qualify under covenant theology? Many try so to do! I raise this because if we say we operate under a particular theology, then are we consistent in applying it? If we only justify infant baptism on the grounds of the existence of a believing parent, then what is the status, validity, and efficacy of the sacrament when a parent is a declared unbeliever? What if, as in the majority of cases, he is a professed theist, but a non-practising Christian? Does it not invalidate the sacrament in that case?

If this notion is reprehensible then some other theology than covenant theology must be found to justify the present practice. I cannot see any alternative to a 'long-fused faith theology' in this case.

I have said that I am essentially wishing to be pragmatic, and hopefully with some pastoral sensitivity. It definitely evokes hostility to be sticky over general baptism if one is trying to work out covenant theology with some integrity, but it is precisely here that a careful baptismal policy should provide the answer. Covenant theology should demand that parents must be brought to a position of professing the faith with integrity first. If they are already in the worshipping body, so much the better. It is ironic that it is precisely those authentic believers today who are *not* asking for baptism for their children, but waiting until later on. It is often the rank outsider who still demands the christening, without conditions.

Can we demand faith of a person? No. But we can evoke a willingness to be open to the teaching of the gospel and the possibility of an appropriate response. A baptismal policy can provide for that possibility if it is carefully constructed. That brings us to evangelism.

Notes

1. J.C.S. Nias, *Gorham and the Bishop of Exeter* (SPCK: 1951), p 98.
2. *Doctrine in the Church of England* (SPCK: 1957), p 230 (first published in 1938). The memorandum then goes on to explore four theories of the nature of sacramental causality.
3. *The Normal Christian Birth* by J.D. Pawson (Hodder & Stoughton, 1989).
4. *A Compendium of the Institutes of the Christian Religion* by John Calvin (Lutterworth, 1965), pp 192–194.

5. G. Kuhrt, *Believing in Baptism* (Mowbray: 1987).
6. E.M.B. Green, *Baptism: Its Purpose, Practice and Power* (Hodder & Stoughton: 1987).

Chapter 11

BAPTISM AND EVANGELISM

In the Diocese of Worcester we are, like every other diocese in the Church of England at the moment, turning our thoughts towards the Decade of Evangelism. It is an interesting exercise to participate in and observe. The Decade of Evangelism is not simply an Anglican prerogative, but is intended to be interdenominational, and co-ordinated ecumenical evangelism is the order of the day. So once again evangelism has arrived on the agendas. It is doing the rounds of the various committees as appropriate, and generally speaking those bodies that need to be aware of the decade and make some response are at least beginning to take up the slack.

But what is evangelism? I note that it is a word which still excites some and instills fear into others. In the parish church at Clifton-on-Teme I have inherited a group of enthusiastic musicians, preachers and testifiers who could be dispatched at a few days notice to any English-speaking part of the world to evangelise it! Some years ago in St Mark's, Bordon we had a similar group. Such people are inclined to be impatient with the tired wrangling of phrases in committee meetings. They want to be out sharing their faith; nothing gives them greater joy. As long as such people exist I am confident that the Christian faith will not die out. I walked with them in the 'March for Jesus' last year through the city centre of Worcester, when 1,500 Christians from Worcester, Hereford, Gloucester and Cheltenham joined forces in a united act of witness... and yet as I looked at the throngs of shoppers that Saturday afternoon in the precincts as we walked through, many scarcely gave us a glance. The greatest impact was on the captive audiences sitting in the buses who had to wait in the traffic jams until the 'Jesus crowd' had passed!

As history shows, evangelism is a difficult business. It is a joy to proclaim, but to turn to Christ in sincerity of heart is a work of grace and free human response. It is more complex than appears on the surface. Our local proclaiming group brings joy to the rector who gains great encouragement from seeing their faith in action, but there are others in the locality who through fear of certain stereotypes might run a mile. It is fear of this kind of approach (which is often badly misrepresented) which tempts evangelism committee members to want to define precisely what evangelism is before committing themselves to any one style of evangelism. One of the first points of discussion was the relation of evangelism to the total mission of the church.

One proven assumption that we might put on the table is that evangelism should be part of the ongoing life of every local church. Where there is spiritual life it should authenticate itself by having a contagious quality. Faith propagation should be perfectly natural. Another fairly well proven assumption is that most people become Christians through personal contact.

In a recent booklet by Gavin Reid for the Decade of Evangelism he says:

A great deal of talk about evangelism seems to assume the normality of sudden conversions either as a result of preaching particular types of sermons or engaging in particular techniques of "personal evangelism". This is a myth that needs exposing.[1] The truth is that the vast majority of Christians become so through prolonged exposure to other Christians. Their faith was not taught but caught.

Gavin then goes on to suggest from results in a recent survey he conducted that relationships play a part in at least 80% of all conversions.

This is true; but I would not want to underestimate the value of the more traditional evangelistic tools in the whole mission portfolio. Nevertheless whether we make much use of preaching, witnessing and guest services or whether we prefer to let evangelism proceed more quietly in a natural way through and out from a congregation, there must be a 'convinced core' at the heart of a congregation. There must be a number of believers who are ready to articulate and share faith. Fire is the simplest analogy. You can have the best laid fire in the street, but if no one strikes a match it will remain simply the best laid fire in the street. 'The church exists by mission as a fire exists by burning.' Many of our churches have not yet begun to emanate the faith that is professed in creed and song. The sad truth is that the Decade of Evangelism for many churches must mean a rediscovering of the faith in a personal way for many within congregations before the fire can burn outwards. Is that such a bad thing?

Even in churches which are 'alive' there is a great deal of nervousness about sharing the faith. Gavin Reid says in his Foreword to *Redescribing Evangelism*:

> Most of us, if we are honest, would admit to being scared of "evangelism". Even within the evangelical tradition, where evangelism is supposed to be a trademark, the truth is that the average man and woman in the pew is more than a little nervous when the church decides to "do it".

Some while ago at St Mark's shared church, Bordon,

we decided to 'do' it. We planned and had a try at a 'mission'. There had been in 1965 a visitation scheme on the first council estate which was very much under a stewardship umbrella. Each house was visited. The baptised were encouraged to come and get confirmed (hallelujah!) and some did. A small church choir was formed which lasted all of a few months and people were encouraged to come to church and make use of the 'facility'. It was a useful exercise from the congregation's point of view, but only a small impact was made on the surrounding community. My expectations of lasting results were not so different in 1985 when the new St Mark's attempted its mission. I expected that the chief result would be the flexing of the congregation's muscles and a degree of confidence gained through the whole exercise. So it turned out to be. A sub-committee was set up some months before the mission to work out the details of what would be the detailed components. It would be based on one special week in the summer, but have a lead-in of several weeks of testimony. Each Sunday in the preceding weeks starting with Easter, someone in the congregation would stand up and give five minutes on 'What my faith means to me'. This created awareness. Then a special edition of the 'Marksman' magazine was printed for the mission and contained a number of stories of how local people had come by their faith. One for example was a schoolmaster. Another was a member of the carnival committee whose name was well known from the local newspaper. Another was a housewife from one of the large council estates who had come to faith a year before and so on. I stole the idea from a mission I had observed in Cambridge years before!

The magazine was then given free to houses we visited on the mission. The visiting was one of the most enjoyable parts of the week. Teams were formed and on two afternoons the three ministers—Anglican, Methodist and United Reformed—walked together around the estates greeting people in the name of St Mark's, giving a copy of the magazine, informing people of the events of the week and enquiring whether there had been a church connection in the previous parish. The secondary agenda of the mission was to attempt to evaluate a number of tasks that could be included as part of an ongoing evangelistic programme of the church. Targeting certain estates was high on the agenda.

Then certain members of the congregation conducted special mission assemblies in the local schools, including the comprehensive. The latter had a very useful consequence: it led to a successful experiment with groups of Christians going into question-and-answer sessions with classes in the local comprehensive school, as part of the humanities department. It was a joy to see previously nervous members of the congregation sitting in small groups with a similar number of teenagers discussing Christian basics in classroom time. For some years previously I had taken a summer session with the fourth year classes in the junior school, usually on the topic 'Who, Where, What is God?'.

On the Saturday we had an open day with the choir and dance group performing throughout the day and free coffee being served. Many of the Saturday shoppers walking through the precinct came in, attracted by the balloons! (I thought this was a crazy idea, but it actually worked.) Saturday was really a shop window, a bit of pre-evangelism, but Sunday was our first attempt at an evangelistic service. Paul Dean, our United Reformed church minister and I had spent time in prayer and preparation. A testimony and some songs were included. Then I preached on Acts chapter 17 (St Paul on Mars Hill) and made an appeal. It was the first time I had ever done so. I asked for people to close their eyes while a prayer of commitment was prayed by Paul and then those who wanted to signal that it was the first time they had ever done such a thing to raise their hands. Several did. The panic and the relief were simultaneous! The Revd John Cherrill took the evening service and made a similar appeal. Again there was a small response. In fact whenever we tried an evangelistic preaching service thereafter, even if the appeal was only in terms of inviting people to come and collect a booklet or have a further chat, people responded.

I noted from this that there is still a need for this kind of opportunity to make a token of response to a message of invitation to commitment. In many cases as we soon discovered it was only skin deep, but I didn't want to judge people. I also had a slight conscience about asking people to respond when I considered I hadn't sufficiently placed enough 'gospel facts' before people. On a few occasions people responded and asked further questions. That mission week came to an end with sighs of relief, because we were venturing into the unknown, but it did have the desired effect: a fresher confidence was born in going 'out', in sharing the faith. The congregation didn't increase immediately afterwards, but the evangelistic muscles had been stretched. It was a church where the fire was lit and so was capable of spreading further. We realised afterwards that evangelism had in fact been gong on all the time in an unconscious, rather haphazard way. It continued afterwards as well, but we saw that there was a place for a 'mission' and an evangelistic service. A lot of water has to flow under the bridge before someone is ready for this kind of response. Is there any reason why the response should not be baptism? This is the pivotal question of this chapter.

Evangelism, if I use the word for the moment to include all the necessary components of bringing a person to Christ, actually involves the will. Whilst grace and even repentance are God-given, the human will is still involved. There is the possibility of not turning to Christ in response to an invitation to follow him, however that invitation is given. A response in repentance and faith may be gradual or sudden. It is more likely to be as a graduated process. However it comes, it involves the human 'say so'.

Evangelists, like salesmen, know that no sale is guaranteed. No technique, however good its track record in persuasion, can override the will if there is resistance or rejection. Much prayer, hard work and witness is necessary before a person can come to Christian discipleship and God, the Holy Spirit, should be in the whole process. The only real pressure should come from the latter. But when the will is given over in discipleship, then it is appropriate that the decision should be signalled to God, the church, and the world. It would seem that baptism is that dominically ordained sacrament for doing this.

In my essay in *Reforming Infant Baptism* I referred to the various response symbols used by the evangelists as 'baptism substitutes'. Raising a hand, signing a decision card, getting up out of one's seat and walking to the front—these are all sub-sacramental in that something other than baptism in water is used for the purpose for which the sacrament was originally given. Those who come to the front at a Billy Graham rally gain great strength from having done so. Their action seals their decision. It is an act of witness before the church and the world and signals a fresh beginning. I am not suggesting for one moment that Billy Graham and other evangelists should cease to use such forms of opportunity of Christian response. I do however make the point that they underline the importance of baptism as the true sacrament of incorporation into the body of Christ. 'By one Spirit we were all baptised into one body.' Yet given the disunity of the church and the still fairly general practice of infant baptism, such substitutes are inevitable.

The disunity of the church leaves the evangelist with little choice but to operate in this way.

It is to the immense credit of Billy Graham, who must in some sense be the pivotal or normative international evangelist, that he always supports and affirms the importance of the local church. He respects the existence of the several denominations and their initiatory practices. All he is concerned to do is to bring people to a faith in Christ and send people back to denominational churches. He indicates certain hallmarks of the kind of churches he suggests people go to, for example they must be 'Bible-believing', but he does not overrule their authority or their responsibility in the matter of nurturing new converts. While the body of Christ remains organisationally divided, the interdenominational ministries which are clearly of God must operate in this way— using their own necessary sub-sacramental actions without knocking over the patterns within the established denominations. This indeed has been the pattern of evangelists like Billy Graham for some time.

The waters have been muddied considerably, however, by the growth of the independent charismatic churches. Generally speaking, they have initiated new converts into their own churches through believers' baptism, with no reference to previous denominational allegiances of enquirers. The tendency of the restoration churches has been to write off the 'dead' denominations as a snare and irrelevance, and to carry on regardless. I am not surprised! One of the saddest phenomena which I have experienced in my ministry is the raising of new Christians in the Anglican Church only to find them slipping out to a newer independent church who have the 'correct' teaching. I often used to feel that we reared sheep to have them inevitably stolen by the 'hotter' churches. Such experiences have been shared by countless other ministers, and we will continue to suffer from them until we in the Church of England tidy up (and that is the mildest phrase I can think of!) our initiation practices.

The publication of *Baptism, Eucharist and Ministry*[3] is a fruit of the ecumenical process to converge towards mutual understanding of initiation practices and to tease out some directions which will steer us towards mutually interchangeable initiatory practices. It is interesting that as the older denominatons draw closer together, the newer churches such as the charismatic independent churches are increasingly marginalising the older denominations in their thinking and practice and going ahead with their own thing. This new division within the body, which is what it is, lies at the bottom of the problem of those who request 're-baptism' as believers after a conversion experience or a 'blessing of the Holy Ghost'. We need to handle the problem with sensitivity. I wonder if the interim rite of immersion with the renewal of baptism vows may be the way through this one for the next generation or two though I doubt whether such a solution will have a smooth theological ride.

But it is also *Baptism, Eucharist and Ministry* which drew attention to the practice of 'apparent indiscriminate baptism' as another source of confusion. If church dis-unity causes the evangelists to continue to use sub-sacramental responses to the gospel, the indiscriminate infant baptism as a normal practice creates arguably the biggest confusing factor in the whole arena of Christian initiation. Becoming a Christian involves the will. Being baptised as a baby does not. If faith and free will are essential components of initiation then a babe in arms is in difficulties. I have supplied enough evidence in this book to show that infant baptism is thought of as a birthrite and fought for as a birthright! If it is thus thought of by the population at large, while the theological assumption of Prayer Book and Articles is that it is the full and complete sacrament of initiation, then we shall always have pastoral problems in the matter. 'Ah!' someone says. 'What about confirmation? Isn't that where it all comes right?'

'Yes' I reply, 'That is where it often does, especially in

the minority who actually get confirmed'. But I would have to add that trying to see confirmation as the effective point of entry into the church isn't the total answer. Confirmation provides the opportunity for willing instruction in the faith and an opportunity to accept or reject discipleship on the part of teenager or adult. I always have started confirmation groups with the proviso that there is a mutual non-commitment clause. Those who join confirmation groups are told that I do not guarantee confirmation at the end unless I think they are ready, neither will any be forced to be confirmed against their will. Thus we start in an atmosphere of free enquiry and this approach over the years has led to several communicant members joining in confirmation groups for a 'refresher'. In practice I have never stopped anyone being confirmed, though several asked to withdraw from the rite at the end of the course when they felt unable to go ahead in discipleship.

This book is principally about infant baptism, but the problems surrounding it cannot be solved unless confirmation is taken into account, for it is only at confirmation that we are able to bring in the personal profession of faith of the candidate and provide the opportunity for the expression of that faith as an act of free choice.

On my priesting retreat I asked the late David Maddocks, former Bishop of Dunwich, what was the church's main theology of confirmation, as I said that the Church of England appeared to have at least three different views on what happened in confirmation. His reply was simply: 'My dear chap, the Church of England hasn't got a clue what it means by confirmation.' He went on to expound the various theologies. I have found indeed as the years have gone by that he was right. Confirmation has appeared to be a rite in search of a theology just as infant baptism itself has so appeared. (Although the champions of 'covenant theology' would protest vehemently.) The basic problem is that the Western church has inherited a fractured rite of initiation and until that is seriously rectified we shall always have to make theological contortions to hang it all together. The Church in Wales Doctrinal Commission in 1971 summed it up well in its report by saying:

> Any separation of baptism, confirmation and first communion either as successively given at different stages in the initiation rite, or as conceivable in isolation from one another, involves grave theological confusion. This is why the disintegrated pattern of Christian Initiation which the Western Church has inherited is theologically unsatisfactory. Such separation leads to pseudo-problems that are insoluble theologically if not in fact meaningless.
>
> In particular, we refer to the impossibility of giving a convincing theology of 'baptism' separated from confirmation, or of 'confirmation' separated from 'baptism'.

Thus if we are to solve the theological problems surrounding infant baptism we need to move it into closer proximity to confirmation and first Communion. This is done already in the Orthodox Church where the three rites are administered to infants. But as the reader might guess this does not provide a satisfactory solution in my opinion, because of the reasons given in the last chapter and this one. There must be the faith and free response element to authenticate the sacrament and to take the Orthodox pattern might actually double the problem. I would rather stay with the present pattern of initiation for another century than try to solve it in a way which would make the latter state worse than the first.

No, I believe that we should move the sacrament of initiation to the point where the candidate is ready to make a sensible and clear Christian commitment. That could be quite young, but certainly not as an infant in arms.

Problems will start to resolve themselves when baptism and confirmation are brought together. The late

Bishop David Brown, former Bishop of Guildford, was discussing initiation with us in our Post Ordination Training group. He was very strongly of the opinion that when any family asked for baptism of an infant they should have that infant baptised without any conditions whatsoever. If I heard him correctly, he went on to say that we had as clergy no right to demand preparation of any kind. We could not insist that the parents read anything or attend anything by way of preparation. As for attending church before a baptism, that was almost an anathema. He would without doubt have been totally against the kind of baptismal preparation groups and church attendance policies that we practised in Bordon.

However, when one turned to his requirements for confirmation preparation in the bishop's notices one discovered that the standards of theological knowledge and understanding of the faith required before confirmation were of the most rigorous kind. I agreed totally with the immensely high standard he expected of confirmation candidates. Yet when I tried to meet those standards, given the educational and social background of many in our parish, I found it difficult, if not impossible, to deliver the goods. If those standards had been enforced throughout the Church of England our modern communicants would have been better grounded in Christian basics than most of those who pass through the rigorous 'membership classes' of the charismatic house churches. When Bishop David preached at confirmation services I was always uplifted by his sermons which came close to an evangelistic challenge. His earlier evangelicalism wasn't so overlaid that it didn't burst out on occasions.

The point I want to make is that if you were to add together his passionate belief in conditionless infant baptism, to his extremely demanding confirmation requirement, the product was an overall initiation demand in excess of anything we tried to extract in our rigorous days. In other words if you see baptism and confirmation together some of the pastoral problems surrounding either start to come into a more balanced perspective.

What then happens in confirmation? I believe that in confirmation the Church of England has received a tradition of precious value from the ancient church, but has somehow lost its meaning. Consequently, various means have been sought to supply a rationale. I think that the traditional understanding that confirmation is a 'strengthening', a confirming, by the Holy Ghost of an earlier work to be the right one. If Anglicans came to confirmations with more faith (ie expecting something more) and bishops prepared to administer confirmation believing that the Holy Spirit would bless the candidates with the Holy Spirit in ways that might be unpredictable, then I believe that confirmation services would take on a wholly different air than they do at present.

I have prepared candidates for, and attended many, confirmation services over the years. I do believe they are improving. However, there are some considerable variations. I recently attended a large confirmation service set in the lovely Georgian parish church of St Mary in the middle of Banbury. The occasion was the annual confirmation for a girls' public school nearby. The clientele was heavily weighted towards the top end of the social spectrum. The service was correct, the address was punctilious, the copes and stoles were splendid, but somehow the ambience of the service had more in common with 'Barchester' than with the bubbling life of St Trinians, which was being well contained down in the pews. The doctrine was faultless (or nearly) the hymns could have been livelier and the bishop might have done better coming down from the pulpit and preaching extempore to such a young audience who were probably well used to watching *Wogan* and *Eastenders* in the school dormitories! I jest slightly, but confirmation services should be magnificent occasions of witness and proclamation of the gospel. At school confirmations parents should go away with a challenge ringing in their ears. The Christian life should be seen to be an option to be decided about seriously. The power of God should be evidenced on these occasions. There is a real danger that the great occasion can be so controlled that the Holy Spirit has no room to do much.

Shortly after the occasion above I attended a rehearsal for a confirmation to be held in our Diocese of Worcester. I was detailed off to stand in for the bishop by sitting in his chair and as each candidate knelt in front of me, I laid hands on his head and said 'Confirm, O Lord, your servant Fred, with your Holy Spirit' and then passed on to the next candidate. That was the rehearsal. But it dawned on me that the time spent by the bishop with each candidate was far too short. It was no more than the time spent by the average parish priest at the communion rail, as he blesses numerous children on the way to the next communicant! On this most solemn occasion a bishop should be given (I am not blaming the bishops) much more time to pray with a candidate for confirmation. Perhaps asking him if he has any special prayer request, finding out his school and job and maybe giving him the chance to say a word about his faith before praying the prayer over the candidate for the strengthening of the Holy Spirit...then who knows what the Holy Spirit might do? Would it matter if a candidate here and there spoke in tongues or merely beamed?

I have witnessed on video an occasion when an unknown diocesan bishop at a combined baptism/confirmation service did take time to begin a personal relationship with the candidates before baptising them. The effect of this in the whole spirit of the service was unmistakable.

There was another occasion when I took two candidates to be confirmed at St John's, Woking, a church not exactly famous for its quiet services. The two candidates were interesting in themselves. One was an ex-Baptist preparing for ordination in the Church of England. The other lady had a remarkable testimony of how she came to put her faith in Jesus Christ. I prayed that the occasion of coming into adult communicant membership of the Church of England would be a lively and meaningful service. I was not disappointed. The choice of music and the vigour of congregational participation was such that had the bishop not been weighted down with vestments, he might have taken off too!

There is evidence around in plenty that the Church of England is slipping out of its somewhat threadbare grave clothes of initiation and seeing the need to relate baptism, confirmation and evangelism more closely. Maybe we should be working towards the day when it really will no longer be necessary to stand by helpless while our members go off to the Baptist or house church to be 're-baptised' and probably join them... or to go down to the latter to have a 'blessing from the Holy Spirit'. These pastoral needs should be ministered to from within our own denomination.

The central plank of such a reform is the re-ordering of infant baptism. To do that the church's rules must change and to that we must now turn.

Notes

1. Gavin Reid: *Redescribing Evangelism* (British Council of Churches: 1989).
2. Buchanan, Owen and Wright, *Reforming Infant Baptism* (Hodder and Stoughton: 1990).
3. The Lima text from the World Council of Churches (Geneva 1982).
4. See Chapter 15 notes.

Chapter 12

DEAR BISHOPS...I'M RE-WRITING THE CANONS

One October afternoon in 1988 I drove to a postbox in the lovely Worcestershire town of Great Malvern and placed inside it fifty or so copies of a letter. Each one was addressed to a member of the House of Bishops of the General Synod of the Church of England. It was the biggest episcopal mailshot I have ever been involved with. The enclosure was a statement that the national committee of the Movement for the Reform of Infant Baptism had agreed the previous afternoon at its meeting in Malvern.

Over the five years that the Movement has been in existence, it has generally been given a fair hearing, though inevitably somewhat misunderstood. MORIB has been an attempt to gather together a range of Anglican opinion from different theological positions, but who are united in a common concern that the traditional way of administrating infant baptism in the Church of England needs to be reformed. Within MORIB one can find everyone from those who passionately defend the baptism of babies of believing parents on a covenant theology basis, to those who have come to a point where they have conscience problems over baptising any infants at all. Many of the latter are happy to carry on with the church's practice as part of their ministry, but remain uneasy about it. That is why the aims of the movement are pragmatic and task-orientated rather than aiming for one singular goal.

The main need for the Church of England that MORIB sees as the call of the hour is to move to discriminate infant baptism. MORIB has not attempted to define precisely what that means, though I have made the attempt in previous chapters. Behind the letter that was sent to the House of Bishops lay hours of committee time and discussion. In the end only one logical conclusion was reached as an achievable goal for the last decade of the century. That was that if parents request baptism for an infant, then at least one of them must be confirmed and a practising communicant or become so.

The text of the letter read as follows:

In order that the Church of England may be better fitted to engage in the 1990s (in accordance with the call issued this year by the Lambeth Conference), the national committee of the Movement for the Reform of Infant Baptism (MORIB), calls upon the Bishops of the Church of England to give public support to the reform of infant baptism.

Fifteen years ago in the debate following the Ely Report on Christian Initiation, General Synod declared that infant baptism should continue to be available for those who requested it and 'were willing and able to make the baptismal promises.' In the ASB service for the Baptism of Children the 'Duties of Parents and Godparents' specify that those bringing children for baptism must be willing that their children should be 'brought up as Christians within the family of the church', and that they should encourage these children, by their example, to be 'faithful in public worship'.

It is a generally accepted estimate that some 26 million persons from the total present population of England have been baptised in the Church of England. Official statistics for 1985 from the Central Board of Finance reveal that only around 691,400 (less than 3%) of these were communicant on an average Sunday. (The total of Easter communicants was some 1,623,800—less than 7%.)

MORIB is concerned about the grave discrepancy between the official membership of the church (measured by baptism), and the reality of active membership in the parishes (measured by communicants). It is clear that most people who present a child for baptism are not themselves active communicant members of the church.

In view of the fact that the ASB describes baptism as 'the sacrament instituted by Christ for those who wish to become members of His church' (ASB, p 212), MORIB therefore calls for a fresh rationale for infant baptism that encourages people to make real their own membership of Christ's church before asking for membership on behalf of another.

MORIB also calls for a review of Canon Law concerning baptism to bring it into line with the clear intentions of the church as expressed by the General Synod and the ASB.

In particular MORIB calls for the Bishops to support those parishes where clergy and PCC's are endeavouring to provide a consistent discipline of baptismal preparation in accordance with the General Synod declaration of 1973 and the rubrics of the ASB. Signed the National MORIB Committee, October 21st 1988.

A copy of the letter was sent to the church press who made passing reference to it and then deafening silence. Maybe we were expecting too much, but we did not receive one comment or even acknowledgement from any member of the House of Bishops. I later learned via one of the several grapevines that it is not the policy of the House of Bishops to respond to open letters. Bishop Colin Buchanan said that open letters were not the best way to proceed and 'Have you seen the size of a bishop's mailbag?'.

Two weeks later I was listening to 'Thought for the Day' when one member of the House of Bishops was giving an excellent address on the programme. I wrote to the bishop concerned to ask for a copy of the address and put in a postscript reminding him that we had sent an open letter on baptism the previous fortnight. Would he be interested to comment?

The text of the radio talk was sent to me, but no comment was received about baptism.

Whatever the reasons behind the episcopal stonewalling I believe it is important that the House of Bishops should note the sane and serious concern that many Anglicans (especially clergy) feel about infant baptism. Those who are concerned have the Church of England at heart and are concerned to see her grow during the Decade of Evangelism and beyond.

The hands of clergy and parishes who are trying to take up the slack in the matter need to be strengthened by changes in agreed discipline and Canon Law. That is why the last paragraph of the letter called for episcopal support in this area.

How ought Canon Law to be revised?

The following is my attempt to amend the present Canons using the existing phraseology as much as possible. To sit down and re-write Canon Law on Christian Initiation with a clean sheet would be an interesting exercise, but it would also be a fantasy to suppose that the Church of England would do the same! I regard it as more likely that any redrawing of Canon Law would take place by amending the present canons. Thus I have attempted the latter exercise. Canon B21 at present reads:

> It is desirable that every minister having a cure of souls shall from time to time administer the sacrament of Holy Baptism upon Sundays or other Holy days at or immediately after public worship when the most people come together, that the congregation there present may witness the receiving of them that be newly baptised into Christ's Church, and be put in remembrance of their own profession made to God in their baptism, nevertheless (if necessity so require) children may be baptised on any other day.

B21 is basically a good Canon. It outlines the important principle that there is value in witnessing a baptism not only from the point of view of the candidate being baptised and his sponsors, but also to be reminded of one's own baptism. If this Canon were followed to the letter, the three o'clock in the afternoon private baptism should not in theory exist. However, as I have said earlier, there is a case for a special baptismal service with hymns, address, etc which could be regarded as a main act of worship. I would therefore suggest: *delete* 'or immediately after' and *add* at the end a new sentence: *'If a baptism cannot take place at an act of public worship, then the regular congregation should be represented at any separate service of baptism by not less than five (say) persons in addition to the minister. If any infant is baptised outside of a normal main act of worship the parent(s) shall bring the infant to the next convenient main service for a prayer of reception.*

In addition I would suggest that the word 'children' be deleted and the word 'candidates' be substituted in the last line, as the general statement about the timing of a baptism should apply to both infants and adults.

CANON B22. Of the baptism of infants.
1. 'Due notice, normally of at least a week, shall be given before a child is brought to the church to be baptised'.

This paragraph needs amending. Emergency baptisms are dealt with under B22.6, but notice is a longer drawn out procedure now than in former times.

I suggest:

'Parents should give due notice to the minister that they are seeking baptism for their child. The notice will be specified in the baptismal policy of the parish'.

2. The present Canon reads: 'If a minister shall refuse or unduly delay to baptise any such infant, the parents or guardian may apply to the Bishop of the Diocese, who

shall, after consultation with the minister, give such directions as he thinks fit'.

This paragraph has been the subject of debate over the years and clergy have made of it what they would. Christopher Wansey, a baptismal reformer of previous days came to a point in his parochial ministry at Roydon in Essex where he felt he could no longer baptise infants at all. In the agreement that he worked out with his diocesan bishop, Canon B22.2. was the ground of authority whereby Christopher was allowed to do this. He says specifically that when the Canon was being formulated, he raised the matter of conscience when the clause was being debated in the Lower House of Canterbury. He received assurance in that debate that no diocesan bishop would instruct an incumbent to act against his conscience in the matter.

It would seem that the immediate sense of the Canon was to allow for those cases where a minister might feel that in all good conscience he could not proceed with a particular infant baptism. To make it a general rule for the non-baptising of infants per se, may not have been in mind when the Canon was drafted. However, there should be I believe some provision (positive provision) made for clergy who come to a point of total unease in the matter. Resignation, or forced resignation, was yesterday's answer to the problem.

Returning to the Canon itself, some provision of appeal should be allowed for parents, but this could be most sensibly dealt with in a parish by the bishop agreeing a particular baptismal policy. Proper consideration should be given to Deanery and Diocesan Policies, so that as far as possible there is uniformity of practice.

I would re-write as follows:

1. 'The minister shall not unduly delay to commence the preparation of the parents of any child in readiness for the infant's baptism. In any case, where the minister feels unable to proceed to the baptism of a child, he is not

*under an obligation to do so. Nevertheless, a refusal shall
not be unreasonably considered...in such cases the parents or guardians may apply to the Bishop of the Diocese,
who shall, after consultation with the minister give such
directions as he thinks fit.'*

This would give room for example for bishop and
minister to look at difficult cases in the light of any
agreed baptismal policy.

Canon B22.3
'The minister shall instruct the parents or guardians of an
infant to be admitted to Holy Baptism that the same
responsibilities rest on them as are in the service of Holy
Baptism required of the godparents.'

There has been with the onward march of liturgical
renewal a progressive shift from focus upon godparents
to focus upon parents in taking responsibilities in Christian upbringing. Series 2,3 and the Alternative Service
Book are clear examples. This Canon makes provision
for this shift. As it stands it smacks of being a provision
after the event of liturgical shift. I would suggest the
following:

*'Preparation for the baptism of an infant will normally
include the preparation of at least one parent for confirmation, if neither parent is yet confirmed. Where such
preparation is not yet desired or is refused, the parents
should be offered the service of "Thanksgiving and Blessing for the Birth of a Child". The acceptance of this
service should not prejudice a later baptism for the child
should the parents change their minds. Parents who are
lapsed communicants should be encouraged to become
regular communicants. A period of familiarisation with
public worship should be regarded as a normal part of
baptism preparation.'*

I have incorporated into this revised Canon the main
provision asked for in the MORIB open letter to the
bishops concerning the 'confirmation of one parent' rule

and an encouragement to become regular communicants. I have also included a clear statement that attendance at worship is part of preparation.

Canon B22.4, at present, is the crucial one which effectively forbids a clergyman to refuse baptism to absolutely anyone *but* goes on to say that he may delay for purpose of instructing parents or godparents. This is the Canon that many clergy try and 'drive a coach and horses through' by their various baptismal policies. It is also the Canon that Bishop Colin Buchanan might have in mind when he implies that by a too liberal interpretation of the word 'preparation' we might be 'pushing against' the Canons a bit.

I would say that it is possible to justify a strict baptismal policy under the above Canon (see the chapter on 'Do we really refuse?'), but that there is a fundamental flaw in it for reasons expounded earlier, namely that baptism goes ahead even if the 'parental horses are unwilling'. The text reads:

> No minister shall refuse or, save for the purpose of preparing or instructing the parents or guardians or godparents, delay to baptise any infant within his cure that is brought to the church to be baptised, provided that due notice has been given and the provisions relating to godparents in these Canons are observed.

I would suggest that as I have covered the points raised elsewhere the present Canon simply be deleted.

> Canon B22.5. A minister who intends to baptise any infant whose parents are residing outside the boundaries of his cure, unless the names of such persons or of one of them be on the church electoral roll of the same, shall not proceed to the baptism without having sought the goodwill of the minister of the parish in which such parents reside.

This is fine as it stands. I would simply add:

The minister involved should agree on how the appropriate preparation should be arranged. The parents should be encouraged to attend the church where they are normally resident.

Canon B22.6,7 and 8 make provision for emergency baptism of infants. I think they are fine as they stand.

The text reads:

6. No minister being informed of the weakness or danger of death of any infant within his cure and therefore desired to go to baptise the same shall either refuse or delay to do so.

7. A minister so baptising a child in a hospital or nursing home, the parents of the child not being resident in his cure, nor their names on the church electoral roll of the same, shall send their names and addresses to the minister of the parish in which they reside.

8. If any infant which is privately baptised do afterwards live, it shall be brought to the church and there, by the minister, received into the congregation of Christ's flock according to the form and manner prescribed in and by the office for Private Baptism in the Book of Common Prayer. (Perhaps we might add 'or its equivalent in the Alternative Service book'.)

Canon B22.9 reads:

9. The minister of every parish shall warn the people that without grave cause and necessity they should not have their children baptised privately in their houses.

I suggest: *Baptisms should not be conducted privately in houses except for grave cause or necessity. Where a baptism is to take place otherwise than in a place of public worship, the bishop should give either a general or particular consent for the alternative location.*

This latter provision should enable baptisms to take place if requested at swimming pools or equivalent places for total immersion.

I suggest including a new Canon B22.10 to do with co-habitation as follows:

Notwithstanding any of the foregoing Canons relating to baptism, parents who request baptism for an infant whilst they are unmarried should furnish the minister with an appropriate assurance that they intend to regularise their relationship at the first convenient opportunity. In particular they should adhere to the Christian doctrine of marriage as outlined in Canon B30.

At present there is such disparate practice surrounding the baptism of infants where the parents are co-habiting that there is a need to seek a unity of policy. Where a single parent requests baptism and there is no possibility of marriage with the other parent because of desertion or some other cause, then I suggest that the single parent be prepared for baptism of her baby as suggested above, being confirmed if necessary. It hardly needs me to say that such pastoral cases need to be handled sensitively. But that by itself does not obviate the need for some consistent guidelines.

B23. Of Godparents and sponsors.
1. For every child to be baptised there shall be not fewer than three godparents, of whom at least two shall be of the same sex as the child and of whom at least one shall be of the opposite sex; save that, when three cannot conveniently be had, one godfather and godmother shall suffice. Parents may be godparents for their own children provided that the child have at least one other godparent.

This needs to be simplified. I suggest:
A child may have up to a maximum of three god-parents of whom the majority should be of the same sex as the child. Parents may be godparents to their own child.

2. The godparents shall be persons who will faithfully fulfil their responsibilities both by their care for the children

committed to their charge and by the example of their own godly living.

I suggest no change!

3. When one who is of riper years is to be baptised he shall choose three, or at least two, to be his sponsors, who shall be ready to present him at the font and afterwards put him in mind of his Christian profession and duties.

I suggest that this is fine, but one simplification might be to say,
'*He shall choose two to be his sponsors...*' and add a new sentence: '*One of these sponsors might conveniently be the minister who prepared him for baptism.*'

At present B22.4 reads:

4. No person shall be admitted to be a sponsor or godparent who has not been baptised and confirmed. Nevertheless the minister shall have power to dispense with the requirement of confirmation in any case in which in his judgement need so requires.

Amend as follows to read: '*...who has not been baptised and confirmed. The minister may accept unconfirmed godparents provided they give assurance that they intend to be prepared for confirmation. Members of communicant status of other Christian denominations may be accepted as godparents.*

B24. Of the baptism of such as are of riper years.
1. When any such person as is of riper years and able to answer for himself is to be baptised, the minister shall instruct such person, or cause him to be instructed, in the principles of the Christian religion, and exhort him so to prepare himself with prayers and fasting that he may receive this holy sacrament with repentance and faith! (Exclamation mine!)

It never ceases to amaze me how we in the Church of England will strain at a gnat in Canon law or rubric to allow infants to be baptised under almost invisible conditions and then in unadorned rigoristic challenge to lay bare the real demands of baptism as in Canon B24 above. Nevertheless I say: 'Hallelujah!' Even the Baptists might find prayer and fasting a bit tough. I would leave that Canon as it stands but might be tempted to add the option of an immersion baptism if requested.

B24.
2. At least a week before any such baptism is to take place, the minister shall give notice thereof to the Bishop of the diocese or whomsoever he shall appoint for the purpose.

I suggest this whole paragraph be now deleted as obsolete.

B24.
3. Every person thus baptised shall be confirmed by the bishop so soon after his baptism as conveniently may be; so that he may be admitted to the Holy Communion.

This is fine. I suggest no change.

I read somewhere in a book on creative writing that he who continually goes back to his prose and amends it, substituting this word for that and tidying up phrases here and there leaves writing that 'smells of oil'. My exercise in amending the baptismal Canons positively reeks of oil! There is a limit to the amount of amending one can do on the back of the existing Canons without running into the need to rewrite the whole lot. However, I hope what I have done above will indicate the kind of work that now needs to be done in the area of clarification of baptismal rules.

I will summarise the principle changes I have made for those who have got lost as follows:

a. Baptism preparation is normal and should include a period of attending public worship.

b. The minister may refuse to baptise an infant if baptism is clearly pastorally inappropriate.

c. A representative sample of the congregation must be present when baptisms take place outside of main worship.

d. At least one baptism parent must be prepared for confirmation if not already of communicant status.

e. Provision should be made for such clergy who have a conscience problem over the baptism of infants.

f. Where baptism parents are co-habiting, they should give a clear intention that they intend to regularise their relationship before the baptism of their infant can proceed.

g. There should be greater liaison between ministers where there is a request for an infant to be baptised other than in its own parish. This applies especially to the appropriate preparation.

Diocesan Policies and Deanery Policies:

Baptismal policies are assumed to be those of parishes, but increasingly deaneries and dioceses are beginning to formulate their own general policies. The need for such was seen in the comments from the Chester Diocesan Survey.

A few years ago I went to speak at Islington Deanery Synod about baptismal reform. Included in the papers I was forwarded before the meeting was a copy of a baptismal policy for Islington Deanery and London Diocese. These were two separate policies drawn up in the 1970s. The deanery one was stricter than the diocesan one. (Do baptismal policies get tougher as one gets closer to the parish?) One clause in the deanery policy referred to co-habiting couples and required a marriage to take place first. The diocesan policy was more general. Both were clearly revisions of the Canons without substantially departing from them or undermining their basic authority. The interesting thing was that at half time one clergyman came up and expressed surprise that a deanery policy actually existed. It is worth noting that any policy forged in the days of the enthusiasts is likely to be lost sight of if it is not continually adhered to. That is why I beleve that the Church of England should keep up its attention to baptismal reform lest the hard work of previous generations is lost sight of and has to be done all over again—unless that is part of the opposing strategy!

In my present deanery, Martley and Worcester West, we have recently debated in Chapter meetings the possibility of a deanery baptismal policy. The main issue we were seeking to address was clearer co-ordination across parish boundaries and in the end we agreed to observe the existing Canon B22.5, which one could hardly call reform! On most other issues the deanery was divided, particularly over how to respond to the problem of co-habitation.

I recently was given sight of a draft in Southwell Diocese concerning the administration of infant baptism. Most of it again is a fairly sound and thorough update of baptismal discipline, but does not go far enough in the direction I am advocating in my revision of Canon Law. The suggested diocesan policy is strong on the need for preparation, urges the service of thanksgiving and blessing as a first step, but again comes back to the overriding consideration that in the end the parents choice must decide the issue. This is where I believe the policy is fundamentally flawed, for until the arm of the local minister is strengthened in this matter, there will always be those who insist on having their infant baptised against all odds.

I am informed that at the present time the House of Bishops are having sight and discussion of an excellent 'position paper' by Canon Martin Reardon. I do hope that the House will have the courage to discern the signs of the times and to take one or two bold steps in the direction I am advocating. If such steps are taken they must be implemented with care, sensitivity and with media awareness; perhaps over a period of time, and giving due notice. But above all let there be courage.

See Appendix 5 for July 1991 update.

Chapter 13

'I DON'T LIKE THE FEEL OF THIS PLACE'

Within a few months of moving to Bordon in July 1976 I started to move into a dimension of spiritual awareness that I had not previously known. It came to me first through the 'feel' of the area covered by the Army village, later to become a new town. It felt a distinctly odd place. I had noticed it way back in 1961 when I travelled the A325 from Petersfield to Farnham. The coach in which I was travelling stopped in Bordon for about fifteen minutes to collect soldiers from the camp and I noticed that the atmosphere in the environs of Bordon felt quite unlike that four miles south or north. As we moved north up the A325, we passed out of the pleasant villages of Liss and Greatham and traversed an area of sandy heathland and pine woods, criss-crossed with tank tracks, military railway lines and army barrack blocks. The dwellings looked shanty-like and out of character with the rest of the surrounding area of North-east Hampshire.

When fifteen years later I became priest in charge of Bordon, I sensed this odd feeling again. At first I put it down to the lack of civil planning and the presence of the Army, but there seemed more to it than that. The ecumenical officer, the Revd Francis Palmer, when describing the place to me said, 'Although it's on the Surrey border, it's extremely scruffy. It even has its own gasworks!' Actually it had one gasholder (so did Farnham for that matter) and that was removed in time. However, Bordon was a place spoken against as a matter of course. When I went to the parish I and my family were warmly welcomed at an official garden party at Headley rectory. The congregation of the parish church were pleasant, welcoming and well-heeled. The tea cups grew emptier, and the initial pleasantries were exchanged, when the tone of the conversation changed. One or two people said to us, 'How long do you think you will stay down there (meaning Bordon)?' 'Will the house be all right?' I began to wonder what I had let myself in for. However, from those clues I began to discern very early on that Bordon was thought a rather different place. It wasn't simply that it was sociologically different, although that was a factor, but it had an odd kind of other planetary feel to it. Neither was it me alone who had this sensitivity to the area; numerous people remarked on it.

'Bordon doesn't feel the same. I could never settle down here!' they might say.

Even the police said the same. I had a number of occasions when I had to discuss matters with the police over the years. On one visit to me a constable said, 'I live in Alton and I always get this odd feeling whenever I come into the police station here.'

'Oh yes,' I replied, 'where do you start to get the feeling?'

'Oh, by Broxhead Common,' said the constable.

Broxhead Common is a high piece of heathland to the north of Bordon. In the drought of 1976 it suffered a large fire, like numerous other places in the vicinity, which left the bracken and gorse charred in a desert-like appearance. Around the area the Ordnance Survey maps showed numerous ancient burial mounds or tumuli. The headmaster of one of the local junior schools[1] had begun a local history and geography project to study the area. He had discovered in his researches that within a two-mile radius of Bordon there were around 150 tumuli or the remains of such. Many had been ploughed out or flattened by tanks on the military training lands. Broxhead Common itself had a tumulus on top and several nearby. At the time I didn't realise the significance of all of this, but through the enlightenment of friends, the idea was put to me that perhaps in some distant age, Bordon may have been a place of ancient worship, rather like Stonehenge. Admittedly no one can quite agree what Stonehenge was originally used for and it almost certainly was not built by the Druids. But it does have this pattern of tumuli arranged around it in a fairly regular form, and spread over all the area of some square miles. The stones of Stonehenge are believed to have come from the Preseli Mountains of South-west Wales. How those ancients did it is a matter of speculation, but the fact that they did it at all and why point to something quite important. There must have been some overriding, all demanding, purpose to set up that ring of stones.

Bordon had no stone circles, but numerous tumuli. The thought was given to me that perhaps at some location in the area there was a woodhenge at one time, which rotted away millenia ago. All this at first reading might seem a total distraction and an irrelevance, but as the years went by at Bordon the conviction grew within me that Bordon's distant spiritual past was linked to its present spiritual uphill struggle! How did that conviction take root? Was it a piece of naive speculation on my part when I ought to have been getting on with my job?

It came out of what I can only call my charismatic methodology. Put simply, I believed that if I was called to minister in a parish, in a church or to a congregation, then God the Holy Spirit knew the way into that situation. A job description might stipulate tasks and strategies: our general approach in Headley and Bordon was 'pastoral evangelism' which may ordinarily include a list of the obvious things that parsons do, like sick visiting, preaching and administration. Yet overriding all of this is the sovereign activity of God breaking into a situation in ways that cannot be discovered in advance. God, the Holy Spirit, springs surprises in the ordinary situations. It is through being prayerful, discerning and watchful that the Holy Spirit will point out the special tasks and obstacles that have to be cleared away in order for God's Kingdom to be established. I could give numerous examples of where the Holy Spirit overruled my own decisions. For example, I felt strongly that it was very important for me to form a link with the comprehensive school and to take the pastoral opportunities offered there. I felt similarly about time spent with certain prayer groups, or with the Air Training Corps. Whatever agenda I might have, I tried to find out what God's agenda was and follow that if I could.

Thus it seemed to me that I was being shown that Bordon's present was conditioned by its distant past. Three other people were influential in my thinking in the early years at Bordon. Richard Inkpen, vicar of Blackmoor, was early interested in the significance of the ancient monuments. There was a large tumulus half a mile from his vicarage and he believed that many of the tree clumps in the district, which had an 'eerie' feel to them, could well have been used for fertility rites as sacred groves in previous generations.[2] Blackmoor vicarage itself looked out over an expanse of almost deserted, damp pine scrub and heathland, which was the Longmoor military ranges. There seemed an interesting connection between military training lands and ancient monuments, particularly tumuli and ancient hillforts.[3]

There was one place which seemed an exception to

the general dark 'feel' of the area...a place which felt like an oasis in a desert.

Set in the centre of Bordon, and originally buried in the woods is Whitehill Chase. 'The Chase' is a Victorian country house of modest size and originally set in a twenty-five acre estate. For much of this century it has been owned by the Knowles family and in 1956, the late Mrs Knowles gave the house into Christian Trust for the ministry of retreats and healing. The house has had many 'ups and downs' over the years, but since 1985 by a mutual arrangement of the Whitehill Chase Trustees and the Acorn Healing Trust, the property has been greatly extended, a new chapel has been built and the house is now a Resource Centre for the Christian Healing Ministry. It was during one of the house's 'downs' in the late 70s, that I fortuitously discovered something that set me wondering about folk religion. The warden at the time was the late Mrs Anna Harper, MBE, and she had been given permission by the trustees to attempt a ministry at Whitehill Chase of 'Caring for the Carers'. Clergy, doctors, nurses and other members of the caring professions would come for a rest. The idea never really took off and the house was let to other groups to supplement income. One of these groups was a TM (Transcendental Meditation) group. We had some debate in our management committee meetings over whether we should accept their booking or not. TM was a slightly suspect group spiritually. In the end they were let in, and they came back twice more.

'Why are they so interested in Whitehill Chase?', I asked the warden.

'It's because of the ley lines that meet in the grounds,' she replied. I was then acquainted with the phenomenon of the ancient ley system which appeared to be a prehistoric system of straight lines connecting up ancient monuments and stone circles. No one seemed to know what precisely these lines were, but that they existed seemed beyond doubt. Mrs Harper herself seemed to be well acquainted with the lines of Glastonbury and the various legends surrounding that place.[4] She assured me of the spiritual reality of these rather odd phenomena and hence the importance of Whitehill Chase.

The third person whom I got to know well at this time was the Head of Geography in the local comprehensive school; a Christian teacher named Martyn Moss. Being a geographer and having noted the phenomenon of ley lines some years before, Martyn had located most of the ancient monuments on the ground and traced the local leys over a radius of ten miles on the two-and-a-half inch Ordnance Survey Map. The pieces of this jigsaw puzzle were slowly fitting together. I then saw how the ancient earthworks in South Bordon lay on a dead straight line with Crooksbury Hill just off the Hogs Back and Butser Hill, south of Petersfield.... All this seemed irrelevant at the time.[5]

Yet the knowledge that a modern esoteric, non-Christian group of TMs believed that by meditating or whatever, they could re-activate these old ley lines, meant that suddenly a pre-Christian religious phenomenon had re-appeared in the late twentieth century before my very eyes. The fact that these lines were claimed to have and transmit some kind of power or spiritual energy made me wonder if they were the reason why Bordon had this strange feel to it. But the oddity was that at and around Whitehill Chase house itself and over the surrounding lawns, there was a totally different feel. It was peaceful, spiritually relaxing, 'light' as opposed to 'dark'. It felt a sanctuary, a place of healing and prayer. There was a definite presence.

It took me some months to adjust to these new awarenesses. I had periods when I wondered if it was me who was deceived and imagining things, but as time went on I became sure that the ancient religion 'hangover' was a serious phenomenon.

One day an old lady in the congregation casually handed me two magazines when I went to visit her. They were back copies of *Sussex Life*. She had never given me magazines before and for no apparent reason she just handed them to me. In one was a feature article on ley lines in Sussex! I learned from this article that in AD 610 Pope Gregory decreed that the Christian churches in this country should be built on the sites of the temples, which were already on ancient sacred sites. The Venerable Bede has preserved a copy of the letter sent to Abbot Mellitus by Pope Gregory which says:

> If these temples are well-built, they must be purified from the worship of demons and dedicated to the service of the true God. In this way, we hope that the people, seeing that their temples are not destroyed, may abandon their error and flocking more readily to their accustomed resorts, may come to know and adore the true God.[6]

Now I realised why Stowmarket parish church had been built on the site of an earlier pagan temple. I also realised why certain church spires in Warwickshire appeared to lie in a straight line across the country. The ancient cathedrals too were believed to have been built over stone circles.

The application of all this to Bordon was at first hard to discern, but we concluded that a possible rationale might be that for some mysterious reason when churches were built over pagan sites they somehow 'clobbered' or neutralised the 'powers of darkness' associated with the pagan shrine. I wondered if there was any biblical evidence for this and without going into great detail believe that there is, in the taking of the Promised Land of Canaan. The Israelites had to smash the pagan altars and build new ones of un-hewn stone and burn the sacred pillars (1 Kings 14: 22–23 and Deuteronomy 12: 1–3). In other words evangelisation was not merely a matter of converting people, something had to be claimed for the territory as well.

On the 1st May, 1983 (a useful pagan festival) at 08.25 on a Sunday, John Cherrill, Martyn Moss and I planted a small wooden cross on the highest point of Broxhead Common accompanied by prayer looking over the whole town. This was a token act to claim the eventual victory of the Lord over the whole area and the building up of a people for himself, in that part of Hampshire. If it sounds odd, is it any different in substance from building churches on the site of previous pagan temples?

There was a real sense in which Bordon was a piece of territory still to be taken in the name of Christ. There had never been a stone-built church in Bordon until St Mark's opened in November 1982. Bordon was virtually uninhabited throughout history (except for the ancients), until the Army came at the end of the last century. Before that just desert. The first churches were either wooden huts or 'tin tabernacles'. The gospel had been preached and Christians had prayed in and around the Army for a century, but there had been no claiming of the territory for God.[7] We felt that prayer was important as the main weapon: not just perfunctory prayer, but a real seeking of God's strategy for the whole place. Until this was done something fundamental would remain untouched.

One night, Richard Inkpen and I arranged a mobile prayer meeting. We took three cars and eight people and encircled the area, praying quietly on the ten-mile circuit, but stopping outside significant places, usually existing churches, and finishing up outside the gates of the comprehensive school where some of the local youths used to hang around on their motor bikes during the lunch hour, to meet girl friends. On the occasion of this exercise none of us could give a rational reason for what we were doing, other than the conviction that we felt it should be done this way. We prayed for God's purposes to be victorious in the area and that any alien forces might be driven back. It was an exercise in faith. As we went we gave thanks to God for the work of past years that had been done in Christ's name and prayed for the future. Were we rediscovering the real significance of the old ceremony of 'beating the bounds?'

The main result as far as I was concerned was that I felt 'hassled' (to use the local jargon) for some days afterwards. I felt as though something was trying to throw a spanner into the ordering of daily life. I suspect our mobile prayer meeting stirred something up.

One other feature of the Bordon area was the high concentration of Romany families. They had other names like 'travellers' or the 'travelling people', but in Bordon they were settled. It was their home.[8] They were on the whole very nice people to get to know, but in general awareness they seemed to belong to an alternative ethnic group. I say this not to make a value judgement, but as a descriptive remark. They were English all right, but somehow belonged to a sub-group that was interbred. It wasn't until I took Romany funerals that I became aware of the phenomenon of alternative religious convictions being worked out under Christian forms. In simpler days I might have labelled this 'superstition', but when a Romany funeral took place, one became conscious of very definite patterns of mourning and release. This is nothing untypical here of any bereavement situation, but with the Romanies it seemed much more carefully ritualised and although they would not have articulated the phenomenon, the rituals appeared to emanate from a deeper set of alternative religious beliefs which were sub- or pre-Christian. One funeral director told me,

'They won't sing at a funeral, sir, but they must have hymns. They must walk in behind the coffin or it isn't right. Whatever you say will comfort them, but they have their own little rituals which you won't change.'

He was right, but above all it was the spiritual 'feel' surrounding the Romanies that first aroused in me the conviction that some alternative religion may be rooted from their ancestry and continuing in their present practice. Furthermore that 'feel' of the Romanies felt entirely congruent with the 'feel' of the area. It really did belong to them.

During our time in Bordon though we made many friends and contacts with the 'travelling' families, hardly any became regular church members, though there were signs that Christmas services were beginning to touch them. It was not until the population doubled and the new town grew with a vast range of new residents, that the old 'feel' of the area started to break up.

Mentioning Christmas of course gives a good lead into perhaps one of the main points I wish to make; that of the Christianising of pagan festivals. It is well known that what we call the Feast of the Incarnation on December 25th had roots in the decision of the Emperor Aurelian in AD 272 to introduce the Festival of the Invincible Sun on the same date. Early in the fourth century in Rome, we have evidence that the Christian festival was established. It is a matter of speculation whether the idea of Christianising a pagan festival was an act of syncretism, an act of take over or cleansing, or merely a counter-attraction, but the Christians of the fourth century decided to handle the problem that way. The historical watershed may have been the Constantinian settlement. Once Christianity had become the official religion of the Roman Empire, baptism into the church was virtually synonymous with membership of the state. The effect of that has obviously hung around for a long time! To be British is to be christened in infancy.

But Christmas still remains an odd mixture of Christian and pre-Christian. Yule logs and evergreens, mistletoe and holly are the outward signs of an old paganism surrounding the winter solstice. Indeed it is worth looking on the calendar to detect those feasts associated with fertility and harvest, noting the common threads running through them which do not depend upon Christian theology to give them a rationale.

Why is it that a large group of people who are not regular attenders at Christian worship feel quite at home in a harvest festival, midnight Communion at Christmas or on Remembrance Sunday (a national religious occasion). Easter appears to be a 'purer' festival, not surrounded by much folk religion, apart from the symbol of the egg.

I am doing no more here than sketching in an area which I think is of crucial importance for understanding the background of the powerful demand for a birthright which is rooted in the folklore as infant christening.

We have to wonder whether the intention of the Constantinian settlement as a notional adherence to Christianity was as much concerned with political peace in the Empire, as it was the intention to genuinely convert the Empire to Christ's religion in serious discipleship. On balance I guess that the former motive was the prevalent one. It has left a legacy of nominal Christianity in nations that have ritually processed their infants into official church membership, without having won them into full discipleship. Indiscriminate infant baptism is the main legacy of this. It puts a Christian label on an individual who may well not embrace that religion, and who may well be opposed to it.

The phenomenon of the use of Christian rituals adapted over the top of an alternative set of sub-Christian beliefs is still powerfully with us. These are chiefly the occasional offices of course, and they do provide opportunity to take the participants a step towards more Christian understanding, but I can see that the underlying belief system remains intact, unless challenged.

Most theologians and Christian ministers long to

understand implicit or 'folk-religion' and there is a tendency to come at this subject from the standpoint of sociology or psychology. This approach must not be dismissed. In *Folk Religion, Friend or Foe?* by Mark Silversides[9] some useful thought is given to identifying the needs at different points in the life cycle. A religious context can confer status and acceptance, for example, and give identity. These insights are important and I would maintain that we could detect the same in our pastoral work implementing our various baptismal policies. However, I do not think that they are the whole story. Behind much sub-Christian and pre-Christian religious beliefs lie other spiritual forces that have a persistance and give off resistance. I heard some while back a television interview in which the subject was white witchcraft. The interviewee said that white witchcraft, being a much older esoteric religion than Christianity, actually had a claim to being a more natural religion for Britain than Christianity (Southern TV).

I do not need to point out that in the new search for meaning and identity, the British have been much more willing to try out alternative faiths, 'isms' and cults than perhaps ever before. People converted to Christ in Britain today are more than likely to have 'dabbled' in some other spiritual system first, before trying out Christianity. Against this background, our evangelism and administration of baptism must mean a cleansing and a break with the past. It must involve a repentance and turning from any alternative religions which are at variance with the demands of being a disciple of Christ. Baptism is in a real sense a cutting off from the past. The prayers for deliverance from darkness and evil are soundly rooted. All this seems to suggest that baptisms must be carried out in the earnest of sincerity and faith and not be allowed to be the continuance of a notional adherance to Christ, which is only that. If any man is in Christ he is a new creature. Old things are to be put away and all things are to be made new (2 Corinthians 5:17). It is interesting how many Christians today are being led to see the importance and possibility of the healing of the memories. Those in the ministries of healing and deliverance will provide abundant testimony to the need for many people to be set free from various bondages before they can be released to grow in the Christian life. All this bears out the notion of spiritual forces that will bind us, given half a chance.

I do not want to labour this point *ad nauseam*, but I did discover in the pastoring of the main congregation at Bordon that several of the problems I encountered had a remarkably recurrent theme to them. I noticed particularly that there appeared to be what I will call a 'spirit(s) of division' over the area. In my dreamier and more enthusiastic days I could have imagined a congregation of several hundred being built up in the course of time. People were coming to faith. We could present the gospel. We had good worship, and house groups, but it seemed that as soon as a person got under way spiritually, they would come under attack, not necessarily from within the church, but possibly from within their family or from some set of adverse circumstances. By attack I mean that they were opposed in their faith to the extent that they ran into serious problems which left them floundering. The reader may have noticed in an earlier chapter how quickly three key converts were moved away from the church to other areas. I felt after a while that something was working against us. Paul said that we fight not against flesh and blood, but against spiritual rulers of darkness, against principalities and powers (Ephesians 6:12). He was right.

More seriously I felt that the church seemed to exhibit the phenomenon of growth up to a point and just as we thought that we had revival in 'the bag', a split would occur over what to me might be the most trivial reasons. I felt for months on end as though I was being 'kept on the run', by an endless succession of pastoral problems, that should never have assumed the importance that they did. Everything from charismatic renewal to fund raising seemed to be a battleground, and from time to time people left the church 'in a huff'. The details are not important, but the phenomenon is. I believe there are many church situations up and down this country where divisons exist and seem to perpetuate themselves over generations.

If such situations do perpetuate themselves and succeeding ministers keep encountering similar problems, then I suspect principalities and powers as the main cause. That is where the battle lies.

By God's grace I believe that we were shown early on that such was the case in Bordon; it was a previously unevangelised area where there had been no permanent habitation previously and where the territory needed 'taking'. We made a start on it. But I emphasise only a start. Only a fool would claim to have done more.

Notes

1. Mr Eric Smart, a former headmaster of Weyford Infant Junior School, Bordon, was quite a keen amateur archivist. His project initially was started for educational purposes but as he progressed his own interest went deeper than that needed for the local children.

2. See W.E. Hudson, *Hampshire Days* (first published by Longman, Green and Co. in 1903. Reprinted OUP, 1980), page 164 of the paperback. Hudson has this interesting passage:

> But the Hollywater Clump in Wolmer Forest as soon as I come in sight of it wakes in me another sense and feeling; and I have found in conversation

with others on this subject that they are affected in the same way. I doubt if anyone can fail to experience such a feeling when looking on that great hill-top grove, a stupendous pillared temple with its dome-like black roof against the sky standing high above and dominating the sombre pine and heath country for miles around.

Hollywater Clump was on the edge of Bordon and definitely felt located within the 'dark' area.

3. This may of course be pure coincidence because military lands generally limit agriculture and are liable to leave an area undisturbed. However the mid south of England, particularly the sweep of Salisbury Plain from Andover and Larkhill through to Warminster, could yield up some interesting secrets.

4. A member of my family visiting Glastonbury Tor for the first time was mysteriously ill for some days afterwards.

5. The principle work on the rediscovery of the ancient leys is: *The Old Straight Track* by Watkins, the son of a Hereford merchant, conceived the existence of leys whilst out walking on the Herefordshire hills in 1934.

6. See *Stones, Bones, and Gods* by R.T. Pearce (Ward Lock Educational: 1982). The *Independent* newspaper recently reported the possible discovery of a huge temple underneath the ancient Avebury circle in Wiltshire. The article referred to a new work *Avebury Reconsidered* by Professor Ucko and three other academics (*Independent* edition of 22 November 1990).

7. I have recently come across one Christian healing ministry centre at Ellel Grange, near Lancaster, that was offering a course of teaching on 'claiming the ground'.

8. This point was forcibly put by a local councillor at a parish meeting of the Whitehill Parish Council when discussing the problem of a large gypsy encampment.

9. *Folk Religion, Friend or Foe?* by Mark Silversides (Grove Books: Nottingham, 1986).

Chapter 14

NATIONAL PRESS

From time to time the subject of baptism gets into the press. Usually it is the local press, and often in a case where an infant is refused baptism (or is claimed to have been refused). The examples contained in Appendix 2 are typical of what I have seen, although the press coverage in the *East Hampshire Post* when we introduced the three-month rule at Headley/Bordon was quite generous. Often the tabloids and some local newspapers thrive on such happenings. I saw a case in Gloucestershire where a vicar delayed a baptism and the ensuing correspondence was full of vitriol. A similar case happened in Warwickshire and another in Derbyshire all within recent years.[1] The reaction says a lot about the deeply rooted folk beliefs that are emotively resistant to challenge.

It is not often, however, that feature articles appear on baptism in the quality newspapers of the national press. I offer two such articles in this chapter both of which are significant signposts to the times in which we live. The first is from *Sunday Telegraph* columnist Minette Marrin, and appeared in the issue of the 8th October 1989:

One of the saddest things about not being a Christian, despite my Anglican upbringing, is that I felt it would be hypocritical to get married in church, and have our children christened. I have always regretted it because marriages and births are times when a solemn and beautiful rite of passage is just what is needed, not to mention a frilly white dress, lace christening gown, *Trumpet Voluntary* and other profane pleasures.

My seven-year-old daughter feels this lack in our life even more intensely than I ever have, and takes a very dim view of the family photographs. Her dearest fantasy is to step into a beautiful bridesmaid's dress, see us properly and romantically married in church, then hurry to the font, her dress doubling up as a christening gown, be christened herself, and then turn round and become godmother at the immediate christening of her little brother. If we delay any longer, she says, he will be old enough to be a pageboy as well.

'We are married,' I protest.

'You just got married in an office,' she always says, censoriously. 'That's not properly married.'

'Yes it is, and you're very lucky we're married at all,' I say feebly. 'There are lots of people these days whose parents aren't married at all.'

She looks incredulous. 'Yes, lots,' I say. 'Just like Natasha's mummy and daddy.'

'Oh, them? They're just as much married as you are,' she says. 'Not properly married.'

Out of the mouths of babes and sucklings, I think wearily.

'Anyway, can't I even get christened?' she always finishes.

This was never a pressing problem, until she received excellent religious education at school. 'Where did Jesse live?' she asked this week during homework. 'Is it something to do with Postman Pat?' I replied and received a quelling look.

'Well, why don't you just write "The Holy Land"?' I said.

'That's not good enough,' she replied, and despatched her unhallowed father off to find out. The result of all this Bible-teaching is that my daughter firmly believes in God, and wishes to go to church.

I think of going to church as a temptation that should be resisted. I miss the old liturgy, the hymns, the organ music, the atmosphere of churches and all those unforgettable incantations and exhortations— Catholic autobiographers always make much of the emotional hold of a Catholic upbringing, but I think the magic of Cranmer's English or Harvest Festival in a country parish is just as potent, and just as haunting to the unbeliever. I usually deny myself these pleasures, because I am not a believer, but I wonder about denying them to my daughter.

Of course I've asked people's advice. They usually say I should let her decide for herself, later on.

The only practical suggestion I got was from the late T.E. Utley, who told me both playfully and seriously that in cases of emergency like mine, lay people have the right to christen infants themselves, under the kitchen tap if need be, and proposed to set about it immediately—a prospect made even more daunting, as he himself agreed, because he was blind.

But people usually can't and don't decide for themselves, either earlier or later. If you encourage a child to believe in God, the chances are that she always will, however vaguely. If you deny a child a religious education, or show your own unbelief clearly, you make it very hard for her to believe in God. He who is not for me is against me, says a voice from my childhood.

Perhaps this is why I am weakening on this front— or it may be just the alarming degree of persistence that my daughter has inherited from her father's side—and I am now even considering the possibility of a christening. My husband disapproves, thinking it is all purely conventional and snobbish, if you don't really believe in it. However, if I didn't choose a pretty church, promise not to enjoy it, and to serve nothing more glamorous afterwards than PG Tips, he might not feel so strongly. But this is not the only problem. There is the consumer dilemma—which church?

Brand loyalty is a powerful force, and the Church of England would therefore be the most natural choice. Apart from anything else, it has the best plant (in the form of the nicest churches in this country), which is an important consideration. On the other hand, I have taken a shine to the local Catholic priest, who christened two of my nieces in two very touching ceremonies, which far surpassed the rather social Anglican dos I have been to in the past.

I feel very ill-equipped to decide these things for someone else. As far as I am concerned, Christianity is a thing of the past; in 1945, 81 per cent of all people born in England were baptised into the Church of England, but in 1985 the figure had dropped to 39 per cent. The estimate for 1995 is only 31 per cent. The proportion of these who go on to get confirmed has also been dropping fast, and even this is often a mere form anyway. And yet there is one curious Church of England statistic which reminds me rather of ourselves.

The great majority of Anglicans are christened as infants, but there is a category of 'others' who get baptised later. While infant baptisms have fallen markedly in this country since the war, the number of 'others' who embrace the Church of England later in life, for some reason, has grown significantly. Only 10,000 in 1940, and there were 45,000 in 1986—a huge increase among the falling numbers. Perhaps it's something to do with going to school and filling in forms. Or perhaps the Church of England still retains some real power to summon back a few lost sheep, such as my children.

I think it is music that keeps people drifting back towards religion. I certainly have always been unable to resist emotional or sentimental church music, like the lovely Nunc Dimittis at the end of television's series of Le Carré's *Smiley's People*.

The actor/director, Kenneth Branagh, is clearly aware of the extraordinary power of religious music, especially, oddly enough, when combined with battle. In his highly emotional film of *Henry V*, Branagh has gone for the jugular, with an unforgettable version of Non nobis Domine, which is played at increasing volume over a heroic four-minute tracking shot of the young king carrying a murdered boy across the blood-soaked fields of Agincourt. What it lacks in refinement it makes up for in raw power. I'm sorry I ever allowed myself to get bored with the idea of Branagh, after all those interviews, because he clearly is quite extraordinary. I wonder if he was brought up as a Catholic.

(Reprinted by courtesy of Minette Marrin and the *Sunday Telegraph*.)

Minette said in a letter to me that she was surprised by the amount of interest shown on the part of readers to the article. She had received a fair number of letters from Christians on the subject and they divided equally between those that recommended christening her daughter as a first step for her (or for Minette herself) into the faith, and those that disapproved of empty conventions in the absence of real faith. How would I respond to her situation?

I have had several such requests over the years, but usually, and I don't mean this derisorily, the requests have come from the less articulate end of the social spectrum. I believe that if a human being is seeking faith, even a seven-year-old, then the Christian church has a pastoral duty to respond. However if the seven-year-old is asking where Jesse lived and is mentally linked to Postman Pat, then I would suggest that baptism may be premature, but instruction and being linked to a church which takes children's instruction seriously could be an important first step. For that to happen it would need some parental approval of a positive kind. It may well cause Mrs Marrin to think again about the basis of the faith and if she should get gently drawn in so much the better.

My first reaction to her article, however, is to give her three cheers (or eight out of ten if you prefer) for her honesty and integrity. She admits to not being a Christian and believes Christianity a thing of the past. Fair enough. I happen to disagree with her but that is not the point. Minette then has the honesty to conclude that she ought to step aside from some of the consequences of assumed Christian belief, such as getting married in church and having children christened. It was when I faced my doubts that my search for spiritual reality took on a direction, but I also admit that it was the thought of not being married in church, especially in naval uniform (swords *et al*) which added spice to my search. The husband in the article does our cause a service by transmitting vibes from the social set where christening has clearly been perceived as a conventional and (slightly?) snobbish ritual. Minette then underlines this by referring to the social Anglican 'dos' she has attended in contrast to the more spiritually sharpened ethos exuded by the Roman Catholic christenings of her nieces. It is interesting that in the *East Hampshire Post* articles, the Roman Catholics were popularly perceived as being a strict church in contrast to we Anglicans who somehow by definition must be all things to all men. Does this lie behind Minette's reference to 'Brand loyalty'?

One of the most powerful paragraphs in the article for me is the one about children being unable to decide for themselves. 'If you show your own unbelief clearly, you make it very hard for her to believe in God.' There are a number of interlocking issues here, but suffice it to say that I think it is healthier for a parent to be honest about its own unbelief with integrity before a child, than to do a roller coaster round the Father Christmas syndrome like so many parents who give a long range consent to an unknown God of whose existence they are doubtful, and do so under a veneer of absolute certainty. That I would maintain is far more blocking to spiritual growth in a child than the stance which is taken in the *Sunday Telegraph* feature by Minette Marrin. The whole theme of this book is the way in which, by failing to discern the motives and level of faith of applicants for infant baptism, we actually aid and abet the 'Father Christmas syndrome' and compound unbelief.

No! Come in honest doubt and search. Hear what the church has to say and if when you decide for or against the faith the decision should be affirmative, then get baptised as a response, with great éclat!

Minette Marrin has done us a service writing this feature. Not only has she touched on some of the key issues but has also 'sussed' one main reason for the growth of the number of other (than infant) baptisms in the Church of England—people like herself!

Clifford Longley, the well known religious affairs correspondent of *The Times*, has written two major articles on baptism in recent years. The first: 'Bridge over troubled baptismal waters' was written in the edition of 29th October 1988 at the time of an approaching motion in General Synod by Roger Godin.[2] The full text of that article I have included in Appendix 4.

The second article was entitled 'Back-to-font reasoning' and that is printed below. It first appeared in the edition of 16th July 1990.

Christenings remain an important social and ceremonial part of the British way of life. A large proportion of the population turns to the Church of England to provide them, as it does for wedding and funeral services, so giving the church a constituency that other parts of its ministrations cannot reach.

Nobody in the church begrudges a church funeral, it seems, no matter how immoral or unbelieving the occupant of the coffin may have been. Except for the divorced, the clergy of the established church are obliged to marry anyone who meets the minimal legal requirements—which say nothing about believing anything in particular about marriage or religion— and no fuss is made about that either. But christenings, which the church prefers to call baptisms, have become deeply controversial. This is a service the church is in the process of withdrawing from the general community.

For a few moments at least, the York meeting of the General Synod last weekend looked about to embark on legislation to ban 'indiscriminate' baptism, confining it to those who take it seriously as a rite of Christian initiation. Parents would have been required to make a solemn promise that they were willing and able to raise their child in the Christian faith, which, by implication, would have restricted christenings to the families of those who are regular members of local congregations.

But before battle had been properly joined, the synod was told that a report on the wider issues was almost ready for publication, and so was persuaded to take the matter no further for the time being. Yet the debate and the proposed legislation were signs of growing pressure within the church to put a stop to indiscriminate baptism. Sooner rather than later, that pressure will prevail. Already fewer than half the number of newly-born children are baptised into the Church of England. Indiscriminate baptism is an embarrassment because it amounts to a public admission by the church that an important religious service may properly be used for purely social and conventional purposes by those who regard its religious content as meaningless. Many vicars refuse to officiate at christenings for non-believing families, and their refusal provokes many a storm in parish teacups.

This is partly the church's own fault. The traditional doctrine of baptism has become meaningless for many inside the church too. There is general agreement only that baptism is a ceremony marking entry into the visible community of the church (which is why so much weight is placed on the importance of parents being regular worshippers). The traditional view was that baptism is far more profound and significant, but it reflected beliefs that are now thoroughly out of fashion. For to believe in the traditional view, it was first necessary to believe in hell, damnation and the devil, in heaven and salvation, and in Christ's atoning sacrifice for sin. Those who still talk like that—except as a metaphor for life's hard knocks—are deemed to be such dyed-in-the-wool conservatives that they are right off the Anglican scale.

Traditionally, baptism was a washing away of original sin, a passage from spiritual death to spiritual life. The unbaptised did not go to heaven when they died, for they were still enslaved to Satan. Baptism was a permanent mark on the soul, showing which were God's own, even as the Israelites marked with blood the immunity of their homes from plague before the exodus from Egypt. To die unbaptised was a fearful thing. To be baptised was to join Christian civilisation.

Such deep feelings linger long, particularly in the rural areas of England and in the rural subconscious of the townsfolk. But they get little support from churchmen, who are inclined to treat them as superstitious. And they do dwindle into superstition when such notions are no longer related to Christian doctrine: not to have a child baptised, it is still widely believed, is to invite bad luck. This is folk religion because the church has moved away from what it originally taught about baptism, while ordinary people have hung on to it in a half-remembered and less-than-half-understood form. But they remember that baptism is a sacrament, while the church now remembers it only as a symbol.

Baptism is more than, even other than, the recruitment of a new member to the local parish church. Taken as merely that, it is meaningless, for no baby or small child can make a lifetime's religious commitment, least of all by the proxy voice of adult parents and godparents. The informed answer to a clergyman who refuses to allow a baptism unless the parents and godparents truly believe the words they have to say is to ask him whether he truly believes them himself. Does he, for instance, believe in the devil?

If traditional doctrine no longer meets the need, the answer is not to translate it into a merely sociological phenomenon that drains away the sacramental richness. That merely throws the font-water out with the baby. The answer is to dig deeper into the sources of doctrine, to find those levels of resonance which were always present but went unheard. Only by recovering a meaning for baptism more momentous than a scout's promise, more profound than putting a child's name down for Eton, will the church know what it is doing and what it ought to be doing. Meanwhile, indiscriminate baptism is as good a policy as any.

(Reprinted by permission of Clifford Longley and *Times Newspapers*.)

Longley (I am sorry not to use the Christian name, but it will serve to avoid confusion with the present author!) starts with the obvious fact: a large proportion of the population seek the occasional offices for rites of passage and hence we have a constituency much wider than our regular congregations. He then notes a distinction in approach between that to baptisms and that to weddings and funerals, noting in particular that while there is a fuss about baptism, no such fuss is apparent over weddings and funerals. This is largely correct. I for one am happy to live with the funerals of most of the population with perhaps some minor amendments to the liturgy. I would almost be inclined to require everyone to undergo a marriage ceremony in church, again if some other amendments were made to the liturgy. Marriage, to my mind, comes under the sphere of 'common grace', whether those entering it realise it or not. The Christian church has a pastoral and prophetic task to uphold the institution of Christian marriage and I believe that it would be possible to so revise the marriage service and liturgy in such a way that it did not make the assumption that the parties to the marriage were professing Christians. I believe that the particular Christian grace which can only come from a relationship of commitment to Christ needed for marriage to rise towards its full potential, but that is a subject beyond the scope of the present book.

But Longley is right here: it is baptism which causes the fuss. He refers to the July Synod of 1990 at York where the 'willing and able' clause was due for a dust off.[3] The point at issue in Synod was a redebate on the propriety of this controversial clause which had arisen in the post-Ely report debates and had been discovered not to have found its way into canonical amendment. The opportunity was taken to defeat this clause by some of its opponents, but before it could happen, discussion was deferred pending the publication and circulation of a discussion paper by Canon Martin Reardon.[4] Mr Longley interprets the existence of the debate at all as a sign that sooner rather than later the pressure to and indiscriminate infant baptism will prevail. I cannot deny that I hope he is right. If you have read as far as this chapter you will know that my colours are nailed to this particular mast. But it is when Mr Longley dives into the doctrinal basis of baptism that for me wires start getting crossed. He seems to suggest that for many within the church (and I assume he primarily means the makers of doctrine and those who follow them) baptism has now become a symbol rather than a sacrament, because the doctrine that made it a sacrament is now no longer believed. Thus we have a symbol in search of a rationale. That rationale is a sociological one of joining the worshipping body, hence the importance of parents being regular worshippers. From this comes the desire to winch baptism in to make it available only to those who guarantee they will play. I may have misunderstood Mr Longley but this is what he seems to say. If I am right then I think he is making a guess which is incorrect.

It is almost certainly true that for a significant proportion of Anglican clergy the 'traditional doctrine' of hell, heaven, salvation and damnation, and Christ's atoning sacrifice for sin still do hold a central place in their theology. For the record: yes, I do believe in the devil Mr Longley! Generally it is the conservatives (I prefer the words 'Traditional orthodoxy') who support baptismal reform rather than the modernists and liberals, to use these latter terms broadly. However Mr Longley is right to dive into the theological arena because that is where the battle must eventually be decided. I like his remarks on folk religion and he is surely right to note the rural subconscious mind of townsfolk (see next chapter), but I think Mr Longley has discerned correctly, or should I say instinctively, the way in which the future lies.

'Baptism is more than, even other than, the recruitment of a new member to the local parish church.' Yes: baptism is something on a higher plane than the one we have allowed it to be dragged down to. Yes, it is questionable to put words into babies mouths. Mr Longley seems to labour under the impression that the clergy are rather naughty for refusing baptisms; the truth is probably otherwise.[5] All in all he has done us a great service also in writing on infant baptism. His last sentence is unfortunate. His penultimate sentence should be woven on a colourful banner and placed over the heads of the next General Synod!

Notes

1. The *Gloucester Citizen* published details of a baptismal problem in Lydney. A tabloid recorded details of a case in Nuneaton, and a Derbyshire local had correspondence on a case near Ashbourne.
2. The details of Roger Godin's motion and its antecedents can be read in the Epilogue to *Reforming Infant Baptism* by Colin Buchanan, Alan Wright and Clifford Owen (Hodder and Stoughton: 1990).
3. See my discussion in Chapter 9 and also my essay 'Grasping the Nettle' in *Reforming Infant Baptism* ([2] above). See also Roger Godin's epilogue (ibid).
4. Canon Martin Reardon's discussion paper should be published by the date of publication of this present book.
5. See again Chapter 9 for the fuller discussion.

Chapter 15

RURAL POSTSCRIPT

In July 1989 we bade farewell to Bordon and moved to
the Diocese of Worcester. The parishes of Clifton-on-
Teme, Lower Sapey and the Shelsleys are among the
most scenically attractive in the land. My predecessor
wrote in his farewell article in the magazine 'surely the
loveliest trio of parishes in all of England'. Lovers of
Devon, Cumbria and many other places will wish to
dispute that claim, but I know what Patrick Hobson
meant. Clifton is set over 700 feet above the beautiful
Teme Valley, as it wends its quiet way from Tenbury
down in a graceful curve to Ankerdine and finally to join
the Severn south of Worcester. From one end of the
village the view takes in the Malverns and Bredon Hill.
The eastern horizon is marked by the northern ridge of
the Cotswolds, while to the south, by craning your neck,
you can see the Black Mountains. To the west loom the
Titterstone and Brown Clee Hills and on a clear day the
Wrekin can be seen alongside Telford new town. Occasionally the steam from Buildwas power station can be
seen too. Nearer at hand, and just in the parish, Woodbury Hill looms large, whilst behind lies Great Witley.
The local folklore says that once upon a time Owain

Glyndywr sat on one hill with his troops, whilst the English sat on Woodbury. They stared at each other for a week and the Welsh went home!

This is the beginning of the Marcher country. It is predominantly rural. Though Hereford and Worcester are now one and the same county, the union is only at Local Government offices. Down in the fields people look to Hereford or Worcester. The old county boundary runs down the edge of the parishes. This part of the country appears to have been sought after in recent years. In many parts of the parish old farm buildings have been converted into highly attractive dwellings and change hands at prices which a few years ago would have seemed ridiculous. Even though the property market has sobered up a little in the last two years, there is still a process of exclusion working against the first-time buyer here for the more exclusive barn conversions. The young marrieds have inevitably to look to Worcester or other more urbanised areas for the starter homes. In one parish however, a well established Housing Association provides accommodation for local people.

Clifton-on-Teme is about one third half-timbered, a little gem of a village, which has (in 1990) won its category of the Britain in Bloom competition. It is a fairly close-knit community where news travels fast and to be a resident is almost like being on stage. Individuals are known by name. Strangers are conspicuous, but ramblers and other tourists are welcome. Shelsley Walsh has a delightful thirteenth-century church with a fine fifteenth-century oak roodscreen, reputed to be the finest in the county. Nearby, three times each summer the famous Shelsley Hill Climb takes place. This is the oldest motor sport event in the world on its original course. Shelsley Walsh, together with its sister hamlets over the river, Shelsley Beauchamp and Shelsley Kings, forms a delectable setting for the fortunate people who live there, but it has just lost its small village shop. With the loss of its school some years previously, Shelsley will in the longer term need to consider how the community can be focused around a centre. It ought to be the church but there is this feeling of being a scattered community largely dependent upon the city ten miles away.

Generally speaking the parishes conform to the patterns outlined in recent studies of life and ministry in rural areas, especially the recently published report of the Archbishop's Commission on Rural Areas (ACORA).[1] Living in the country after an absence of thirty years has put me in touch again with my childhood roots. Living in a Warwickshire village of no more than 300, it was an assumption of life that you knew everyone and all the local gossip too. Everyone had an opinion about the parson whether they went to church or not, and most felt that they knew what was expected of him. Coming back into the country has meant a change of gear. Thirty years of urbanisation meant that I could walk down the street, even with a dog collar on, largely ignored by the crowds. In the village one is expected to show awareness of everybody else. One needs to slow down and reduce the pace of life a little, to allow room for casual conversations and greetings which can easily provide some vital piece of pastoral information.... Yet there are still myths about the countryside which will evaporate after a few months of living in a small community. Bishop Colin Buchanan said that villages nowadays are 'thinned out bits of suburbia'. They are exactly that. Modern mass communication and the media has meant that villagers are pretty well in touch with the world over the horizon. The majority of those who work commute; some even as far as Birmingham.

The local parish churches attract on an average Sunday approximately 10% of the local population. With attendance at Festivals and the occasional offices, I would hazard a guess that up to 50% of the population has passed through one of the churches during my first year. Curiously enough I have found that the boundary between the church and the rest of the community to be much clearer and more distinct than I would have imagined. There is a grey penumbra around the church, but parishioners are quite ready to own the fact that they are not practising Christians, that they do not 'believe', or that they are pleased with the presence of the church, but do not attend out of conviction. I actually welcome this as I believe it makes ministry easier.

Within the church congregation we have virtually the whole range, from those who believe that heaven cannot be reached without the Book of Common Prayer, to those who believe it a hindrance, and from the Matins and Evensong 'once-a-monthers' to the Praise and Worship charismatics. A pattern of services has emerged over the years which attempts to satisfy the whole range. I have no plans to change this pattern. I think it important in a rural parish church to have variety and to cater for the needs of the populace, as they cannot run down the road to the Catholic or Evangelical church. With the exception of the Roman Catholics, who do travel into Worcester, the parish church has to host Methodists and other Free Church members as well. Conducting and organising the worship needs a sensitive ear to all these requirements. But somehow my goal is exactly the same here as it was in my other very different parishes; to bring people to a faith in Jesus Christ and to build up the faith of those inside and encourage those outside to draw nearer.

The task of evangelism in Clifton, as far as the children are concerned, is made considerably easier by the presence of the village school. The headmaster, Ron Maddocks, is a member of a Free Evangelical church in Worcester, and an accomplished preacher. His primary school assemblies are up to the best I have seen in biblical teaching at children's level. Closer links between church and school are an obvious area of growth.

It is in this community that I have attempted to administer baptism. With the background of my experience outlined in this book, I naturally began to think about how I would tackle infant baptism before I moved into these parishes.

I worked out that I would move from point 3 on my Richter scale to point 2—'Open Policy' (see Chapter 7). To have jumped straight in with the kind of policy that we were working in Bordon would have been to commit pastoral suicide. So I decided, that while I would insist on some clear form of preparation before baptising any infants, all would be 'done' for the time being, without too much pressure from me in the way of additional hoops. I also felt it was important to begin in a totally new community from a position that could establish itself and from where no one would want to push me back. I have furnished plenty of evidence already that if too strong a line is taken on baptism and you 'lose', then it sets back the work pastorally by some years. I say this with sincere conviction, not out of a sense of wanting to acquiesce in a position that ideally I wouldn't want to be in, but out of sheer common sense. If anything, I am feeling slightly guilty that I have weakened the preceding baptismal policy a little by allowing a number of baptisms to be in the afternoon, and thus in a sense private baptisms. Where this has happened, however, we have arranged for the parents to bring the infant to a separate service for the giving of the card and the reception prayer.

Yes, the country is different, but it is basically the dynamics of a small community that make the difference rather than any fundamental difference in approach by people to christenings. The numbers being fewer mean that virtually every baptismal request is dealt with personally and preparation also. I have not yet tried experimenting with group preparations, because the infrequency of requests so far has made it inconvenient to arrange it. However, that could come in time.

I have conducted ten infant baptisms during the first fifteen months here. Four who formerly lived in the parishes had come back to have babies baptised. In each case the appropriate incumbent was approached and in one case the home incumbent did the preparation. Of the other six, it would be true to say that although I have seen all the parents in church on occasions, none are yet regular attenders.

The preparation has consisted of my home visit to the family, the discussion of the nature of baptism, the listening to my original tape (cassette) and a going through the service. Most people seem to have raised no objections to this. One or two mentioned that they 'hadn't met this before' and in a couple of cases I detected 'signs of smoke' at having to stop and think about what baptism is.

I have baptised no adults yet. But there lies an interesting tale. I have said that before I came to the parish I worked out where I would start off my baptismal policy for infants, but one day I received a telephone call from these new parishes to enquire what my line would be on an adult immersion taking place, after an experience of 'renewal'. I replied with explanation that while I would be delighted to baptise adults who were going under for the first time, I had no authority to sanction re-baptisms. If on the other hand candidates felt that they wanted to renew their baptismal vows in water, whilst leaving the authenticity of their infant baptism intact, then I would be happier to approve of that provided they didn't ask me to do them! I further hoped that whatever was to happen would have happened before I came to the parish!

In the event it did not. I found myself speaking at an occasion in December 1989 at which a number of adults renewed their vows in water (two or three were being baptised for the first time) and the ceremony was conducted by a house church leader from Worcester, Dr Rick Thomas. It was a 'hybrid' occasion—not officially ecumenical and of course slightly *sub judice*. I do wish that we could have an approved rite for such occasions as these which doesn't force people to 'go round the back'.[2] However, the occasion passed peacefully and joyfully and there have been to date no further requests for anything similar.

As secretary of MORIB, we were asked to supply any thoughts we might have about baptism in rural areas for ACORA, the Archbishop's Report on the Church in the Countryside. The request came too late to do a substantial survey, but there was time to sound out quickly some incumbents in rural areas. Including myself, there were five of us in Worcester Diocese and one each from Lincoln, Hereford and Derby dioceses.

The summary that I submitted read as follows:

There seemed to be a general consensus that each of the five incumbents felt that even though they would have worked or did work a more rigorist baptismal policy in an urban area, somehow the countryside was different. The identifiable difference was the sense of community. The community expectation was that infant baptism was primarily seen as a rite of passage and belonged to the whole community. Therefore to fence it around with too many conditions was seen as an infringement of personal rights!

'Any attempt therefore to work any kind of baptismal discipline had to be done carefully, sensibly and with utmost patience. Problems over baptismal rigorism were part of community "bad news" and the negative publicity attaching to any single pastoral case took a long while to live down. Nevertheless, each incumbent felt that they had to take at least the minimum of preparational steps when couples asked for infant baptism.

I found on investigation that some of the policies were quite brave!

One vicar insisted on at least one church attendance before the baptism as well as a visit to the vicarage and another hour visiting the parents' home. He also urged at least a four-week gap between enquiry and the event to allow time to think. The Hereford diocese incumbent expected church attendance before and after, but made it non-conditional to having the child baptised. He also urged strongly that if a parent was a lapsed communicant, then attendance at Holy Communion was expected at least once before the baptism.

One incumbent based his preparation on an audio-cassette he had made. One insisted that all baptisms should take place within a main act of worship, others felt this a little impractical. One was urging attendance at a family service after the baptism for the purpose of the welcome into the congregation and the giving of the baptismal card.

The common threads of the five incumbents in their baptismal approach were:

1. *Patience.* Often baptismal instruction had to begin at 'Square One'.[3] It was the long-term goal that was important.
2. *Church growth.* All incumbents felt that time spent in baptismal preparation was important for church growth. The pastoral relationship with the parents seemed crucial as well as being the key to growth.
3. *The tension.* There was a real tension experienced between the earnest desire to instruct parents, and the recognition that too strict a discipline, however legitimate, was interpreted as unjust or even as a refusal to baptise. One incumbent said he baptised virtually indiscriminately, but it left him with a heavy heart.
4. *The quality of worship.* This was taken as a point in favour of a cautious approach to jockeying people along to worship too quickly. What would they find as

the natural feed-in point for a new family? If one did not exist then there was a natural reason to start one.
5. *Being a welcoming church.* Being positive in a sincere welcome was seen as the crucial first step in responding to baptismal enquirers.

It is obvious that the vast majority of parishioners in the country have never seriously thought about baptism, its theology or even remotely become aware that the practice of general infant baptism causes difficulties to some vicars. I put most of the blame for this state of affairs at the feet of the clergy ourselves. Baptism is very rarely preached on as a subject, even at baptisms. Confirmation is not mentioned much apart from preparing candidates. Such straight evangelistic preaching as we have makes little reference to baptism and confirmation, except to almost undermine them. I went back through my own sermon file and to my shame could find no clear teaching sermons on baptism.

I am saying that before reform can be started there has to be a change of climate, and step one towards that change is teaching. Congregations need to be taught about initiation and all its components in clear unambiguous language. It may take quite a while for this to happen. If the Decade of Evangelism does no more in some quarters than teach people what it essentially means to be a Christian and how to become one, we will have achieved a great deal. Ten years is actually quite a short time. Only this week a lady going out of the door from eight o'clock Communion said 'You know, on the whole Anglicans really do not understand the basic essentials of the faith.' Who will say she is wrong?

So how do I expect baptismal change to come in the countryside? My reply is: after a period of teaching, when the climate is right, when a significant portion of PCC and congregation want to move forward in the matter. Meanwhile I am re-doing my preparation materials. I hope before long the PCC might agree, at the very least, to encourage in writing the regular attendance at church of families who seek baptism for their infants. But it is in the countryside in particular that if baptismal reform is to 'stick' it needs the clear support of Canon Law (revised as in Chapter 12). When families know that the church expects at least one of them to be a regular communicant and at the end of the day I have authority to delay baptism for a long time, then there is an authoritative basis to move ahead. In the meantime I will quietly work away at Point 2 on the Richter scale.

In *Reforming Infant Baptism* I mentioned Alec Vidler, who wrote in 1940, as a possible father of modern baptismal reform.[4] It was interesting to note that in the first edition of E.J. Bicknell's *Theological Introduction to the Thirty Nine Articles*, published in 1919, the problem of indiscriminate baptism is already mentioned. Part of the chapter on holy baptism reads:

> So the baptised infant requires food and nursing for its soul if it is to grow up spiritually sound. The Christian child is to come to self-consciousness within the Church. He is to be taught all that his life means and the grand possibilities that it contains. Hence the need of godparents, who in the name of the Church promise to train the child. Accordingly, teaching on baptismal regeneration must never be separated from the thought of the Church as God's family in which the new life is to be realised. The gift of God in baptism implies as its background His gifts to the Church as a whole. *It is very doubtful whether it is right to baptise infants indiscriminately as is too often done to-day* when there is no real security that they will be brought up as the Prayer Book directs. Godparents are too often selected, not for spiritual, but for worldly reasons. As a result, baptism comes to be regarded either as a mere form or else as having a vague magic efficacy! (Italics mine.)

Bicknell goes on a little later:

> Much as we deplore the refusal of the Baptists to administer

baptism to infants, at least their position witnesses to the fact that baptism means a great deal. That is a truth that the Church of England needs to restore to its due prominence.

Bicknell then adds a footnote which is quite significant:

The importance of baptism is also obscured by the custom, *in defiance of all Prayer Book rules*, of administering it in a hole-and-corner fashion instead of in the presence of the congregation. The whole idea of admission to Christian fellowship is lost. We have substituted 'Private Baptism' in church for public baptism. (Italics mine.)

All this has a familiar ring about it. While I am encouraged that the issues I have been grappling with in this book were coming over the horizon early on in the century, I am confounded that it has taken so long for the gauntlet of reform to be picked up. Let us pray that the Church of our Lord in the year of our Lord of 2,000 and beyond (DV) will have courage to grasp the baptismal nettle once and for all.

I close these chapters with a quotation from Dietrich Bonhoeffer's *The Cost of Discipleship*, and with it my case rests.

Cheap grace and costly grace.

Cheap grace is the deadly enemy of our Church. We are fighting today for costly grace, Cheap grace means grace sold on the market, like cheap-jack's wares. The sacraments, the forgiveness of sin, and the consolations of religion are thrown away at cut prices. Grace is represented as the Church's inexhaustible treasury, from which she showers blessing with generous hands, without asking questions or fixing limits...cheap grace is the preaching of forgiveness without requiring repentance, baptism without church discipline, communion without confession, absolution without personal confession. Cheap grace is grace without discipleship, grace without the cross, grace without Jesus Christ, living and incarnate.

Costly grace is the treasure hidden in the field; for the sake of it a man will gladly go and sell all that he has. It is the pearl of great price to buy which the merchant will sell all his goods. It is the kingly rule of Christ, for whose sake a man will pluck out the eye which causes him to stumble, it is the call of Jesus Christ at which the disciple leaves his nets and follows him.

Costly grace is the Gospel which must be sought again and again, the gift which must be asked for, the door at which a man must knock.

Such grace is costly, because it calls us to follow, and it is grace because it calls us to follow Jesus Christ. It is costly because it costs a man his life, and it is grace because it gives a man the only true life. It is costly because it condemns sin, and grace because it justifies the sinner. Above all it is costly because it cost God the life of his Son: 'ye were bought at a price,' and what has cost God much cannot be cheap for us.

Notes

1. In addition to ACORA see *Rural Anglicanism* by Leslie Francis (Collins: 1985), and *The Country Parish* by Anthony Russell (SPCK: 1986). See also *A Place in the Country* by Nigel Duckers and Huw Davies (Penguin Group: 1990). This latter book is an excellent portrayal of modern country life based on the 'old' county of Rutland.

2. I have come across two rites, or more correctly one rite and one special occasion. The first comes from the Doctrine Commission of the Presbyterian Church of New Zealand. I do not know whether it has found its way into general use in that country.

   The occasion was that of a service of Joint Baptism and Confirmation in an Anglican/Baptist Local Ecumenical Project at Binley Woods, Coventry (June 1989). There was provision in the service for those who were being baptised 'for the first time' to do so by immersion and in addition for the renewal of vows standing in water followed by an immersion using the words: 'Receive now immersion in this water as a reminder of your baptism.'

3. I am aware that the Church Pastoral Aid Society (CPAS) have a baptismal preparation course under that very title: *Square One*. I have yet to try that course in a parish.

4. *Reforming Infant Baptism* by Buchanan, Wright and Owen (Hodder & Stoughton: 1990).

EPILOGUE

by Colin Buchanan, Honorary Assistant
Bishop in the Diocese of Rochester, President
of the Movement for the Reform of Infant
Baptism

I am delighted to add a reflection upon Clifford Owen's delightful and personal account of how he found his way, partly by trial and error, partly through an instinct for the light, through the tangled and dark undergrowth of the English baptismal sub-culture out into a clearing sunlit by scriptural principles. I can enjoy it all the more because I know and honour Clifford Owen the man, and because I found myself saying 'Yes, yes' to myself as I read through the book in typescript.

I do not, however, abandon all critical faculties simply because I am being carried along by a tide which is so evidently flowing in the right direction. And here I suppose I can best contribute not by seeking items to query, but instead by filling in a couple of gaps. One of these relates to the national background to the issues thought through in Bordon, and I hope this will be seen to give a context to his personal story. There is also, perhaps to my surprise, one other gap which yawns hungrily in the book, one which I had not expected to find. So I now supply from my own experience that which, when I first picked up the book, I had honestly hoped I would be able to read from his viewpoint. It is a story in which he has stood at the centre of events; it is a story which relates naturally to his theme throughout this book; and yet it is a story which hardly emerges in his pages. I attempt to make good that lack without further apology—but can of course only do so from my own rather more limited standpoint.

To what do I refer? Why, to the very movement which Clifford has so nobly helped to pilot into existence and into effectiveness—the Movement for the Reform of Infant Baptism (MORIB). And if Clifford can be autobiographical, so can I, though I hope to restrict my self-exposure to simply the themes raised by Clifford Owen's account. I do, however, have the same problem as he does, that baptismal issues cannot be narrowly isolated and then resolved as though they were unconnected with other doctrinal, pastoral, and constitutional issues. This emerges time and again in his treatment, and it is exactly what the biblical handling of baptism would lead us to expect.

A personal theological pilgrimage

I came in on the issue both as an undergraduate in the 1950s and as a young clergyman in the 1960s with a sense that the Church of England—and particularly the evangelicals in the Church of England—did not know why they baptised infants. There was a kind of inherited notion that we baptised infants because that was the tradition of the church, a lawful development from the apostolic use of baptism; and because we were the established church in the land, it was right and proper for us to baptise all infants brought to us. If the more rigorous and searching questions were asked, particularly as to whether such a post-apostolic development could be held to be binding on a supposedly scriptural church, then the average Anglican was at a loss. The general answers available from those who did give their minds to it included the following: the self-authenticating character of tradition; the prevenient grace of God; a supposed basis in 'the faith of the church'; the general 'necessity' of the sacrament; and the pastoral importance of having our doors wide open. This would not of course satisfy the more trenchant evangelicals, not only because in the 1950s and 1960s they were endeavouring to get their own intellectual act together, but also because they were in constant contact with Baptist and Anabaptist streams of thought. It was the vague cobbling together of arguments to justify existing practice which both caused some people to become Baptists, and undermined the confidence in infant baptism of those who did not.

In the 1950s there was said to be a four-page folding tract being spread around at the Keswick Convention, on the front cover of which appeared the title 'ALL THAT THE BIBLE TEACHES ABOUT INFANT BAPTISM'. The other three pages were all blank—a very cheap and effective form of propaganda. I also recall at Oxford around 1956 the Bishop Jewel Society advertised a 'Bible-Reading' on infant baptism. This led a Baptist friend of mine to protest 'There cannot be such an exercise—I can imagine a lecture, or a debate, or a survey, or *anything* except a Bible-Reading, on this subject.'

It was very clear that evangelical Anglicans would need better arguments than those listed above if they were to remain Anglicans with a good conscience.

The literature available at the time was perhaps of interest. The best biblical defence of infant baptism was Marcel's *The Biblical Doctrine of Infant Baptism* (ET, Jas. Clarke, 1953), which proceeded like a river of lava from the higher ground to the lower, beginning with the covenant of grace, and pressing inexorably downward in the second half of the book through circumcision to baptism, and in the last quarter through baptism to infant baptism. It was a great encouragement to those

Calvinists who already wanted to be Pedobaptists, and certainly gave a sense of weighty literature at our backs—though of course it did not untangle Anglican complications.

The field became much wider open academically when the Jeremias/Aland controversy appeared in English through the good offices of the SCM Press.[1] This was much more like an *a posteriori* enquiry—ie, an investigation into *what actually happened* in apostolic and post-apostolic terms. It demonstrated that Pedobaptists need not be wrong-footed before the argument starts, though the argument also became slightly academically esoteric. And it helped those who wanted to argue responsibly from Scripture to see that they had a case there, in which Jeremias' handling of 'the *oikos* formula' added enormously to their confidence.

It was at this time that I asked an American Baptist what was the best statement he knew against infant baptism and he put me on to Paul King Jewett, whose lecture 'syllabus' from Fuller, dated around 1960, I still have (and it has since become a book). Reading this, I detected more clearly than ever before the areas where the debate had to be conducted, but it also came home to me very strongly that the debate could only refer in principle to the propriety of baptising the children *of believers*. And in 1965–66 I actually began to write a major book on baptism, some long-hand chapters of which I still possess, an earnest of work I deemed necessary but discovered, for time reasons, to be impossible.

The broader pastoral scene

This sense that the biblical case could not be made to run beyond the children of believers was, in the 1960s, starting to affect parish life. It is worth noting also that the 1662 liturgy for infant baptism, the only legal rite around until 1966, had its own part to play in this. The phrase 'seeing... that this child is regenerate' was beginning to stick in various throats. While the usual instinctive reaction by evangelicals was to call for the softening of the phrase,[2] a more reflective one was to wonder about the appropriateness of the candidates, or of some of them. Certainly, if calls for a softened phrase in the liturgy had ever succeeded,[3] most clergy would hardly have hesitated to use a liturgical text which in effect said 'I throw some water at you in the name of the Trinity and hope it does you some good.' It was the very wording of the rite which was stirring an unease among the clergy.[4]

It is difficult to tie down the detailed history of the transition from indiscriminate baptism to a reforming practice, such as is so widely desired even if not fully implemented today. There is a kind of pre-history most notably associated with Roland Allen; Clifford Owen himself traces origins in history back to 1940; further seeds were sown in the Parish and People Movement in the 1950s; a thoroughgoing *ballon d'essai* was inaugurated by Christopher Wansey in Woodford in the same decade; 'indiscriminate baptism' was the title of a chapter in the 1965 Swanwick Conference report, *Crisis for Baptism*; Michael Botting and his PCC introduced a fairly demanding policy; 'baptismal discipline' was a phrase used in the Keele report in 1967; and the issue was part of the terms of reference of the 'Ely' Commission appointed in 1969.

Around 1970 bishops started to omit from their institution services questions about 'seeking out the unbaptised', and some signs of conflict also arose. One of these latter came, interestingly enough, around the year 1970 in the parish of St Christopher's, Leicester, where, as this book shows, Avis, Clifford's wife, was brought up. Whether the incumbent concerned was moderate or extreme, wise or foolish, I do not know— but it is certain that in Bishop Ronnie Williams he was up against an episcopal power which would not brook any discrimination at all, and would always favour complaining parents. If I mistake not the man resigned his living.

The synodical farces

In 1972 R.R. Osborn produced his book *Forbid Them Not*, which even at that stage, nineteen years before I now write, fell upon us like a relic of Queen Victoria. In the debate on the Ely Report in General Synod in February 1974, I ventured to read a short extract from Osborn:

> Baptized Christians in a Christian commonwealth can never become mere numbers in a totalitarian or fully mechanized State. George Orwell's *1984* is no more than an impossible nightmare to Englishmen.[5]

Why so? Why, says Osborn, because universal infant baptism is a defence against every form of unjust power, including the might of the Trades Unions and every other 'nightmare'. The Synod fell about laughing at the absurdity of the advocacy, but (typically) still voted for something like an Osborn programme when it came to decision-taking.

I say 'something like'. What in fact it favoured was a motion

> That the General Synod adheres to the view that Infant Baptism should continue to be available to the children of all parents who request it and are willing and able to make the requisite promises, asks that the Liturgical Commission should note this expression of view, together with the requirements of Canons B.21, B.22 and B.23, in the framing of any new baptismal services, and commends, in particular, paragraphs 4 to 21 of the Working Paper for study in the dioceses.

Contemporary inspection and subsequent sad experience reveal that this motion was full to the brim with inconsistencies, timebombs, and stumbling-blocks.[6] For the sake of giving a national background to Clifford Owen's local pilgrimage, perhaps I could now summarise these nonsenses.

The first problem arising from this motion was that it became, through the addition as an amendment of the last seventeen words, part of the reference of the initiation issues to the dioceses. It was an interim expression of an opinion. It gave a lead to the dioceses, but it had no other force. The reference to the dioceses did not include a particular form of mandatory question to which they had to reply, and they were free to pass motions or not. In the event, my own diocesan synod, Southwell, sent up a motion:

> That this Synod, endorsing the forms of interrogation in Series 2 and draft Series 3 Infant Baptism Services, desires that there should be a re-examination of the conditions upon which infants are accepted for baptism.

I moved this Southwell diocesan motion in General Synod in November 1976 as part of the final decision-taking on the Ely Report after the responses had been received from the dioceses. The General Synod that day accepted the Southwell motion by 170 votes to 151. *This* was its last word on the Ely material, but we have had another chapter of accidents arising from it—including, it seems, a persuasion by the Standing Committee of 1985 to 1990 that they had in 1974–76 put 'willing and able' into the Canons (which they had not), a persuasion when they discovered they had not that they should have (which they should not have), and a further persuasion that 'willing and able' referred to godparents (which it did not). What the Standing Committee had actually done in 1976 was to ask Bishop Knapp-Fisher to write a one-man report on the issue of infant baptism. He did so, (and it is a very poor report), but the Standing Committee never introduced the report to the Synod— so I conclude that the 'conditions upon which infants are accepted for baptism' are *still* (nearly fifteen years later) *sub judice* in the Church of England.

The second problem of the 1974 motion was that it took an impossible procedural line. It referred an issue to the Liturgical Commission for action, while simultaneously referring the whole matter to the dioceses for reconsideration, acceptance or rejection. Clearly, the Liturgical Commission could take no notice of such an instruction. In fact, when it drafted Series 3 in May 1975, the Liturgical Commission actually strengthened the wording of its baptismal interrogations from Series 2. In Series 2 the interrogation was preceded by this run-in:

> Those who bring children to be baptised must affirm their allegiance to Christ...

and the antecedent of 'their' was left unresolved. The February 1974 motion had been drafted on the basis that 'their' referred back to 'Those who...', though in fact the formal nature of the vows rather favoured the view that the antecedent was 'children'! This ambiguity was overlooked and the Synod was asked to deprecate the form of the vows as being inconsistent with the parents being 'willing to make the requisite promises'. However, in the 1975 draft form of Series 3 the matter was wholly resolved by the Liturgical Commission, and deliberately went in the opposite direction from that implied by the 1974 motion:

> Those who bring children to be baptised must affirm their allegiance to Christ.... You must answer both for yourselves and for these children.

It was this form which the Synod endorsed in the Southwell motion in November 1976, and this form which now appears in the ASB. So the Liturgical Commission were not only procedurally correct in ignoring the 1974 motion, but were also substantially justified by events, in that the Synod, when it came to address baptismal rites, showed that it did want a fully Christian personal profession from the parents.

The third problem arising from this motion was that the Synod was afflicted by this nonsense of 'willing and able'. The 'and able' was a late-in-the-day amendment moved by Christopher Wansey without a speech. In point of fact he was being wholly cynical, for he did not himself believe *any* parent to be 'able' to make vicarious vows. The Synod, it seems, seized upon his amendment as giving some very slight weighting towards discrimination, such as to relieve the members of the possible opprobrium of having gone for wholly indiscriminate baptism. However, they opened a can full of worms for later sessions of General Synod. This, of course, would not have occurred if the Standing Committee had resolutely stuck to the point that the 'willing and able' motion had been superseded by the Southwell one in November 1976. The Synod has been constantly allowed to yield to the temptation to refer back to this interim, superseded, facing-two-ways, and desperately muddled motion, as though it had some standing or authority in the Church of England. Well, let us assume for a minute that it has. What is its problem?

It looks as though the easy reading of 'willing and able' is supposed to yield as its meaning that 'willingness' is tested solely by the parents themselves, whereas 'ability' is tested by the church. Thus, on this reading, parents might declare themselves 'willing' to frame the baptismal declarations, but a clergyman or church body might still declare them not 'able' to. If this means *anything*, it means *everything*—that 'and able' sets up a kind of judicial enquiry into the parents concerned, an enquiry which can properly conclude that they are not serious in what they are 'willing' to profess, and thus they must be deferred.

This rendering would provide the basis of the toughest possible pattern of rejection by the church. It is of course hardly likely to be what the words truly mean, and any parents appealing from it to a bishop would probably then find that a 'charitable' bishop would rule in their favour rather than the parish's. There would be no sound basis for a discriminating policy here. If of course the parents are themselves to adjudicate on the question as to whether they are 'able' to make the requisite promises, it is certain that any who already saw themselves as 'willing' would have no difficulty in adding 'and able' to their 'willingness'. The Church of England would be not one whit further forward. So 'and able' either adds far too much or nothing at all to 'willing'. My own estimate would be that if either 'willing' or 'able' has concealed within it the moral commitment to Christ required, then both have—and if either does not have such moral commitment concealed within it, then both do not. Then again 'and able' does precisely nothing to clarify or give limits to 'willing'. It is a false trail.

The fourth nonsense of this motion is that, though quite unnoticed in the brouhaha at the time, there are *no* requisite promises! Why so? Ah, because in the Book of Common Prayer the parents promise *nothing*—all the vows are taken by proxy on behalf of the candidate by godparents. Peter Cornwell, who drafted the report which underlay the Synod motion, had clearly got 'hooked' on the Series 2 forms, and there was no Mark Dalby in the Synod to rise and point out that the 'requisite promises' in the platform motion were an absurdity.[7] This was only finally discovered in Summer 1990 when the (abortive) attempt was being made to incorporate 'willing and able to make the requisite promises' into the Canons.

So much for the dreadful fumbling in the dark in

General Synod—it is only the most visible tenth of the
story, but is probably too wearisome as even that much.
The synodical background may be fogbound, but some
clearly distinguishable events, with Clifford Owen
involved in them, have been happening in the fore-
ground. To them I now return.

MORIB

I wrote an early Grove Booklet on Ministry and Worship
about this subject—no. 3, *Baptismal Discipline*, first
published in March 1972, and going to a second edition
in 1974. Other baptismal writings undergirded it after a
while, but when it itself went out of print a second time
in the late 1970s, I decided to revise it more thoroughly,
though I had to wait years to find the opportunity. Thus
in January 1987 I produced Worship Series no. 98, *Policies for Infant Baptism*. I reflect ruefully nowadays upon
these words which I then wrote:

> Opposition to infant baptism at intervals leads to calls
> within the Church of England to abolish infant baptism
> altogether. A new group wishing to achieve this is launching
> itself as I write...[8]

That 'group' proved to be the Movement for the
Reform of Infant Baptism, of which Clifford Owen was
the founding secretary in autumn 1986. However, from
my standpoint at the time, it sounded like a maverick
organisation—or at least one engaged in maverick public pronouncements. I now know it included both those
who wanted to reform the practice of infant baptism, *and*
those who wanted to abolish it. The former had the
advantage in the name of the movement and in its stated
aims, whilst the latter seemed to have the headlines and
the eye-catching publicity. Thus I had myself concluded,
as can be seen from the quotation from my booklet
above, that, whatever its title, it was in effect an organ-

isation for the abolition of infant baptism. If I had been told that, no, it was in fact only committed to reforming practice, I guess I would simply have replied that as far as I could see the revolutionaries were using a moderate public front in order to knock the bottom out of the boat, but that every now and again I could spot their true colours. I actually thought the venture would go away.

Well, the reverse happened. The MORIB committee asked me to speak at their Annual General Meeting at Shrewsbury in May 1988. I did so, and, having listened in the morning to a then committee member reading a paper of which the drift was unmistakeably abolitionist, in my own paper I warned that the movement needed to sort itself out fast, or it could not enjoy confidence from the great majority of reforming Anglicans. That was that: it was easy to be blunt, and I went my way home glad to have met interesting people (and to have sold a few books) but still fairly sure the movement's committee was digging its own grave.

Then came the surprise. The committee wrote courteously to me and asked me if I would take up a role as 'President' of MORIB. I demurred and asked to see them. At the meeting I warned them that if I accepted the role then, if the committee gave public vent to abolitionist policies—which would go far beyond the stated reforming aims—then I would have to dissociate myself from the movement on the spot. I would in such a case both resign and denounce them, and therefore I urged them to re-consider the invitation to me to be their president. The committee went away, held a residential meeting, and renewed the invitation to me. I then accepted the role, whilst reiterating my warning that it would be far better that I should never take up this presidency than that they or I should find ourselves in an embarrassing position, such as a public division of opinion as to the purpose of the movement further down the road. They accepted me on those terms and I became president and started to attend committee meetings from early 1989.

There then occurred exactly that which I had predicted, though it occurred by action rather than word. The then chairman of the committee in August 1989 underwent a public submersion which he described as baptism. I immediately set before him the very point I had made but a few months before—that I could no longer stay with a committee so compromised. He himself very honourably resigned from the committee, and was succeeded by Paul Kirby, the vicar of Bidston in the Wirral. The committee has reflected further upon its task, and has both clarified the aims of the movement (with the agreement of the some hundreds of members) and has agreed that its own tasks should be to serve the aims as stated. I detect myself a growing confidence round the country that such a movement will well serve the needs of a missionary church of the 1990s, and it is for the sake of its mission that baptismal issues are pursued.

One further comment is worth adding. In 1989 Clifford Owen arranged for the writing of a symposium on infant baptismal issues, in which the three main contributors were to be himself, myself, and the then chairman of MORIB, Alan Wright. It was deliberately agreed that this was *not* an officially sponsored MORIB publication. As a result, when Alan Wright underwent the submersion mentioned above, although his position in MORIB was immediately in question, his role as a contributor to the symposium was not. Thus it is that a book entitled *Reforming Infant Baptism* (Hodder and Stoughton, 1989) includes a chapter called 'A Parish Priest looks at Infant Baptism', which, on inspection, is a call for the abolition of infant baptism. This in my view has unbalanced the book, and given a somewhat disintegrated character to it, though I would opine that it nevertheless contains valuable material, not least Clifford Owen's first public mulling over of the issues.

A MORIB book as such is still awaited. Meanwhile Clifford's delightful unfolding of a tale of both a parish and a personality will lead many into an appreciation of the whole purpose of a reforming movement. Indeed, because he is the secretary of the movement, I suggest that readers now write to him (The Rectory, Clifton-on-Teme, Worcestershire WR6 6DJ) both to congratulate him on his book, and to join MORIB. There could be few better ways into a Decade of Evangelism.

Notes

1. J. Jeremias, *Infant Baptism in the First Four Centuries* (ET, 1960); K. Aland, *Did the Early Church Baptize Infants?* (ET, 1963); and J. Jeremias, *The Origins of Infant Baptism* (ET, 1963). I now observe that in my *A Case for Infant Baptism* (Grove Books, 1973) I have called this controversy 'dry' (footnote to page 4), but on reflection I reckon it assisted considerably in getting the argument onto all fours in biblical terms.
2. This was first found at the Savoy Conference in 1661, and was echoed at intervals thereafter, right up to and including the Keele Congress in 1967.
3. The nearest approach to such excision or alteration came in the moves for Prayer Book Revision in the nineteenth century. None of these revisions succeeded within the established church, nor even in the 1878 Book of the newly disestablished Church of Ireland (though there it became the subject of discussion in the Preface). They were, however, incorporated in the Book of Common Prayer of the Reformed Church of England and other such Books (see R.C.D. Jasper *Prayer Book Revision 1800–1900*).

4. Personally, I have always viewed the 'categorical' language of baptismal regeneration as being necessary in a sacramental liturgy. Our problem is that we have been so swamped by a pastorally eccentric situation that it is has been difficult to see the liturgy straight, as it should be used in 'proper' circumstances. In particular I have defended the 'categorical' language in my *Liturgy for Initiation: The Series 3 Services* (Grove Booklet on Ministry and Worship no. 65, 1979)—a commentary which in substance covers the whole of the 1980 ASB initiation rites also, as they are virtually unchanged from the Series 3 rites of 1979.

5. This is from *Forbid Them Not*. page 84. The quotation itself makes clear how 'established' a concept of the Church of England Osborn had. No one today could talk about this land as a 'Christian commonwealth', could they? So perhaps we have moved a little.

6. I refrain from reflecting here on the arbitrary choice by the Standing Committee of an 'indiscriminate' form of motion to be moved from the platform, let alone upon the destructive procedural trap into which I innocently ran when trying to amend it.

7. Why Mark Dalby? Because he is nowadays a member of General Synod, and he recently published his extraordinarily backward-looking manifesto *Open Baptism* (SPCK, 1989), in which he fairly revels in the fact that the parents make no promises and give no undertakings in the BCP infant baptismal rites. There are of course requirements made of parents in the Canons, but they cannot be properly called 'promises'.

8. *Policies for Infant Baptism* (Grove Books, 1987) page 5, footnote 2.

APPENDIX 1

PAVING THE WAY FOR A TOUGHER BAPTISMAL POLICY

Articles in the Headley/Bordon Parish Magazine, October 1988

A. From the Rector

Very often, the first words I hear when I answer my study phone are, 'I want the baby baptised, Vicar.' My usual response is, 'Why?' After a short pause, back comes the reply,

'Well, it's the right thing to do, isn't it?' Another reply I often hear is, 'Gran says I must in case something should happen to the baby.' Such a phone call will end by my arranging to visit the family, to talk to them about just what it is they are asking for.

Such home visits have long since failed to surprise me at the ignorance of the people who are asking for this sacrament of the Holy Church—BAPTISM. Much of their thinking is tied up with superstition and old wives' tales.

However, their ignorance is not their fault; it is ours, the clergy. We have, I believe, failed in our calling as teachers of the faith for many, many years, if not for centuries.

When we look back to the beginnings of the Christian church, we find that people (that is, adults) who came for baptism underwent a three-year period of instruction. However, the baptism of infants has been the practice of the church from fairly early times, but has no certain evidence in the New Testament. St Mark chapter 10 verses 14 and 15 *must* be taken along with verse 16— 'And he took the children in his arms, put his hands on them and blessed them.' He *blessed* them, he did not *baptise* them. And when we consider the practice of infant baptism, we must also remember that it was administered to children of committed Christians and it was *never* the intention of the church to allow the practice to be administered to the children of parents who had no intention of bringing them up as Christians within the family of the church. Neither is it right to allow children to be bound by promises which they have no reasonable chance of fulfilling, or to admit to the church large numbers of paper Christians. This deplorably common practice has, I believe, done more than anything else to weaken the sense of church membership.

My colleagues and I have spent many hours of discussion and prayer, reading and thinking, as you will see from their articles which follow, on this same subject. Like me, they agree that it is not the fault of the enquirers that baptism of infants has been made so easy. However, we must remember that Jesus likens baptism to being 'born again' (St John 3, verses 3 and 5) and as a result of this, we have come to the decision that we—as the church—must instruct the enquirer on just what it is they are asking for.

Parents have some nine months in which to prepare themselves for the birth of their baby and no doubt, during that time, they will attend classes to prepare them for this very special event, and for the care and nurture of the baby after its birth. We are asking all baptism enquirers to attend a course of instruction, in order to help them understand the Christian faith, and to understand the very important commitment they will be making at the baptism, should this still be their desire after that course of instruction.

My colleagues and I believe that we are helping them to come to what we hope will be the right response to the questions God is putting to them, both for their child and for their own conscience.

Yours in the service of the risen Lord.

B. From Revd Clifford Owen

Twenty years ago, if a parson refused to baptise an infant, it would probably have made the national press. Nowadays so many more people are aware that the church is trying to say something, it is less likely to cause a stir. Over the years in Headley-Bordon, I have heard remarks like:

'I never knew there was so much hassle to get a baby christened,' or, 'When my friend went to Revd So-and So, he just did it.' On the other hand, I have had clergy telephone me from other parishes to say they were most unhappy that we were apparently going to baptise an infant from their parish, when the real reason was that the family were looking for an 'easier ride'.

There is no need for me to elaborate on the main problem that the modern clergy have to face when baptism requests come in a secular society. Most of us are caught in the often unbearable tension between making a positive relationship with a family, and knowing that there is precious little on which to begin baptismal preparation. True baptism is a marvellous pastoral opportunity for explaining the gospel but, in the majority of cases, after the gospel has been explained parents show no interest in it, or are mildly hostile but still insist on baptism for their infant.

I have long puzzled why this should be so. After all, most parents are intelligent, rational beings and I would be the last person to want to push them into Christian commitment they were unwilling to make. Why should they still want to press ahead with a solemn sacrament of the gospel which involves them in making a profession of faith and an act of repentance, when they do not have any intention of living out that professed faith? I believe in these circumstances we are close to dealing with a religion which masquerades as Christianity, but in reality, falls far short of the genuine article. If this is not the case, then please explain to me why the vast majority of infant baptisms never result in confirmation?

Why indeed? First of all there is theological confusion, much of it of the church's own making. The Church in Wales Doctrinal Commission in 1973 concluded: 'any separation of baptism, confirmation and first communion *either* as successively given at different stages in the initiation rite, *or* as conceivable in isolation from one another, involves grave theological confusion... such separation leads to pseudo-problems that are insoluble theologically, if not in fact meaningless.'

In simpler language, no one ought properly to call himself a Christian until he/she has made a personal response to Jesus Christ, been through water baptism (sprinkling, pouring or immersion) and received the laying on of hands for the empowering of the Holy Spirit. This means that in the popular way in which we administer infant baptism today, it cannot at best be more than a first step in Christian initiation. The problem comes when we put everything onto an infant sprinkling, insisting that this in itself is sufficient for salvation. When this is coupled to the idea that you can be a Christian without going near the local congregation for participation in its life and worship, you have the formula that lies behind the popular approach to christening.

If it weren't so dangerous a notion perhaps we could pass it by, but at its heart is a measure of delusion. Immunisation has as its mechanism the injection of a small dose of the disease to prevent the catching of the real thing. This is often what happens with christening. Because we believe that the time has come for the church in its pastoral approach to the sacrament to make some of these issues clear, we have been working for some years now in the Headley-Bordon parish a stricter pattern of baptismal preparation. With the choice that parents now have of the service for thanksgiving for the birth of a child, there has been much more thought surrounding this whole issue, and I might add, a good deal of positive spiritual fruit.

C. From Revd John Cherrill

You may read your Bible in English with no fear of being burnt alive! This was not so in the 15th and 16th centuries or before. Many were put to death for saying the Lord's Prayer in English. The freedom you have to read your Bible in English has been gained for you at the expense of men's lives. These were men prepared to seek for the truth, and state the truth openly. St Francis embarrassed the church by suggesting that instead of persecuting the non-Christian people of North Africa, should they not preach the gospel to them! The institutionalised church seems always to be so reluctant to involve itself in reform; yet continual reform must be the very essence of the church as it strives to grow nearer to the image of the body of Christ.

The Preface to the recent Crockford's *Clerical Directory* is an example of one Church of England priest clarifying the areas he saw in need of reform. What a tragedy that has proved to be.

A most problematic area needing much careful thought, and about which the church needs to seek for the truth, is that of infant baptism, where the loss rate to the Church of England is some 97.4%. The majority of parents who make enquiries about baptism for their babies will adamantly assert that there is no need to go to church to be a Christian. Unfortunately the church has far too long acquiesed in their assertion without presenting them with the truth, and pointing out the consequences of their decision.

If a building surveyor is negligent in his professional duties when surveying a building, and that negligence leads to structural deterioration or collapse, then that surveyor can be sued for professional negligence. If a minister of the church does not warn the Lord's people of the consequences of their decisions, then he too is guilty of professional negligence. He has, however, to give an account of his ministry to God. Small wonder those ministers who take their ministry seriously find they must speak the truth, often at the expense of their own popularity, their livelihood and, in some instances, their lives.

When a baby is baptised according to the rite in the Book of Common Prayer, the parents and godparents promise God that the child will:

a) renounce evil
b) believe God's Holy Word
c) obediently keep God's will and commandments all his/her life, also
d) hear sermons
e) learn the creed, the Lord's Prayer, the ten commandments, the catechism and all other things necessary,
f) be confirmed.

This is in order that the child might know the solemn vow, promise and profession *he hath made*. When the baby is then asked if he will be baptised in this faith, the parents reply that it is the baby's desire!

Similarly, if a baby is baptised according to the new rite (ASB), the parents and godparents are asked to state publicly that they will ensure the child is:

a) brought up *within* the family of the church
b) brought to confirmation

and the purpose is to learn public worship, private prayer, trust in God. Since they declare this will be achieved by their *example*, they are declaring their intention to be *within* the family of the church—ie present in church.

The parents and godparents also affirm that the child:

a) *does* turn to Christ
b) *does* repent of his/her sins
c) *does* renounce evil
d) *does* believe and trust in God the Father, God the Son and God the Holy Spirit.

APPENDIX 2

RESPONSE OF THE PETERSFIELD POST TO THE NEW POLICY

A. Suffer the little children

Clergy in Bordon are taking a tougher line with people who use the church for christenings but who have no real commitment to the church.

Christine Ryan spoke to young mothers about the new policy.

A crackdown on 'paper Christians' who want their children baptised but are not regular church-goers has met with a mixture of anger and disbelief in Bordon.

The Post went along to the Forest Centre and asked a cross-section of parents what they thought about Team Rector the Revd Michael Powell's decision not to baptise babies until their parents had attended an instruction course.

We could not find anyone who agreed with Mr Powell and the Team Vicar, the Revd Cliff Owen, but we did discover that the measures have already been introduced elsewhere in neighbouring parishes.

Marian Clarke of Blackthorn Close said: 'When I saw the story in *The Post* I thought "those churchmen are talking a lot of rubbish." I think they are trying to create too much of a strict church, more like the Catholic Church.'

She added that the church at Bordon had refused to baptise her son, Shane (3), and commented: 'Why should it make any difference to him whether I go to church? I think anyone

274

should be able to have their child baptised, even if they are not regular church goers.'

She said: 'A lot of the people in Bordon are travellers, and the church is trying to shut them out. It is going over the top—the church should do more for the people in the area.'

Sisters Stephanie Gates from Liss and Karen Turner from Bordon have both been told they cannot have their children baptised because they do not regularly attend church.

Stephanie, who is a single parent, explained that they had wanted to have her son Edward (22 months) and Karen's daughter, Filipa baptised together.

She added: 'I agree that the children can make up their own mind up about religion when they are older, but not all parents think like that. They should have the right to have their children baptised without having to go to church regularly themselves. I think the vicars have the totally wrong attitude on this.'

Gillian Hicks of Blue Timbers Close, Bordon had to go to a church in a different area to have her son, Stewart (14 months) baptised, when she was turned down at her own church in Farnham.

Stewart was Christened in Guildford, where his sister, Kerry (4) had been baptised previously.

Gillian said: 'They shouldn't take it out on the children if the parents don't go to church regularly, after all it does say in the Bible "Suffer little children to come to me." When they are older, they can choose for themselves, but they should have been given that start.'

Another mum who does not attend church regularly, but had her four-year-old daughter baptised is Angela Knight.

She said: 'I believe in God, and I know he is up there, watching over Jemma as well as me. I don't think anyone has the right to tell others what to believe—I will guide my daughter and tell her what I think, but once she is old enough she will make up her own mind anyway.'

Angela added: 'You have them Christened because that is your own personal view, and because you want to set them on the right road. I can see the rector's point, but I don't have time to attend church regularly.

'Jemma will eventually make her own choice—but I would

hate for anything to happen to her before she was old enough
to decide for herself that she wanted to be Christened.'

B. Letters in response to the article

'Baptism is not for those without faith'

'Suffer the little children' the headline ran in last week's
Bordon Post; an often abused quote and here it is rolled out yet
again.

The topic of the article was infant baptism and various
mother's responses to the Anglican Church which is trying to
come to its senses over indiscriminate infant baptism. At least
three of the four mothers mentioned appeared not to attend
church regularly and by implication neither do their children.
Who then is 'suffering the little children' to come unto Christ
Jesus?

The blatant ignorance of people mentioned by the three
Headley and Bordon Clergy is evidenced by the views
expressed. These are people who presumably do not know one
end of the faith from the other.

The tragedy is that it has been the Church that has allowed,
or even propagated, some of this thinking for centuries. Let me
say straight and clear that it is not biblical to baptise those who
have not first expressed true faith.

Let me quote another scripture: 'Let us not give up meeting
together, as some are in the habit of doing, but let us encourage
one another and all the more as you see the Day approaching'
(NIV Heb. 10 v 25). It is central to the message of Jesus that we
are baptised into Him and become part of His one body the
Church. It is our duty and our joy to meet together to worship
Him and encourage one another.

I am compelled to ask if parents are so concerned about the
eternal destiny of their children why are they not keen to
discover the only route God has made available to reach that
goal?

Kevin Lewis
2, Birch Grove,
Whitehill.

Infant baptism: no biblical grounds

With reference to your Talking Point article 'Suffer the little children,' I should like to point out that having read the Bible cover to cover, I find the baptism of babies to have no biblical foundation at all. The New Testament standpoint is that we should believe and be baptised (in that order!).

Indeed Jesus did say 'Suffer the little children to come unto me,' but that was in the context of parents bringing their children to Him to bless. We read that He took them in His arms and blessed them, but not that He sprinkled them with water and pronounced them to have been born again as of that moment. The pattern of baptism endorsed by Jesus was the total immersion of the repentant sinner. In fact the sprinkling of water on babies has its roots in the ancient Babylonian occult religion and was carried over into some parts of the Church when Constantine proclaimed Christianity the official state religion several hundred years after the time of Christ.

There is a significant body of support for this view within the ranks of the Anglican clergy and a preference amongst them for infants to be dedicated to God. But such dedication necessarily implies an active role by parents in teaching the Christian faith to their growing children, and most importantly through personal demonstration in their own lives. They cannot, however, 'make' Christians of them, since each individual must choose for himself whether or not to live as he pleases or allow Jesus Christ to live in him.

I hope these comments will provide food for thought.

Sheila Burton (Mrs)
Tegdown,
Petersfield.

Petty tyranny

I see in last week's Talking Point in the *Petersfield Post* that the clergy in Bordon will not baptise children unless the parents attend an instruction course.

This is an extreme example of petty tyranny. They are attempting to degrade baptism to some kind of admission ticket to a church club. Baptism is a holy sacrament between Christ and the baptised child only. It is not a prize for the parents' theological knowledge, or for their promise of attending at some particular church. It is quite irrelevant where it is held, whether it is in a private room, or before a congregation.

The clergy who discriminate in this way by rejecting some and admitting others, have a great deal to answer for. Many of those they choose to reject may probably never be baptised. This means that they can never come to Confirmation which is the completion of baptism, and this, of course, means that they will never receive Holy Communion. Have they really studied all the consequences of their pernicious policy?

I would strongly advise the rejected parents to seek elsewhere. There are many Anglican churches in this Diocese that welcome children for baptism without imposing these conditions upon them.

Nobody, whether clergy or laity, can ever fully comprehend the mystery of baptism, and the greatest wrong one person can inflict upon another is to prevent them being received by Christ.

> Patrick J. Lamport
> 112, The Causeway,
> Petersfield.

Promises should be kept

Dear young mothers of Whitehill. I read your report in the local paper with great sadness. I am a baptised, confirmed member of the Christian family.

Before you condemn the clergy in your parishes please sit down quietly and read the baptism service through. In that service you have promises to make to God for these children, through the priest, and in the presence of the Christian family. Are you and the godparents prepared to make these promises that you may have difficulty in keeping? Are you going to lie to God and expect the priest to baptise your baby he knowing full well that you will not bring that child up regularly in the Christian faith and family? Remember at his own ordination he made huge promises, are you asking him to break his promises to God?

Confused

How can you bring the child up in the Christian faith to confirmation, if you don't come regularly to worship with the family? The child will not know which way to go, and will only be confused. One always finds time for the really important things in life. You will see I am a mum and grandmother.

Jean Pay,
Shotterfield Terrace,
Liss.

He died for all

I found the report in last week's *Post* about baptism both disturbing and sad. There seems to be a most important principle at stake.

As I understand it, the Church has always provided for the baptism of dying infants by anyone. Are we now to assume that this is to be denied to despairing parents unless they first have a course of instruction? If this is not the case we are being told that what God can do for a dying child He will only do for anyone else in certain circumstances. Is it for us to decide what God can or cannot do?

Of course, it is desirable that promises should be made and kept, and that instruction should be given whenever possible, but all down the ages the Church has baptised and given the sacraments to simple folk who could not understand or were unable to attend for instruction.

There are still many such with us (see the recent Mori Poll on educational standards). Is it proposed that the Church shall now restrict the sacraments to the amenable, educated middle classes?

I believe that, in the words of Charles Wesley 'For all, for all my saviour died, for ALL my Lord was crucified!' When it comes to the gift of God's Holy Spirit in baptism any legalistic restrictions are quite irrelevant.

John Warren
Hatch Farm
Standford,
Bordon.

APPENDIX 3

QUESTIONS FOR GROUP DISCUSSION

The groups should last about 45 minutes and there are three questions for discussion. Question 3 really leads on from 1 and 2.

1. You meet a middle-aged female acquaintance one day in the street. You are near the church. In the course of the conversation she says:

   'Well, you know I don't go to church apart from weddings and so on, but I do believe in it. I had all my kids christened and I want my daughter to get hers christened. They should be brought up right, shouldn't they?'

   How would you wish to continue the conversation?

2. Three years ago you attended a Billy Graham meeting and you came to understand what Christianity was about and made a commitment. You attended your local Anglican church and completed a follow-up course and then you were confirmed. Your next door neighbours whom you know quite well think you have

gone a bit 'over the top' with religion. They hardly ever darken the doors of the church.

Those same neighbours have recently had a new baby and the Revd Ian Splashall has agreed to baptise it one afternoon in your church. Your neighbours have invited you to the christening and the party afterwards.

Do you:

a. Find an excuse to refuse?
b. Buy the baby a Bible and set of tracts for his christening present?
c. Attend the party and join in the fun like everyone else?
d. Write a long letter to them explaining that until they make a commitment to Christ you cannot in all good conscience attend?
e. Attend and stay miserable all the way through the proceedings, scowling where appropriate?

3. You are a member of the PCC at St Winemalls. The Vicar, the Revd Ernest Catchem, believes the time has come to work out a baptismal policy for the church. How would you set about it and what would you like to see in it?

APPENDIX 4

Bridge over troubled baptismal waters

Although the national average is about a third, something like half the babies born in the rural areas of England are still christened in church. And woe is the lot of any rural clergyman who fails to perform on demand at the baptismal font on the grounds that the parents' attachment to the faith of the church is too much lacking.

This is the general picture to emerge from a study of baptism in rural communities published by the Movement for the Reform of Infant Baptism. In many cases, vicars have found coldness or even hostility and anger in their parishes when they have tried to pursue a policy of restrictive baptism, and not just from offended parents. Villages have been split as parishioners take sides, more often than not against the vicar. Even hesitation, or just the suggestion that they talk about it first, often sends the parents straight off to some neighbouring church where no questions are asked.

Some appear to have overcome at least part of the initial resentment, and have found it possible to reach a compromise with the parish. But often they had a rough ride getting there. The Movement for the Reform of Infant Baptism nevertheless represents a growing trend away from universal or indiscriminate baptism in the Church of England, and 123 members of the General Synod have signed, at least as deserving debate, a private members' motion which says as much.

It calls on the House of Bishops to prepare a report for the synod, and it is likely to be discussed at next month's synod meeting. The resolution, to be proposed by Mr Roger Godin, of Southwark diocese, 'calls attention to the concerned over apparent indiscriminate baptism...increasingly shared by many people of differing theological persuasions in the Church of England.'

These are highly sensitive matters. While the tendency in the church itself has been to regard baptism as the rite of initiation into church membership, with all that that implies, baptism also clearly serves an important purpose in the community as a rite of initiation of another more secular, or at least less Christian, sort. Otherwise the anger makes no sense at all.

Many of the parents angered by a vicar's refusal to baptise their children do not want to attend his church, nor do they want their children to do so; and they are unlikely to hold, or even to know about, the Christian doctrine of baptismal regeneration. They want a christening for their babies just as they want to give or receive birthday presents, decorate their homes at Christmas, tie old boots to the back of a newly-wed's car, and celebrate 21st birthdays. It is part of their culture: it does not have to have a reason.

Part of the explanation is contained in the Bishop of Salisbury's address to his diocesan synod last weekend, when he referred to the general level of ignorance, among ordinary church-goers and in the community at large, about the Christian faith. Dr John Baker spoke of 'confusion and lack of assurance about what it means to be a Christian' which led to 'humiliating anxiety hidden from their fellow-worshippers and most of all from the vicar.' For it is in just such a climate of ignorance that clergy and parents will be at most cross-purposes about baptism. It is entirely possible that parents will dismiss a vicar who started to talk to them about Christian initiation as 'some sort of crank.'

But if the folk do not understand the clergy, the clergy do not quite understand the folk. There are two alternative anthropological understandings in collision. As in the case of church marriage, the service provided by the clergy is seen from the community as being akin to a public utility, available to all as of right. The refusal of the vicar to sprinkle babies on demand is therefore as incomprehensible as a refusal of the water authority to connect up the mains.

There may well be profound reasons for this: it is not simply an unfortunate by-product of a policy of indiscriminate baptism in the past. The community, particularly if it is rural, likes to regard the local parish church as its property, a shared asset jointly owned. An incumbent who wants to make changes the community does not like will quickly find himself up against solid resistance, as if he was no more than a passing tenant or caretaker who had impertinently started to act as if he was the proprietor.

In most contexts, the Anglican parish clergy rejoice in this sense of belonging to everyone, and try to enhance it whenever possible. They treat the parish as the same as the village, parishioner and villager as interchangeable terms. But discrimination between those parishioners whose children he will baptise, and those villagers whose children he will not, is a contradiction of this whole pastoral ethos; which is the local version of the concept of the Church of England as the established church of the nation rather than the church of a separate denomination called Anglican.

That it has already become the latter is presumably the view taken by that half of the rural population which do not seek to have their children christened; and it is also the view which, unwittingly or not, the Movement for the Reform of Infant Baptism is encouraging.

In various ways including this one, the present difficulties of the Church of England arise from it being in a slow transitional phase, gradually changing from being the unique English 'community church' to being one denomination among many. Baptismal policy is the perfect case study of what is ultimately an irresistible change, which will meanwhile be very tricky to handle without causing much distress and anger.

On the one hand a Christian church cannot go on administering a Christian sacrament to those to whom it is meaningless in such terms; on the other hand if it stops doing so, it will be withdrawing itself from providing a much-loved ceremony at a most important moment of people's lives. And they will not like it.

Clifford Longley
The Times
Saturday, October 29th 1988

APPENDIX 5

July 1991 Update

The General Synod debate on Initiation has come and gone with mixed results. The motion that the initiation legislation should be amended to incorporate 'willing and able' and 'be not proceeded with' was carried overwhelmingly. This now means that it is unlikely that we shall see another major debate in General Synod on baptism for around ten years. On the other hand, the House of Bishops urged in the same session that the general pattern of 'no communion before confirmation' should remain. This recommendation was carried, and so the fence technically remains around the communion table rather than the font. This pleases me as the drift of this book urges that there must be a fence somewhere!

Colin Buchanan in a recent letter to me says: 'In general, I want to emphasise that although there was an emotional 'open baptism' direction to the General Synod debate, there was no canonical change at all, and we are just where we were before.'

Where do we go from here?

I believe a lot of the heat could be taken out of the present situation in many parishes if the House of Bishops were to give a try to the idea of sanctioning the baptismal policies of individual parishes on (say) a five year term. This would mean that when a vicar and PCC formulate a baptismal policy, they would have it discussed and agreed with the Diocesan Bishop, who would then support it.

In 1980 The House of Bishops produced a Code of Practice for conduct in Local Ecumenical Projects. This served well as a guide and forerunner until the new Ecumenical Canons B43 and B44 came along in 1990. Something like this is needed now to enable parishes to have episcopal support for their baptismal preparation from the outset; rather than having to wait for some test case from an angry parishioner.

In July 1991 I attended the first gathering of the national forum of Churches Together in England. Baptism came up for discussion in my sub-group of mixed denominational representatives. It may yet be that it will be from an Ecumenical pressure point that baptismal reform will be urged upon the Church of England.

The Church Down Our Street

by Michael Wooderson

Michael Wooderson's booklet Good News Down the Street has pulled thousands of Christians out of their pews to share the Gospel of Christ . The Church Down Our Street brings Michael's account up to date and helps us to grasp his vision for down-to-earth local evangelism.

Michael helps congregations bridge the gap between church and community. As he tells his own story, he shows how he learned to choose, set up and monitor an evangelistic team. In his easy, humerous style, he spreads before us a feast of ideas and anecdotes.

It was in France that Michael first met Christians who fired him with enthusiasm for a ministry of hospitality, friendship and preaching. Later, having taught in West Africa, he returned to Britain to train as an Anglican minister. He is now Vicar of Chasetown, West Midlands, where the Good News of Jesus continues to spread down the street.

MARC
Monarch Publications